GIRLS' STUDIES

Girls' Studies

Published by
Seal Press
A Member of the Perseus Books Group
1700 Fourth Street
Berkeley, California

Library of Congress Cataloging-in-Publication Data

Lipkin, Elline.
  Girls' studies / Elline Lipkin.
    p. cm. -- (Seal studies ; 6)
  Includes bibliographical references and index.
  ISBN 978-1-58005-248-1 (alk. paper)
  1. Girls. 2. Girls--Study and teaching. I. Title.
  HQ798.L55 2009
  305.23082'0973--dc22
                                        2009027283

Cover design by Kate Basart, Union Pageworks
Cover illustration © Lauren Simkin Berke c/o rileyillustration.com
Interior design by Michael Walters
Printed in the United States of America by by Edwards Brothers
Distributed by Publishers Group West

GIRLS' STUDIES

ELLINE LIPKIN

SEAL
Studies

For my nieces, Claire Mary and Tessa Nicole, and my nephew, Benjamin Isaac, and for the next generation.

CONTENTS

PROLOGUE

IN THE MID-1990S, specifically the summer of 1995, I was working at one of my first editorial jobs when I walked by a stack of newspapers. The lead story on the front page caught my eye: "When Typical Teen-Agers Are Awesome Elders; Super Supy Girls Are Those Who Pass the Traditions Down to the Younger Ones." The image presented, of a preteen girl at summer camp, stopped me in my tracks. I remember wondering, *What was this article about and what was it doing on the front page of* The New York Times? I picked up the paper and began to read.

The article was about a girls' summer camp in upstate New York; it was about the bonds and rituals that had become emotionally essential to the girls who attended every year; it was about the transitions and milestones and uncertainties the girls experienced as they made their way from their elementary to their high school years; it was about the nuances of girlhood—baffling, energizing, changing almost by the minute as these girls tried to figure out who they were and what they were doing. And it was in *The New York Times*. On the front page. Of the Sunday edition. Furthermore, I realized, this wasn't just an isolated article. It was one of a four-part series. As I stood there taking this in, I felt stunned.

How could this be? was my immediate reaction. *Was this really considered "news"? Wasn't this prime newspaper space reserved for Important Stories?* Yet the more I read the more I felt an almost electrical reaction as I saw aspects of my own teen years represented, and a kind of credence given to the experiences that I knew would resonate for others but would probably never be acknowledged beyond their peers. I felt a curious combination of being both shocked and moved.

When I reread the series of articles now I feel emotional all over again, not just because of the content matter covered—the poignancies, triumphs, and intricacies of these girls' bonds—but because what the series communicated is that these girls' lives mattered. Their concerns and their visions for their futures *are* news. The mere existence of the series stated that the public *should* care about how girls are shaped by popular culture and how the stamp of femininity is pressed upon them. It was a revelation to me to see this in a paper of national reputation in the mid-1990s, and I'm grateful that I don't think this series would seem such a radical act now.

Unbeknown to me at that time, the field of girls' studies was just being born, usually the offspring of gender and women's studies departments. Energy gathered in the early '90s around the Riot Grrrls movement and the AAUW's key reports about girls' experiences in school, alongside the fast rise of popular books that brought to light girls' drop in self-esteem around the time of early adolescence. All of a sudden, in both the popular press and in the academic world, there was serious study about how girlhood was defined, which experiences most shaped girls and into what kind of mold. Although there has always been concern about how to turn girls into "young ladies," looking at how ideas about femininity constructed—and constricted—girls suddenly became a topic of new importance.

In the years since, concern about girls has swung a wide pendulum: Some voices maintain their self-esteem is ever in peril, others insist that girls have never been as strong and outspoken as they are now; some voices decry that girls are sexualized too soon, others claim it's great that they feel ownership of their bodies in ways previously disallowed. And rather than girls being taught silence, girls' voices are now heard shouting through the distance. Through zines, websites, lyrics, blogs, videos, among other outlets, girls now have greater visibility in expressing their concerns and making their points of view heard. Yet in an ever more media-saturated world, these additional resources can also be places where girls feel even more pressure to fulfill set expectations and to perform a certain type of femininity.

As a field, girls' studies is very much still in its own girlhood. Mention of its mere existence can still astonish. I see in my own students' reactions to learning that this field exists at all the same wonder and revelation that I felt when I first picked up *The New York Times* article about camp. They are amazed that their lives are considered worthy of examination, that it is legitimate to recognize the forces pressing on them through their girlhood years, and that, alongside other academic disciplines, this also matters. This stunning thought alone brings a sense of validation and excitement into the classroom that is deeply energizing.

However, girls' studies is hardly a centralized, unified field. In a university setting, finding classes can be difficult, if they exist at all. Much of the debate over gender differences between girls and boys has moved into discussion of differences around learning and the value of single-sex education. Education departments have often pursued this focus, while, for example, classes within an English department might center around the figure of the girl in literature. No matter in which department study about girls is found, chances are bringing this topic to the fore is still new. As this field develops it has experienced the growing pains any adolescent does—including debate about its necessity and concern that promotion of girls means that boys are unfairly being left out of the equation. Proponents of girls' studies will often advocate that this is exactly why the field needs to exist—to counter the unspoken assumptions that use boys' experiences as the baseline in studies about youth or adolescence.

One interesting aspect I've noted about this field is how powerfully it dips and swerves into public consciousness. Debate about girls plays out in popular newsmagazines, television shows, school policies. As I carried the books I was reading around with me this past year—on planes, in coffee shops, or just out on walks—it almost never failed that a woman who asked me what I was reading, and why, would react with the same profound recognition that I first had in understanding that girlhood is worthy of study. After I explained the rise of this new field, there was often a long pause as I could see some measure of emotion collecting behind the questions asked, or buried within the stories that burst forth about their daughters, or rising within a moment's recollection of a girlhood hurt, or a special bond, or an unexpected legacy whose impression lingers. The power felt in those moments was palpable, and often contained, again, the breathtaking realization that their girlhoods were considered important—worthy of study, of consideration, even just of mention.

There is now deep concern about girls in the world. Seeing popular culture follow the waves of interest in "mean girls," crest to the catchphrase "girl power," and then ricochet off to new directions has led me to realize how deeply American culture cares about its girls—and also how fraught that concern can be. Similarly, I was glad to discover how many organizations now exist to promote girls in developing countries, often with the realization that helping a girl finish her schooling, for example, can have a significant impact on her entire family, or even her whole village. It is heartening to know there is new recognition of how central a girl's value is, not only to her family but to an entire social system, even if much work remains to have this more widely acknowledged and accepted.

The passion that exploring issues of gender often incites is still very much present. When I teach, I often hear students, male and female, say that there's no need for feminism any longer—it's all "solved"—the doors to any choice have been thrown open and all paths are clear. Yet when I bring up discrepancies in how many women hold positions of power or wage equity, or more subtle differences in expectations for their futures, the conversation often takes new turns. Debate also often quickly sparks around how girls outpace boys with grades, college admissions, or GPAs once on campus, hence the seeming lack of a "self-esteem problem" for girls these days. But when coaxed to look beyond these figures to how this success translates to later life empowerment, students' arguments often grow thin. And yet, the concept of girlhood as a troubled time isn't one that most students, male or female, want to have clouding near them. They are often quick to point out how pressured they feel, often with no neutral ground on which to stand as they negotiate the conflicting messages they are given about girlhood—be athletic but not too tomboyish, or attractive but, not too sexual, assertive but not transgressively angry, or, alarmingly still, intelligent but don't look too smart. Stories about injustice against girls because they are girls still abound in the news, and toy stores divide neatly along gender lines.

Not too long ago, after a move, I unpacked several boxes of childhood juvenilia. I was amazed to see favorite toys, series of books, stuffed animals emerge from what felt like a time-warped (and wrapped) pink cocoon. Much of what was buried inside seemed just as appropriate to give a girl today, the realization of which I wasn't sure what to make. As I unpacked, I found myself remembering Toni Morrison's *Sula*, an old favorite, and turned instantly to the book's closing lines, just as Nel recognizes how much she's been missing her childhood friend, Sula. Morrison writes, "'We was girls together,' she said as though explaining something. 'O Lord, Sula,' she cried, 'girl, girl, girlgirlgirl.'" The emotion Nel expresses, in her ringing cry for the girlhood friendship she shared, is described as having no bottom or top, just "circles and circles of sorrow," and seems to stand in for the coiled mysteries of girlhood itself—some of triumph, some of pain—that release in a spiral toward womanhood, that very much, as Morrison says, has no end. I hope this book will bring better understanding of the circles of girlhood, overlapping, concentric, and expanding outward, individually, collectively, toward the future.

© CORBIS

Two teenage girls doing their makeup in the bathroom.

CHAPTER 1

LEARNING TO BE A GIRL, LEARNING TO BE A WOMAN

THE PINK CAP IS PUT ON SHORTLY AFTER BIRTH. In a still-common practice in hospitals, babies are identified by their bodies, and then sorted into two simple categories—blue for boys, pink for girls— within minutes of their entrance into the world. When and how the traits associated with being female then enter each girl's head is harder to pin down, but the imprint of gender is usually pressed onto her right from the start. Brought home from the hospital, she may be dressed in pink clothing or wrapped in a blanket decorated with flowers. A doll will likely be among her first gifts.

Learning to play, she may enjoy solving puzzles or building with blocks, learning to identify objects and then putting together phrases from words. But will she be told not to be aggressive if she takes toys from other children? Not to be too "bossy" if she orders other kids around? She most likely will, since most kids are taught to control their impulses—but will it be less permissible because "that's not how a little girl" should act? Will she be allowed to participate in Little League soccer or baseball, or instead will she learn to dance? And at what age will she first learn that there are "boys' toys"—GI Joes, race cars, helicopters, Lego robots, Nerf guns, sports video games—opposed to "girls' toys"? Will she receive unwelcome looks from teachers, parents, or friends if she reaches for the wrong pile?

As girls grow, they learn from the messages they see around them. If *Sesame Street* has only a few female Muppets on the show, children

1

absorb the absence, although they might not understand why. If adults reflexively refer to all gender-nonspecific animals and creatures as "he," that too is absorbed. If cartoon characters most often feature boys who are rescuing girls, or who are big and brawny, while the female characters are petite, this also filters into young girls' minds. Children learn what is considered "normal" by observing the world around them—whether it's that mothers care for kids while fathers (if present) leave in the morning to go to work, or the other way around. These are the messages their open minds take in.

Whispered secrets, sleepovers, and shared stories are just some of the ways young girls learn how to bond with each other. And girls also learn that excluding another girl can be powerful, and that not acting or looking or dressing a certain way can make you unpopular. Whether they pick out their own clothing or someone provides it, girls are likely to be presented with clothing options that, even in elementary school, show off some part of their bodies. Will girls run as well in short skirts and sparkly flip-flops during recess, or will they already realize clothing can restrict and influence their behavior?

At young ages, girls absorb messages about their bodies—usually that thinness and being small fits best with the archetypes of femininity. Loving candy and ice cream is pretty typical for most kids, but will a young girl be told sooner than her brother that keeping herself slim is important? Will she be sent off to dance class while he goes to tae kwon do, and would it be okay if their roles were switched?

As girls mature into young women and enter adolescence, the physical changes of teenhood accelerate them into awareness of the body as a site of sexuality. Will this girl be proud of her changing body's size and shape? Will she be catcalled on sidewalks, or in the school hallway, as a matter of course? Will she be able to sit anywhere she wants in the lunchroom at school, or will some groups be unwelcoming? And will she be safe walking home alone at night, or will she be more at risk than her brother simply because she is a girl?

If she's good at school, will her decision about which field to pursue be nudged one direction or another because certain fields, such as literature, seem more available to girls? Will she have role models in her math and science classes or see other women who are making strides in these disciplines? Will she be told, subtly or overtly, by her family that going to college doesn't matter so much because they can't afford to send her, or because her real destiny is to become a mother? Will it be uncomfortable for her to be too ambitious or too smart?

Television commercials don't feature men talking about how a cleaning product allowed them to get the sink cleaner than it has ever been before. Newspaper photos of a summit of world leaders feature few, if any, women in the room. Children hear terms such as "fireman" and "waitress," but they may never hear a female pilot make the announcement that a plane is on course. These are just a few of the subtle ways in which girls learn how their gender (broadly defined as the sets of behaviors, expectations, and limitations imposed by culture on girls and boys simply because they are female or male) defines the roles available to them. The messages start in infancy, and they continue steadily, filtering into girls' consciousnesses so that they think these definitions simply seem to be just "the way that things are."

But how did these messages get there, and why do they seem to be the status quo? Why does pink persist? Why "sugar and spice and everything nice," as the old-fashioned, but still recited, verse goes? How *do* we define what it means to be a girl? What remains to define girlhood if there are no barriers to achievement or restrictions left, as girls are now often told—and is that statement actually true? At a time when many people think that we're "beyond" gender restrictiveness—that the glass ceiling has been shattered and girls can do anything—it's important to look closely at how understandings of gender have been shaped, and whether they have shifted from traditional expectations into new definitions, or whether they are just slightly changed variations.

This book looks specifically at the "gendering" experiences of girls in the United States, starting at the earliest moments of their lives and continuing into their transformations to young women, and then women. (The word "girls" will be used to encompass anyone between the ages of zero and eighteen who is born with female secondary

Why Study Girls?

Girls' studies is an academic field that specifically considers the experience of gendering girls, starting at the earliest moments of their lives and continuing into their transformation to young women. Historically, studies that explore "childhood" broadly, or the experience of growing up generally, have often been biased to represent the experiences of boys. Separating out the realities within girls' lives uncovers new issues, topics, and concerns that are unique to being female and brings attention to experiences that might otherwise be subsumed into what are considered "standard" experiences of childhood, which presume the experience of boys to be the norm.

In the 1950s, phrases such as "date rape," "domestic violence," and "sexual harassment" weren't part of contemporary America's lexicon (though many women experienced these things). As women's experiences were brought to the fore by feminists in the 1960s and 1970s, names for these phenomena entered the public's vocabulary. So it is with the many feminist perspectives on girlhood, which are united in recognizing that the experiences of girls are unique compared to those of boys, though they are often subsumed into broader categories that ignore the specifics of gender. Attention to girls has brought new focus on classroom dynamics—for example, how often boys call out answers without raising their hands, or interrupt and cut off conversation, and how teachers too

sexual characteristics, or who identifies herself as female.) There are no clear lines of demarcation between these stages, which can vary greatly from culture to subculture; the passage from childhood to adulthood—whether male or female—can differ so widely that it would be impossible to pinpoint or categorize all the variations here. Even within the United States there is a huge range of cultural markers that separate girlhood from womanhood, varying from a bat mitzvah to a *quinceañera* to a debutante ball to a sweet sixteen celebration. When girls feel "grown up," or they're told they are, is also another matter. When they are allowed to wear makeup, get a tattoo, babysit, hold a job, often let this pass as "normal" while girls in the same classroom might not receive equal time. Scholars and writers have focused further on the "gendering" of certain fields—such as math and science—and how often students are informed (usually subtly) that one area is more suited to one gender than another.

Thinking through how girls interact differently from how boys do—in a broad sense—has opened up a conversation about what the needs of girls are and the unique joys they also experience as they move from childhood through adolescence. There's never one prescription for this, but separating girls out for study has spotlighted some areas that were long disregarded, such as girls' risk for eating disorders, or the ways that media and cultural sexualization of women harms girls' self-esteem. It has also highlighted other important realities of girls' lives—how resilient girls can be, how much they often take on, how important female friendship is, how they learn to grow an emotional center within themselves as they meet challenges, and the place they hold within their families.

Still young, the field of girls' studies is a new one—as of 2009, it's less than twenty years old, still in the range of its own girlhood. It is generally considered to be a subfield of gender studies and women's studies, and scholars who study girlhood are often found among a range of departments: history, popular studies, or the social sciences. A college course on this topic might be found in the gender and women's studies department, or history, or American studies, or with a focus on literature for girls in English.

go on dates, or take on new responsibilities, such as parenting, varies widely. The process of moving from girl to woman is often traveled by meeting challenges and finding rewards as girls gain independence and learn what their changing bodies and changing roles mean—for each girl individually as well as within the varied cultures in which she participates and her identity as a woman is formed.

Lauren Greenfield's 2002 photo-essay book *Girl Culture* includes images of girls of all ages, from across America, representing different facets of the complicated prism of contemporary girlhood. Greenfield's book explores girlhood years from multiple angles: She examines what popularity looks like as she photographs cliques in a middle school cafeteria, and she asks what it means to be attractive through images of hooting men gesturing toward a bikini-clad girl on a spring break boardwalk. A rail-thin nineteen-year-old white teenager in New York City explains that her parents value education over looks, but she wants to explore how far she can go within the world of modeling, and she knows some boys want her on their arms for the prestige she adds. Mary Cady, a white, upper-class, eighteen-year-old self-described "Southern belle," insists that her future husband will make all the decisions in their marriage because she's "a typical Southern girl. A lady." Nkechi, an eighteen-year-old Los Angeles girl whose parents emigrated from Nigeria, is pictured after a prom makeover she was selected for. "Looks are important to American girls," she comments. "I'm glad I was raised in a different culture, because my mother kept emphasizing that [looks are] not that important. . . . If you're brought up here, you're taught that you have to look good to succeed, that beauty gets you what you want and gets you where you need to go. I don't worry about being beautiful, because I just make myself feel beautiful. Whatever I wear, I make sure I feel good in it. It's the way you carry yourself."

These girls reveal how stereotypical feminine values, despite variation from cultural region to region, have been stamped into their psyches, and consequently, into their bodies and into their future expectations for themselves. This book will further explore what that means—how the power and danger of female sexuality has been engraved into girls' minds before adolescence even begins to change their bodies, as seen in the image of four-year-old Allegra, posing with her hand on her hip, microphone to her mouth, as she "plays" at being a provocative singer in a skimpy, glittery outfit. A simple walk to a local mall to look at the slogans found on T-shirts for girls—Precious; Sweet & Sassy; Pop Star; Girls Rule, Boys Drool—raises the question: Why these messages? And no matter how "innocent" it might seem to show these slogans to the world, what inner impressions on girls, and the world at large, do they leave?

A walk down the aisles at any toy store reveals how toys are assigned to genders and what activities are then encouraged or discouraged. Why is there still no cookware set advertised with a boy serving a make-believe dinner? Why do toy companies market makeup kits and nail polish to preschool-aged girls? And if some stores offer chemistry lab sets and beginner toolboxes geared toward girls, why are they packaged in shades of purple and pink? Why make them gender specific at all?

Lessons in Toys: The Socialization of Girls

A doll. A truck. An Easy-Bake oven or an erector set. The Hardy Boys or Nancy Drew. Bratz or Thomas the Tank Engine.

One of the common beliefs about childhood is that it's a time in which children are free—free to use their imaginations to think up anything, free to try on different identities, free to roam in their play, habits, dress, to experiment and figure out who they are as they experience the world openly.

Yet from the time a parent acquires the first toy or article of clothing for a baby, a gender script is already being imposed, often unconsciously, by adults who replicate standards and assumptions that seem too common to question. Even before a baby's birth, when parents post a registry or attend a baby shower for their child-to-be, presents flow in (or are picked out) in preset gender schemes. If, more rarely these days, parents don't want to know the child's sex, a color that is deemed "acceptable" for either might be picked: yellow, perhaps white or green, but the mere concept that colors are sorted out into preassigned designations for boy or girl reveals a gender coding already at work. When girls' blankets and baby clothes come embellished with flowers, and boys' with tiny symbols of maleness (a wrench, truck, or hammer), does the newly minted child truly ever explore his or her own desires? Roughly $12 billion per year in the United States is spent on advertising and marketing to children: According to sociologist Juliet B. Schor's *Born to Buy: The Commercialized Child and the New Consumer Culture*, advertisers spend more than $150 per boy and girl in the United States.

Some parents will argue that a set of XY chromosomes or XX predetermine who has the "truck gene" and who has the "doll gene"—an essentialist attitude (meaning that certain qualities are naturally intrinsic to each gender), which means girls simply are one way and boys another. Those who study gender and think through its development as a social construct tend to disagree. What can be measured, however, is not inherent genetic predilection, but rather what children are given to play with, exposed to, offered, and encouraged to participate with when considering how they form their likes and dislikes, preferences and refusals. Marketers, advertisers, and the media are all invested in offering gender-specific toys, games, and myriad other products to increase revenue and convince parents that their children's play cannot be unisex. And adults, whether consciously or unconsciously, replicate gender typing and encourage differences that lead to the development of gender awareness. The "choices" that children may seem to make when left alone with a roomful of toys can be realized as nonchoices in light of how much gender scripting they have, at remarkably early ages, already absorbed.

Sharon Lamb and Lyn Mikel Brown, in their instructive book *Packaging Girlhood: Rescuing Our Daughters from Marketers' Schemes,* cite a flyer for a Fisher Price dollhouse from 2002: "Little girls love to play with dollhouses. . . . It's their way of learning about who they are and who they might be someday!" The text continues, "Making decisions about what kind of furniture she likes and where it should go puts your little girl in control. . . . The road to imaginative fun and adventure is just ahead . . . recreating the familiar—like running errands around town. . . . Make her house a home with lots of Loving Family accessories."

What does this tell girls other than that they are bound to be keepers of the domestic sphere? When "the road to imaginative fun" is followed by the phrase "recreating the familiar," the assumption is that girls/women run errands around town by day rather than working at their careers. Historically, children have always been given gender-specific toys, often alongside the message that the toy was preparation for the adult roles they were expected to fulfill: for girls, motherhood (hence dolls) and domestic duties (hence play cookware or decorating/ decorative sets), and for boys, building blocks or cars and trucks, building or erector sets, sports gear, action figures.

A quick browse through the aisles marked for girls at almost any store reveals that pink and purple (in a variety of shades) are the dominant colors used for packaging and marketing, with flowers, stars, and sometimes rainbows often used for adornment and embellishment. The theme of motherhood is pervasive—girls have the option of a multitude of dolls to choose from (with more ethnicities represented than ever before, but still a minority), but preparation for motherhood is a central tenet: Dolls are made to be fed, have diapers changed, are in need of strollers, bibs, high chairs, and more. Girls are taught to take pride in nurturing at this early age, and that this is their expected role.

It's worth noting that gender typing is more restricted for boys at this juncture. A girl is often told (and allowed) to cross over to some "boys' activities," even if gender coding is still embedded into the products themselves—often through color choice and detail; for example, she might play with a hot-pink truck or flower-decorated cars. But boys are, generally speaking, still disallowed from having dolls or using the many home maintenance sets girls are offered. The mere fact that in a toy store, whether large or small, or in online shopping, toys for children are categorized into "boys'" and "girls'" reveals how divided American culture is over what can and should be offered for play and development. The taboo that boys still feel about crossing over the aisle, or what girls might feel about a "boys" toy, is simple proof that these stereotypes still prevail.

The emphasis on girls' appearance also begins when they are shockingly young. Girls are offered brushes, "makeup," hair accessories, nail polish, and other grooming kits from a very young age, all with the implicit (and explicit) message that this is one way in which to fulfill their femininity and that attention to one's looks is a worthy pastime, one that is appropriate to "play" at in preparation for a lifetime of brushing on mascara and "playing" with one's hair. Similarly, purses, jewelry, and other accessories are offered to girls at a remarkably young age as they receive the message that these are an expected part of a feminine "costume" and well-dressed experience. The ubiquitous princess is another distinct marker for girls' toys and marketing, selling the idea that girls are princesses and should consider themselves as such (with all the attendant themes that accompany this narrative—a prince to the rescue, socialized passivity, and the need for saving in the first place). Crafts are considered an acceptable way for girls to play and a range of kits that often connect to the domestic sphere are available: soap making, beading, jewelry making, sewing, and frame making, to name but a few. The dollhouse is another symbol through which girls learn an association: They can decorate, move their dolls around to enact a narrative of home life, and thereby learn that caretaking of a home is their responsibility. In parallel form, toys for cooking, cleaning, and entertaining are often available. Girls' cook sets, toy stoves, shopping carts, or miniature vacuum cleaners, mops, brooms, and dustpans are offered to girls along with dishes for the stereotypical tea party.

Few toys offered to girls offer intellectual challenges, emphasize exploration or adventure, assume leadership, or goad girls into action. This conditioning seeps in and in a world where the refrain "but all opportunities are open to girls now" is heard, it's important to think back to how messages (and which messages) are first imprinted and to the preparation for what kinds of roles these toys serve.

A 1997 study produced at the Renfrew Center argues that toys for girls are often damaging to their self-esteem. The report references "an electronic phone game where the object is to find the perfect boyfriend, to accessory toys in which the winner succeeds by putting on the most makeup or jewelry in the fastest time" and "The message that kids are getting at an early age from these toys is that this is what women and girls do best," says Adrienne Ressler, body image specialist for the Renfrew Center, nationally known as the country's first residential facility for adolescents and adult women with eating disorders. "Shopping for clothes, applying makeup and jewelry, or dating to meet a husband is often the object of the toy or game. This type of activity, combined with cultural messages about beauty that we receive from magazines and television, . . . can promote thinking that sets the stage for addictions or patterns of disordered eating." Clinicians found that "90 percent of the toys and dolls surveyed for girls ages two to ten years emphasize beauty, shopping, and dating. In one shopping mall game surveyed, the stores include a beauty salon, a bridal shop, a store with glamorous gowns, and one for pretty ballerinas. In another game, the object is for the girls to buy the most items in the shortest amount of time." And all of this comes at a time when many people would deny that there is still a glass ceiling for women, or that gender discrepancy is still a legitimate concern.

Mixed Messages: What's a Girl To Think?

Looking at how stereotypical femininity is taught to girls across a range of topics shows some of the more subtle ways in which this engraving process works. Conduct manuals are no longer offered to "developing young ladies" as they were a century ago, but American culture is adept at communicating its lessons of stereotypical femininity just as effectively, if not more insidiously. In the 2006 *New York Times* article "What's Wrong with Cinderella?" journalist Peggy Orenstein explores how impossible it is to shield her young Japanese-Jewish daughter from the (often Aryan-centric) "princess culture" that pervades the products, as well as the subtle and overt messages that her daughter is presented with. Her own desire to provide her child with stronger role models than princesses who need saving is met with resistance from a culture that, at large, wants to promote the stereotypical feminine values Disney princesses represent. Orenstein writes, "There are no studies proving that playing princess directly damages girls' self-esteem or dampens other aspirations. Yet there is evidence that young women who hold the most conventionally feminine beliefs—who avoid conflict and think they should be perpetually nice and pretty—are more likely to be depressed than others and less likely to use contraception. What's more, the 23 percent decline in girls' participation in sports and other vigorous activity between middle and high school has been linked to their sense that athletics is unfeminine." She also cites a study by the advocacy organization Girls, Inc. that underscores the pressure many girls feel to be "perfect": not only to get good grades and be leaders, but also to be pleasing to everyone, attractive, and well liked.

The messages given to girls in America are often deeply conflicted. They are told they can and should be sexy and attractive—but they are condemned for being sexually active or a "slut" while boys are lauded for their prowess. Girls are told they can be leaders and it's okay to be smart, but they may then be critiqued for being too ambitious or pushy, a process that doesn't necessarily stop when they grow into women. For example, during the 2008 election year, U.S. Senator Hillary Clinton's presidential campaign was closely watched for signs of sexist media coverage and the public's response to it. Clinton was scrutinized on levels many thought her male counterparts were not: Her style was called "aggressive" or her personality "bitchy," while these traits, often given different labels, were likely to be seen as positives in her male counterparts. Clinton's laugh was called an offensive "cackle," and her style of dress, hair, and personal appearance were often subject to levels of attention and criticism that her male peers never experienced. A novelty nutcracker in the shape of her body came onto the market, with the implication that she would crush nuts—as in, male testicles—handily between her legs. The nutcracker was sold widely online and in shops as a "gag" gift item, albeit one that "played" with Clinton's ability to wield political power, which seemed to make some people uncomfortable and others proud to see such a powerful female candidate. It often wasn't Clinton's platform that generated discussion as much as the mere fact of her presence—a strong woman candidate who would not conform to certain stereotypical expectations, as shown by the discussion around merely having a female candidate—proof that this is not yet the expectation or the "norm."

Girls are bombarded with contradictory messages. Accept and embrace your body and sexuality, they are told—but within a society that follows a heterosexist script. Love your body as it is, girls are reminded—but images in magazines and advertisements consistently celebrate white, able-bodied, rail-thin women. Be proud of your ambition and your intellect—but being too aggressive will scare off boys, and it's not acceptable to brag. Decades of social gains have been made through the civil rights and feminist movements, but the world into which girls are born is still shaped by systemic sexism, homophobia, racism, classism, and ableism.

Told that they can do and be anything, girls later enter a job market where as women they are still not, dollar for dollar, paid equally with men. Told that motherhood and working need not be exclusive or even difficult, they still live within a country without clear or generous maternity leave. Told that their leadership is welcome, they still live in a system that has yet to elect its first female president, where governmental representation is lopsided by gender, and where the business world still claims scant few female CEOs.

The mixed messages girls are given can act like a vise. Turn one way and certain restrictions tighten; turn the other, and a different hook catches—often making adolescence a treacherous path to navigate with few ways to turn.

Investigating Girlhood

In the early 1990s, newfound attention was being paid to girls. It was more than 20 years past the peak years of the civil rights movement and the "second wave" of the feminist movement, and assumptions about gender roles had, for many Americans, moved from the polarized positions that had firmly fixed "male" and "female" at different ends of a spectrum. The roles men and women inhabited had begun to shift, with more doors opening for women—in education, in the workforce, in maintaining a career alongside a family, if they chose—and there was a more general expectation that men, if they had kids, would be involved parents and might not want to commit themselves only to their careers. Fields that had once been divided by gender had begun to show more flexibility, although more change was still ahead.

In 1972 the album *Free to Be . . . You and Me* was released, followed two years later by a television special. The album was created by

The Politics of Language: What Does "Girl" Mean?

"Girl." "Woman." "Lady." "Young woman." "Little lady." What makes the difference between these words? In women's studies and gender classes I've taught, I like to do an exercise with my students in which we describe what we envision when we hear each of these terms. Not surprisingly, a "lady" seems older, better dressed, more prim and proper in her physical appearance and her demeanor. A woman might be a mother, my students often say; she holds a job, and she could be anywhere from twenty-one to a much older age.

But who's a girl? This term often gathers the widest responses—a girl might be your teenage younger sister, newborn niece, or your grandmother who likes to hang out on the porch of her apartment complex with her friends, "the girls." "Girls' night out" might apply to people in their twenties, or a "girls' weekend away" might mean middle-aged moms getting together while their partners babysit. "She decided to go to an 'all-girls' college'" is something you might hear, in contrast to "he went to a men's college."

"Have your girl contact my girl" once would have been commonly heard in business contexts; "the girls in the office" wasn't an unusual way to hear adult secretaries and assistants referred to, with the presumption being that support staff were female, and bosses were male.

Does language matter? And to whom? Do the ways in which we label people, events, instances in our lives change the way we think or feel about them? What happens when we clarify things through our words and take on the associations and nuances that words confer through cultural context?

To that end, when does it become important to call someone a woman, rather than a girl? And what defines a lady? What happens when men and boys call each other girls or women (as California Governor Arnold Schwarzenegger has done for comic effect in his political career)? Why is it so shaming? If a boy tells another boy "You throw like a girl," why is it an insult?

Many girls call each other "guys" or "dude," but boys or men are usually insulted if called "girls" or "women." The use of the "universal he" as the default pronoun for all people is still considered standard. And while a "mailman" is just as likely to be female these days, "mailwoman" isn't usually heard. How does it affect the public's mind, knowing that women are subsumed through language into a male standard? Would it seem strange if every place the word "man" was used to mean all people was switched out with "women"? What does this say about how the category of being female is considered?

In August of 2007 the AP reported in a story titled "Thai Police to Sport 'Hello Kitty' Armbands" (it ran on MSNBC) that the police department in Bangkok, Thailand, implemented use of a bright-pink "Hello Kitty" armband as a punishment technique for officers who broke rules. If an officer was late to work or parked in the wrong place, among other offenses, he was made to wear the armband as a sign of humiliation. "This new twist is expected to make them feel guilt and shame and prevent them from repeating the offense, no matter how minor," said Pongpat Chayaphan, acting chief of the Crime Suppression Division in Bangkok, explaining, "Kitty is a cute icon for young girls. It's not something macho police officers want covering their biceps."

Why is it humiliating for a man to don a pink armband marketed to girls, and why is it an insult for men to be called "girls"? Are there equivalent embarrassments for girls or women, or, again, is it okay for them to be called by male names? ("Hi, you guys!") Boys know that being called a girl is being called "less than." Reflecting on the power of naming and the ways in which certain labels are considered acceptable and others are considered insulting reveals the ways gender stereotypes influence our cultural mores.

Lebanese-Italian American actress and children's author Marlo Thomas, who wanted to teach her young niece that it was okay to eschew traditional stereotypes, particularly those presented in children's books at that time. The songs on the album included "William's Doll," the tale of a boy who wants his own doll, and "Parents Are People," which introduced nonstereotypical jobs for moms and dads, and an ironic tune, "Ladies First," that satirized the idea that girls should always be first in line. The album was a hit, and its songs—and more significantly, their messages—became part of a new consciousness that advocated edging away from traditional gender stereotypes.

With the reverberations of the social justice movements behind them, in the 1980s and 1990s new generations were still seeking ways to redefine gender and bring stereotypes into new focus. Different groups of academics began to ask: What happened to girls before they became women? Was boys' behavior considered the standard in education— just as in medical research, what was once generally considered right for men's bodies was broadly considered simply applicable to women's bodies as well? Was the experience of girlhood radically different from boyhood, and did writing about "childhood" and the educational experiences of children presume male bias?

A report commissioned and then published by the American Association of University Women (AAUW) in 1991—titled *Shortchanging Girls, Shortchanging America*—attempted to address these questions and to bring public attention to the experiences of girls. Beginning in 1990, the *Shortchanging Girls* researchers interviewed nearly three thousand boys and girls, between nine and fifteen years old, of a variety of races and ethnicities and from a variety of regions, to examine "the comparative self-esteem levels, career aspirations, educational experiences, and math/science interests of American girls and boys" and ascertain "the impact of gender on their self-confidence, academic interests, and career goals." According to the organization's website, *Shortchanging Girls* "was the first national survey to link the sharp drop in self-esteem suffered by pre-adolescent and adolescent American girls to what they learn in the classroom"; the results "shook

America's consciousness" and paved the way for later AAUW studies such as *How Schools Shortchange Girls: The AAUW Report*, which synthesized data from more than thirteen hundred published studies on girls in school.

The landmark 1991 study linked the drop in self-esteem that girls experience as they reach adolescence to their experiences in the classroom. The poll also confirmed a growing body of research that indicates that girls are systematically, if unintentionally, discouraged from a wide range of academic pursuits—particularly in math and science.

The *Shortchanging Girls* researchers examined the differences between girls' and boys' perceptions of themselves and their futures and identified how adolescents develop self-esteem and identity. Researchers also considered how and when loss of self-esteem translates into loss of action—girls simply not doing things at all or feeling that they couldn't do things well. They asked adolescents about physical changes, and whether they perceived them positively or negatively, and found that boys were more likely to view physical changes positively—and girls less so, as they absorbed the message that their physical appearance was important. Researchers considered the development of adolescents' aspirations and the part schools play in forming adolescents' career choices, expectations, and perceptions of gender roles. And finally, the survey examined the relationship of math and science skills to the self-esteem and career goals of the girls and boys.

In *Shortchanging Girls, Shortchanging America,* researchers found that boys were far more likely to say that they were "pretty good at a lot of things" and twice as likely to name their talents as the thing they liked most about themselves. They also discovered that girls were more likely than boys to say that they were "not smart enough" or "not good enough" to realize their dreams. And according to the report's executive summary, researchers also found that issues of race influence girls' self-assessment and confidence. They found that from elementary through high school, black girls showed high levels of self-esteem and personal importance because of strong family and community reinforcement, although their positive feelings about school and their teachers dropped. Meanwhile, "Hispanic girls are much less confident and positive than black girls and go through a crisis in some ways even more profound than that of white girls. While Hispanic girls start with significantly higher levels of self-esteem than white girls, their confidence plummets in their appearance, family relationships, school ability, talents, and importance. Between elementary school and high school, their personal self-esteem drops 38 points, more than the drop for any other group of girls."

Why all of these deflating findings? And how did they come to be? *Shortchanging Girls, Shortchanging America* connects girls' drop in self-esteem and lower aspirations to a popular culture that marginalizes women and stereotypes their roles. "Unintentionally," the authors state in the report's summary, "schools collude in the process by systematically cheating girls of classroom attention, by stressing competitive—rather than cooperative—learning, by presenting texts and lessons devoid of women as role models, and by reinforcing negative stereotypes about girls' abilities. Unconsciously, teachers and school counselors also dampen girls' aspirations, particularly in math and science." The report revealed that sexist practices were at work in the classroom, with girls often called on less frequently than boys, and their responses not taken as seriously. "Routine behaviors" within the classroom—such as boys calling out answers and gaining a teacher's attention, in contrast to girls who called out being told to raise their hands if they wanted to speak—were highlighted in the report, along with gender-insensitive curriculum, testing, and other policies shown to disadvantage girls in ways not previously recognized because they were so routine. The AAUW cites the work of education specialists Myra and David Sadker, who note that teachers more often initiated interactions with boys, "strengthening boys' sense of importance," and tended to praise boys for "the intellectual content and quality of their work" while girls were more often praised for neatness and form. The Sadkers also mention that when boys performed poorly, teachers were more likely to attribute this to lack of effort, whereas girls subtly received the message that effort would not improve their results. The drop in self-esteem that girls experienced, along with institutionalized sexism, had, unsurprisingly, long-lasting impact. Girls were both overtly and covertly discouraged from pursuit of hard sciences and math, researchers found, and the report predicted long-lasting consequences for gender equity in these fields, never mind the loss of opportunity for girls who want to begin careers within them.

Suddenly, focus on girls' lives—their self-esteem and ambition, expectations they kept for themselves and those that society held out for them—was of critical concern. Following on the heels of its first study, in 1992 the AAUW released another, titled *How Schools Shortchange Girls*. The authors stated that their work was prompted in part by the fact that in 1990 and 1991, broad educational goals and plans advanced by both the National Governors Association and the Department of Education failed to make "any mention of providing girls equitable opportunities in the nation's public schools." Girls were being left out of consideration for educational reform, despite the establishment of routinized gender bias in the classroom. In this new study AAUW researchers examined the educational experiences of girls from kindergarten through twelfth grade, revealing more startling inequities and asking for further educational reform from a system that, they posited, incorporated routine gender bias against girls, resulting in an educational experience that was far from equal. They reemphasized the lack of attention girls received in favor of boys, and they provided more data about gender gaps in math and the sciences. The study also found that "African American girls are more likely than white girls to be rebuffed by teachers; curricula ignore or stereotype women; reports of sexual harassment of girls are increasing; and many standardized tests contain elements of gender bias." All of these factors again were determined to contribute to the undermining of girls' sense of self-esteem and to serve as a deterrent to their academic success, especially within the fields of math and science.

How Schools Shortchange Girls again cites Myra and David Sadker's work on education as proof of educational inequities, stating: "Even when boys do not volunteer, teachers are more likely to encourage them to give an answer or an opinion than they are to encourage girls. Research reveals a tendency, beginning at the preschool level, for educators to choose classroom activities that appeal to boys' interests and to select presentation formats in which boys excel. The teacher-student interaction patterns in science classes are often particularly biased."

According to the report, researchers Sandra Damico, Elois Scott, and Linda Grant found "that African-American girls have fewer interactions with teachers than do white girls, even though they attempted to initiate interaction more often." "Furthermore," these researchers' findings show, "when African-American girls do as well as white boys in school, teachers often attribute their success to hard work while assuming that the white boys are not working up to their potential." The result, the report concluded, was that girls were not graduating from school with the same degree of confidence and self-esteem as boys, and their educations were not equal.

How Schools Shortchange Girls also brought attention to the "routinizing" of sexual harassment: "When sexual harassment is treated casually, as in 'boys will be boys,' both girls and boys get a dangerous, damaging message: 'girls are not worthy of respect; appropriate behavior for boys includes exerting power over girls.'" The report emphasized the need for a representative and diverse curriculum, coining the term "evaded curriculum" to draw attention to the diversity absent in the texts offered to students: "Curriculum delivers the central messages of education," the report explains. "It can strengthen or decrease student motivation for engagement, effort, growth, and development through the images it gives to students about themselves and the world. When the curriculum does not reflect the diversity of students' lives and cultures, it delivers an incomplete message."

In a subsection of the executive summary of *How Schools Shortchange Girls* titled "How Do Race/Ethnicity and Socioeconomic Status Affect Achievement in School?" the authors report that girls from low-income families face particularly severe obstacles. "Socioeconomic status, more than any other variable, affects access to school resources and educational outcomes," they write, continuing, "Test scores of low-socioeconomic-status girls are somewhat better than for boys from the same background in the lower grades, but by high school these differences disappear. Among high-socioeconomic status students, boys generally outperform girls regardless of race/ethnicity."

How Schools Shortchange Girls also called for attention to be given to issues of gender and power, explaining that girls grow and graduate into a culture that "both idealizes and exploits the sexuality of young women while assigning them roles that are clearly less valued than male roles." The authors continue, "If we do not begin to discuss more openly the ways in which ascribed power—whether on the basis of race, sex, class, sexual orientation, or religion—affects individual lives, we cannot truly prepare our students for responsible citizenship."

Again, the ways in which girls were shortchanged by schools were met with growing concern, as it came to light that the girl sitting quietly in a corner of the class, although not openly looking distressed, might be in need of help. The revelation of institutionalized expectations for girls—the belief that they would excel in language arts, not sciences; the perception that they "needed less" than boys academically, and hence were often shortchanged; the fact that they were subtly rewarded for passive behavior that muted their questions and quelled their exuberance (while boys' disruptions were considered "standard behavior")—prompted new critical views of the American classroom among parents and teachers, and especially among feminist scholars, who realized the stereotypical behavior that many girls were rewarded for—being quiet, obedient, unquestioning, and unargumentative—was at odds with receiving the full education they deserved. By 1994, concern sparked by the *Shortchanging Girls* poll and later research had helped promote heightened sensitivity to the needs of girls, manifesting in such developments as Take Our Daughters to Work Day—and the AAUW's research on girls resulted in gender equity provisions being included in the 1994 U.S. federal education reform act.

The two AAUW reports were followed shortly thereafter by two key texts by psychologists: the reissuing of Carol Gilligan's *In a*

Intersectionality

The category of "girl," of course, can mean many different things. Girls come in all shapes and sizes and from many backgrounds. Within the United States itself are multiple ethnicities and identities that form the melting pot that is America. Although girls all share the experience of being gendered, how other elements combine in their lives, such as ethnicity and personal ability, or class and race, is highly individual. In academic circles the understanding that each individual's experiences within the world intertwine, sometimes harmoniously, and sometimes disynchronously, is called "intersectionality theory," a term first attributed to Kimberlé Crenshaw and made better known by Patricia Hill Collins.

The history of feminism is long and varied, but the idea that historically, mainly white middle-class women have been at the foundation of this movement is one that began to be questioned in the 1960s and 1970s. Women began to consider how to be more inclusive of women of different backgrounds and ethnicities and to recognize that the experiences women have are hardly homogenous, and that concentric imprints of identity make up each individual. Any person will feel the influence of gender, race, sexual orientation, class, religion, ability, ethnicity, and possibly more as she brings together all the parts that compose her life and identity. How these

Different Voice in 1993 and Mary Pipher's *Reviving Ophelia* in 1994. Author Peggy Orenstein's book *Schoolgirls: Young Women, Self-Esteem, and the Confidence Gap*, published in 1994 (in association with the AAUW), also had a large impact. Each brought newfound attention to the plight of girls in educational contexts and sudden awareness of their emotional transitions through adolescence.

Both AAUW reports had related girls' loss of a sense of competence and drop in self-esteem to their environments—particularly within the dynamics of the classroom and institution of school. Gilligan's work, and Pipher's, revealed more explicitly how girls stopped themselves from reaching toward their dreams and aspirations, often to meet a code of feminine behavior they felt obligated to hew to more closely influences interact with one another, sometimes in overlapping systems of oppression, is another way of understanding intersectionality.

When thinking about girls in America, it's important to keep this in mind. "American girl" can mean so many things—there is no one standard. Some girls are part of an ethnic majority, some a minority, some are walking a line between traditions they want to honor that might conflict with contemporary teenage values. Some girls, who were not originally born in the United States but who emigrated might feel caught between countries with differing national and cultural traditions. Thinking about where a girl feels comfortable, and where she can feel wholly herself, is critical for determining perspective—does she feel that she's at the margins of her school's social circles, and why? Is she comfortable at the center? When experts speak or write about the plight of the "American girl," it's important to consider how inclusive the study is. Does it include girls from diverse geographic regions or socioeconomic classes? If not, can it be considered a representative study? Feminist writers, such as the African American scholar bell hooks, or the Chicana theorist Gloria Anzaldúa, have brought deeper awareness of how race and ethnicity intertwine with gender as they write about what it is like to hold a position of identity situated outside or at the border of traditional American society—and how complex, sometimes conflicted, and yet enriching, this can feel.

in adolescence. As girls move into their teenage years, Gilligan and Pipher asserted, they encounter a more specific script—one in which their achievements are not necessarily celebrated nor their ambition rewarded. Rather, in adopting the traits of traditional femininity, girls realize they must mute certain behaviors, and their understanding that they must take on these new traits often leaves girls feeling confused as they realize they might have to leave parts of their previous identity behind as they adapt to new roles.

Both psychologists' books, Pipher's *Reviving Ophelia* and Gilligan's *In a Different Voice,* describe adolescent girls losing the sense of power they experience when younger. The AAUW research corroborated these findings, looking particularly at how they manifest within school

Girls and Poverty in the United States

Within the United States, girls live in many different socioeconomic brackets and within many different family arrangements. Socioeconomic status affects children's access to schools and educational resources and can have a great impact on the educational level they reach. The National Center for Children in Poverty, a research and advocacy organization, puts the percentage of children in low-income families at 39 percent, explaining: "Most of these children have parents who work, but low wages and unstable employment leave their families struggling to make ends meet. Poverty can impede children's ability to learn and contribute to social, emotional, and behavioral problems. Poverty also can contribute to poor health and mental health. Risks are greatest for children who experience poverty when they are young and/or deep and persistent poverty."

In the 1992 AAUW report *How Schools Shortchange Girls*, researchers report, "In a recent study, 37 percent of the female dropouts compared to only 5 percent of the male dropouts cited 'family-related problems' as the reason they left high school. Traditional gender roles place greater family responsibilities on adolescent girls than on their brothers. Girls are often expected to 'help out' with caretaking responsibilities; boys rarely encounter this expectation."

ChildStats.gov, the website for the Federal Interagency Forum on Child and Family Statistics, comprises a "working group of federal agencies that collect, analyze, and report data on issues related to children and families." It paints a bleak picture of how many children in the United States are facing serious economic difficulties: In 2004 and 2005, 18 percent of all children ages 0–17 lived in poverty, and more black and Hispanic than white children did so. In 2005, 10 percent of white, 28 percent of Hispanic, and 35 percent of black children lived in poverty.

settings: As girls in the study grew into adolescence, for example, rather than saying they were good at things—and risking the "unfeminine" act of bragging about or exaggerating their merits—they were more likely to diminish their accomplishments or to back away from competitive activities and avoid seeking out achievement. Downwardly spiraling self-esteem left girls undermining their skills and succumbing to a blanket sense that their powers were best not mentioned, whereas boys were far more likely to see their skills through an inflated lens. A constellation of influences, some overt, most covert, seemed to conspire to tell girls that boys were more central—and a world of cultural expectations, with sources in popular culture, family, religion, and elsewhere, tacitly complied with this vision.

In 1994, journalist Peggy Orenstein published *Schoolgirls: Young Women, Self-Esteem, and the Confidence Gap,* in which she used the AAUW reports as a starting point to see if their findings were borne out in two California middle schools, which she visited for a year to do original research. The simple answer? Yes. As Orenstein spent time in the eighth-grade classrooms of the two public schools—both with diverse economic and racial compositions, one in a suburban and one in an urban setting—she realized that "the strands that make up the self are intricately interwoven. They include school, but they also include family life. They encompass the ways boys treat girls as well as girls' reaction to emerging sexual desire and new consciousness of sexual exploitation and abuse." Orenstein writes that when the girls in the AAUW survey entered adolescence and began the process of becoming women, they discovered "in a new and profound way that boys are still central in every aspect of the culture. I began to wonder, if girls feel a reduced sense of self, how is that expressed in their attitudes towards all the vital threads of their lives?"

Orenstein's book creates a narrative for the AAUW reports' findings as she sees the reported statistics played out in girls who are struggling with success and failure, coasting waves of self-esteem and self-doubt, and even more significantly, caught in a conflicted nexus of family expectations for daughters, classroom dynamics with teachers, and sexual tensions found within the school.

Gilligan's *In a Different Voice,* originally published in 1982 and described by Harvard University Press as "the little book that started a revolution," was, in part, a response to the work of psychologist Lawrence Kohlberg, who put forth an influential theory of "stages of moral development" within children. While teaching at Harvard, Gilligan worked with Kohlberg as his research assistant and became familiar with his theories, in response to which she began to develop her own as she realized that girls needed broader representation within the field of psychology. Among other, more commonly cited findings, Kohlberg's research on the issue had concluded that women, on average, reached a lower level of moral development than men did. Gilligan pointed out that the participants in Kohlberg's basic study were largely male, and that the scoring method Kohlberg used tended to favor a way of reasoning that was more common to boys, using argumentation, rather than focusing on relationships, which was more common to girls. The psychological development of girls, Gilligan posited in her book, was different from that of boys, and she put forward that their voices—on multiple levels—went unheard. Her research came to be seen as part of a theoretical foundation that insisted that women's development and reasoning centered around issues different from those of men, and that had to that point been unconsidered.

In a 1993 preface to the book, Gilligan recounts the milestones of the late 1960s and early 1970s, such as the Supreme Court ruling in *Roe v. Wade,* and the gradual realization by many women that they had a voice that didn't have to go unheard in favor of the voices of men. Yet, she said, many women hesitated to exercise their voices against a cultural onus that still told them that their words were not important. "Women often sensed that it was dangerous to say or even to know what they wanted or thought—upsetting to others and therefore carrying with it the threat of abandonment or retaliation," she writes. Her work began to focus on why women kept themselves from speaking out, and how they were told it wasn't permissible to do so.

In the preface, Gilligan also discusses working with educational researcher and activist Lyn Mikel Brown and psychologist Annie Rogers on the Harvard Project on Women's Psychology and the Development of Girls. Taking the voices of adult women as a starting point, they initiated a five-year study of girls aged seven to eighteen, examining how their voices were heard, or not. Their results were published in

1992 by Harvard University Press in *Meeting at the Crossroads: Women's Psychology and Girls' Development*. Gilligan and Brown developed a way of listening to girls that took into account what girls said, in part, by the way they said it—whether they spoke with confidence and assertiveness or not. The considered how girls both literally and figuratively "lost their voices" by not saying things that they felt were now culturally disallowed, but also how a note of confidence or assertion left their speech as they instead experienced disconnection or disassociation from themselves as they faced oncoming adulthood as young women. As Brown, Rogers, and Gilligan accumulated their data, they realized girls were coming "face to face with a social construction of reality that is at odds with their experience." Because girls' passage into adulthood occurs "in a world psychologically rooted and historically anchored in the experiences of powerful men," Gilligan writes in *In a Different Voice*'s 1993 preface, they begin to experience *dissociation,* or "difficulty in hearing or listening to one's voice, the disconnection between mind and body, thoughts and feelings, and the use of one's voice to cover rather than to convey one's inner world." In her work, Gilligan strives to bring these dissociative experiences to light and, as she writes, to confront "a patriarchal order that can remain in place only through the continuing eclipse of women's experience." Gilligan emphasizes that keeping women's experiences at the forefront of awareness—in all fields—is essential to changing what had existed as "set" understandings within many academic areas in which the "standard" set was one of male experience. In the opening up of new understanding to women's ways of being in the world, paradigms can shift. She writes, "Bringing the experiences of girls and women to full light, although in one sense perfectly straightforward, becomes a radical endeavor."

In 1994, also shortly after publication of the AAUW's two key reports, another important book made its way into the national consciousness—psychologist Mary Pipher's *Reviving Ophelia*. Years before the AAUW reports came out, Pipher was gathering case studies about girls' transitions into adolescence through her private practice in Lincoln, Nebraska. Her findings, gathered in *Reviving Ophelia,* catapulted her to fame as another chronicler of the transitional difficulties girls encounter in adolescence. In chapters such as "Drugs and Alcohol: If Ophelia Were Alive Today," and "Worshiping the Gods of Thinness," and "Within the Hurricane—Depression," Pipher summarizes her observations and experiences.

Working primarily, but not exclusively, with the middle-class, mostly white girls Pipher saw in her private practice and at the school where she taught, her research reflects a narrower sample, as well as a pre-Internet, pre–cell phone era. Because her students and clients were primarily from the Midwest, and not ethnically diverse, her findings reflect the localized sample from which she drew her research and may not apply to girls in more urban environments or to girls of differing socioeconomic backgrounds. But the sense of difficulty she reports is nonetheless considered by many to be relevant for numerous girls. "In early adolescence," she writes, "studies show that girls' IQ scores drop and their math and science scores plummet. They lose their resiliency and optimism and become less curious and inclined to take risks. They lose their assertive, energetic and 'tomboyish' personalities and become more deferential, self-critical and depressed. They report great unhappiness with their own bodies."

Interspersing case studies with clinical summaries that articulate girls' lack of resources and the constricting and conflicting messages girls are often sent, Pipher highlights dysfunction that is often systemic, revealing the widespread and long-lasting effects of a culture that denies girls agency, boxes them into uncomfortable squares of traditional femininity, and then also blames them for their constriction. Pipher uses the dramatic figure of Ophelia, from Shakespeare's play *Hamlet,* for her title and as a metaphor and symbol for all girls: Ophelia, happy until adolescence, loses herself as she falls in love with Hamlet, living only for his approval. When she is spurned she goes mad with grief, eventually drowning herself in a stream filled with flowers, weighed down by her elegant clothes.

Pipher has continued to be known as a foundational expert on girls, and her work has opened discussions and further investigations about what girls experience. She writes in the book's preface, "As I looked at the culture that girls enter as they come of age, I was struck by what a girl-poisoning culture it was. . . . America today limits girls' development, truncates their wholeness and leaves many of them traumatized." Pipher explains that American culture "smack[s] girls on the head in early adolescence . . . when they move into a broader culture that is rife with girl-hurting 'isms,' such as sexism, capitalism and lookism, which is the evaluation of a person based solely on the basis of appearance." She articulates one of the essential arguments made for the study of girls—that preadolescent girls are often filled with brash, glorious self-confidence and a sense of grand and unlimited potential. The zest, she states, with which most healthy girls lead their young lives represents a sense of wholeness that becomes gradually fractured as they advance into adolescence—the first chip in their armature irrevocably made when they sense the changing roles ahead of them. Girls' communication becomes "more tentative and less articulate," Pipher writes, as part of their retraining into an adulthood in which women are expected to tamp down their power and self-abnegate, focusing on pleasing others. She refers to the issue as a "problem with no name"—because this process of socialization is regarded as the norm, and those who resist it are the exceptions. Her last chapter reveals examples of girls who navigate the waters of adolescence buoyed by a sense of personal resilience; she also offers prescriptive advice on how to cultivate this resilience for girls, suggesting a move toward more "androgynous" behavior between parents—fathers who do housework, mothers who mow lawns—to teach girls that a spectrum of behaviors and roles is available to every human and not limited by gender.

Observing the disconnect between the traits expected of most women and the traits of assertive girls, Pipher articulates the conflict "between [girls'] autonomous selves and their need to be feminine, between their status as human beings and their vocation as females." Throughout much literature on girlhood, this theme reverberates: the loss of a powerful, confident, fearless childhood self, and the assumption of the mantle of sexualization along with the mores, fears, and expectations of cultural femininity—and for many girls, the sense of a diminished vision of their potential.

So much of the world seems changed since the 1990s, when the AAUW, Pipher, Orenstein, and others published their groundbreaking analyses of American girls' lives. And so much seems the same. On May 1, 2008, columnist Tara Parker-Pope reported in *The New York Times* that 35 percent of middle- and high-school students who were surveyed reported experiencing sexual harassment from their classmates, and that among gay and lesbian students, victimization was as high as 70 percent. Citing a study by Dr. Susan Fineran and James Gruber that surveyed 522 children aged eleven to eighteen, Parker-Pope explained that peer sexual harassment—whether unwanted touching or via mediated means, such as comments on webpages and texting—was "often largely dismissed as normal student behavior by school officials." But, Fineran and Gruber's study concluded, "the emotional toll of sexual harassment by school kids appears to be even worse than physical bullying." Surprisingly, Parker-Pope reported, the researchers found that boys and girls reported equal levels of harassment; unsurprisingly, Fineran and Gruber also concluded that "girls and sexual minorities were far more upset by [the harassment], suffering from lower self-esteem, poorer mental and physical health, and more trauma symptoms." The effects of harassment, while different for each individual, can be long lasting. Boys are more likely to be told or taught to brush off hurtful behavior, while girls are more likely to internalize insults or feel the effects differently. When students who are part of a sexual minority are teased or harassed at school, chances are they are also receiving wider messages from society at large about how their choices deviate from the "standard" and are, therefore, deviant, in a way that leaves them with little support. In the context of the larger culture, harassment at school may just be one part of a circle of affronts that deepen feelings of inadequacy or angst about personal appearance, choices, or lifestyle.

"Schools often focus on general bullying problems," Parker-Pope writes. "But Drs. Fineran and Gruber argue that sexual harassment is a distinct problem that should be addressed separately, in part because laws, particularly the education law known as Title IX, already exists to protect students from sexual discrimination and harassment at school." Fineran elaborates, "Title IX protects everybody in school against this kind of behavior, but as soon as you call something 'bullying,' then it's just viewed as ill behavior that one student does to another student. . . . The school needs to do something about stopping sexual harassment because they're legally bound to."

What About the Boys?

It seemed inevitable. Not long after the publication of *Shortchanging Girls, Shortchanging America* in the early 1990s, voices began to rise asking about the plight of boys. And not long after that, the attention girls were receiving began to be viewed as attention that shortchanged boys, or at least shifted the focus in a way that some saw as unfair.

Many feminists responded simply that this is precisely *why* girl empowerment was needed—because boys routinely receive more attention within a patriarchal society (that is, a society that holds male behavior and needs as standard or higher)—and because construing girls' advancement as detrimental to boys reinforces a polarizing argument positing that advancing one gender comes at the expense of the other. To many girls' advocates, the newfound focus on girls was foremost a way to even out the score and then try to change the game altogether, leveling the playing field (or creating a separate one for girls where none existed before, as with Title IX). To conservative pundits and policymakers, the girls' movement was the work of a handful of feminists who were digging unfairly at a traditional structure and incapacitating and demonizing boys' behavior. Cries of "sexist" switched from girls' advocates to those who now thought that boys were being discriminated against.

No matter which side of the political line, critics routinely agree that the gap between how girls and boys perform in school is closing, with girls pulling ahead of boys in some areas. A June 2006 report from the independent education policy think tank, Education Sector, titled "The Evidence Suggests Otherwise: The Truth About Boys and Girls" and written by Sara Mead, provides recent evidence that girls have narrowed "or even closed some academic gaps that previously favored boys, while other long-standing gaps that favored girls have widened, [such as with reading skills] leading to the belief that boys are falling behind." Yet the report says, "There's no doubt that some groups of boys—particularly Hispanic and black boys and boys from low-income homes—are in real trouble. But the predominant issues for them are race and class, not gender. Closing racial and economic gaps would help poor and minority boys more than closing gender gaps, and focusing on gender gaps may distract attention from the bigger problems facing these youngsters." Ultimately, the report concludes, "The real story is not bad news about boys doing worse; it's good news about girls doing better."

According to the Education Sector's report, boys are less likely to attend and then complete college than girls, and they are far more often diagnosed with attention deficit disorder, labeled as emotionally disturbed, and disciplined within a school setting. Girls' gains that reach ahead of boys in an educational setting seem to be both applauded and condemned by conservatives who see their gains as either demoralizing to boys or derogatory to them, or both. Girls have long outpaced boys in reading and humanities subjects, and the gap is beginning to close in the hard sciences and math, causing acknowledgment of what some want to call "the reverse gap," in which boys now lag behind girls academically and therefore deserve special attention.

In 1994, Congress passed the Gender Equity in Education Act to ban discrimination against girls in school—an important moment that made at least attempting gender parity a law. In rapid response, critics of girl empowerment began to question whether or not the crisis of girls' adolescence was even real. Christina Hoff Sommers, in her 2000 *Atlantic Monthly* article "The War Against Boys," poked what holes she could at the AAUW studies, *Shortchanging Girls, Shortchanging America* and *How Schools Shortchange Girls*, and at other foundational work on girls' self-esteem; if there once was a gender inequality, she posited, it's long been solved. The mere fact that girls outperformed boys academically in some areas reinforced to Sommers that there was, in fact, now no crisis at all and that it was boys who suffered academically and received critically less attention because of the compensatory focus on girls.

Although girls outpace boys in some areas of education, there are a host of other factors to be considered. Boys often outscore girls on standardized tests such as the SAT, and although fewer graduate from college, those who do are bound to earn more than their female peers, since the wage gap is far from being closed, never mind the gender distribution within upper-management positions of power.

The argument gets stickier when one examines the issues behind success in school. Most educational systems reward self-control, concentration, diligence: qualities that girls are taught and assume more often than boys. The "call-out" gap that the AAUW study pointed out reveals how boys are less likely to adhere to "traditional model student behavior" and yet aren't necessarily punished, while girls who defy this code are. Girls' diligence in school may pay off in better grades, but does it come at the cost of reinforcing a stereotypical femininity that works against them once they are out of the school system?

The claim that boys' particular needs aren't being met—a need for more kinetic learning, the chance to move around the classroom more—and that they are punished for their essential "boyness" and stigmatized in a model that praises stereotypical girl behavior is a fraught one. The article "Lost Boys" (written by Amy Benfer and published on Salon.com), covers the rising debate about how boyhood is being viewed, that is, whether or not boys need saving from a traditional patriarchal model that some see as limited or are they just hard-wired to be a certain way. In it, Sommers, a conservative pundit, comments that English classrooms (most often led by female teachers) now often select literature that is of little interest to boys. "Boys love adventure stories with male heroes," says Sommers in "Lost Boys." "Many would love books by Stephen Ambrose and Tom Clancy. Since they are so far behind in reading, why not give them texts they enjoy? Some teachers are promoting political correctness at the expense of the basic literacy of their male students." Sommers describes her tenth-grade son as struggling through Amy Tan's *The Joy Luck Club* and says that it was "full of annoying psychobabble about women and their self-esteem struggles. He disliked it. If teachers are going to assign books in popular literature, they should consider the needs and interests of boys." She leaves out the fact that in previous years reading lists ignored female authors altogether—and the fact that there are boys who enjoy narratives about interpersonal relationships, and girls who like sci-fi. Where the argument, again, becomes muddy is in its rigid essentializing—in this case, the idea that boys simply are one way and learn one way, and girls another.

The "girls are ahead, boys are behind" or "girls are promoted, boys are penalized" argument has most recently spun out into issues of single-sex education and its merits. Boys' advocates, such as Sommers or Michael Gurian, author of *The Wonder of Boys* (and *The Wonder of Girls)*, have argued for single-sex environments and skewing lesson plans toward subjects that "naturally" interest boys more and interacting with them in ways that err from the traditional classroom model, thereby not punishing their "essential" behavior. In the article "Lost Boys," Gurian is reported as taking the idea of single-sex education even further and in his 1998 book, *A Fine Young Man,* proposing that Title IX be revoked, as he maintains that gender differences between the sexes must be respected. Tom Mortenson, a scholar at the Pell Institute for the Study of Opportunity in Higher Education, a Washington think tank, among other positions, is also cited in the "Lost Boys" article as saying, "If I were teaching, I would get boys out of the classroom. Take them to a swamp, dig through the muck, look for pollywogs. Then maybe take them back and have them look at pond water through slides and write up a lab report. They need hands-on activities. They get bored and distracted if you ask them to sit down and read a chapter and write up a paragraph— the kind of work that girls excel at." Again, he reinforces the idea that boys naturally act one way and yearn for certain types of activities, while girls yearn for another, a position that others eschew, hence complicating the debate about how to best "accommodate" the learning needs of boys, and particularly within what some call a "boys' crisis" in education.

Other scholars—most notably feminist psychologist and girls' scholar Carol Gilligan, who has turned her focus to boys' behavior in work such as *The Birth of Pleasure*—often argue for moving the model boys are presented with from a traditional, patriarchal one to more gender-neutral ground, stating that both boys and girls, and hence men and women, benefit from moving boys away from socialization that valorizes hiding their feelings and emotional vulnerability.

Gilligan argues that early on boys and girls learn to associate math and science with masculinity, and that so-called "hard-wired" differences are more often learned. She also points out that buoying up girls in subjects that have traditionally been associated with boys (math, science) has been regarded as far more acceptable than socializing boys to embrace subjects more traditionally associated with femininity and girls, such as strong verbal and writing skills. Moving both boys and girls to a more "gender-neutral" space, Gilligan and others conclude, is beneficial to allowing individuals' preferences and talents to emerge.

Whether boys are trailing girls academically, and what this means, seems largely dependent on who is looking at the path that's being cut. But without question, squinting to see who is ahead and who behind as girls and boys pace themselves through the educational system depends on how the terms of the "race" are defined.

Have Girls Gained Ground?

Now that more than twenty years have passed since the AAUW reports came to light, has the revolution been won? Or is it being fought on new territory, still inching forward from the ground that's been newly gained? Technological advances have intensified the pressures many girls feel—to look good in a social networking photo, to be aware of being caught on a camera-phone and having an image quickly broadcast—but the fundamental contradictions girls suffer still seem consistent within these media, rather than despite them. Schools now have harassment policies in place, as do most workplaces, and the pressure of "political correctness" can keep certain kinds of discrimination from being as blatantly expressed as it once was. But discrepancies and disparities still exist, sometimes now only in a more underground or coded form. And the evidence of institutionalized sexism persists.

In January of 2005, then-president of Harvard University, Lawrence Summers, during a speech for the National Bureau for Economic Research conference, suggested that "innate differences" between men and women help explain the lack of top-level female professionals in science and engineering. He also offered two other reasons why there might be discrepancies within these fields: One was that since women want to have children, they don't put in the kinds of eighty-hour workweeks that would make them competitive with their male peers, and that discrimination discourages women from pursuing science and engineering past their undergraduate educations. It was a year in which Harvard had tenured a strikingly small number of women compared to the number of men who were granted tenure that year. Summers's remarks played exactly back into the culturally accepted impression that girls and women just aren't as naturally strong in certain fields.

It was the suggestion that women are inherently less capable within these fields, and hence don't rise to the top, that caused an uproar; Summers's remarks were seen as reinforcing an old idea—that girls and boys are simply "naturally" better at some fields than others, and that math and science fields in particular are shaped by innate ability rather than by hard work.

Among the protesters who first heard his remarks, many thought that Summers was outrageously quick to ignore years of evidence that it's not innate or natural ability that sets men up for advancement in these fields and disadvantages women, but that social factors—the way girls are influenced against or face discrimination in pursuing certain paths—affect women's performance and representation.

A few months after his remarks were made public, the faculty at Harvard passed a "no confidence" vote in Summers's ability to lead, and not long afterward, he stepped down as president. Purportedly, Summers said, "I hope to be proven wrong" at the end of his remarks, not yet knowing the maelstrom that would ensue. Thinking about how education and gender expectations intertwine, from the work that was begun by educational reformers decades ago, to the new awarenesses that have arisen within the past twenty years, to the work that lies ahead, makes it clear that much still needs to change.

Elsewhere, concern about gender equity in classroom has only continued, with real interest in uncovering how things could yet change. The 2001 AAUW study *Beyond the "Gender Wars": A Conversation About Girls, Boys, and Education* documents the conversations of scholars from many disciplines who gathered in mid-September 2000. Participants discussed a range of issues, checking in on where the conversation has turned since the initial early-1990s focus on girls first broke upon the national scene, paying particular attention to what has changed in the educational system, and to the idea that the "gender wars" means one side wins while the other loses. Early on in the summary, Barrie Thorne, professor at UC Berkeley, brings up a nuanced development in gender research: closer attention to race and socioeconomic status, correcting the reductive compression of many levels of differences among girls and boys into two categories. "One has to ask, which girls, which boys?" she states. "For example, the needs and problems of low-income African American boys and girls are quite different in some ways from the needs and problems of white, middle-class girls and boys."

An emphasis on educational reform that serves all students—male or female—often emerges in the report's summary. More freedom for both genders is also a recurrent theme—if boys are restricted to areas that are "acceptably masculine" and girls to "stereotypically feminine," the panelists agree, neither side benefits. Likewise, for girls to gain entry into previously male-dominated fields while boys continue to avoid traditionally female-specified ones—such as nursing or daycare, for example—doesn't help shift the spectrum of gendered behavior. Scholar Michael Kimmel of State University of New York at Stony Brook comments in the summary, "I can think of no trait whatsoever that only boys categorically have and girls don't or that girls categorically have and boys don't. What we know is that girls as well as boys are hardwired to be competent, creative, and competitive. What we know is that boys as well as girls are hardwired to be caring, nurturing, and compassionate. . . . The question is which [hardwired traits] we value and nurture in which gender that makes these relatively related people seem so different."

The 2001 report explores how far the focus on gender in the classroom has come since the initial breakthrough of attention to it, and also which steps make sense to take next. Ultimately, the researchers advocate for an equitable and enriching classroom environment for every child, regardless of gender, and avoiding gender stereotyping through career path or even labeling behavior ("boys will be boys" and "girls will be girls"). Leaving "zero-sum game" thinking behind—that is, if girls are ahead, boys must be losing, or if boys are ahead, girls must be losing—allows for more collaboration on how to make classroom spaces richer for all.

What Does "Feminism" Mean for Girls, Anyway?

"Feminism" is a term with many meanings and many interpretations. Fundamentally, it's a movement, a philosophy, a way of approaching the world that holds that all genders should be treated equally and given equal rights. In a traditionally patriarchal society, women are considered subordinate to men, with patriarchal traditions reiterating this in sometimes obvious ways, and sometimes in more subtle ones. Consider the tradition of children being given their father's last name— why is patrilineal descent privileged?—that is, continuing the father's family line, rather than the mother's?

People who support and believe in feminism seek ways to create greater equality between the genders. An early, key moment in the feminist movement was the gathering in Seneca Falls, New York, on July 19 and 20, 1848, of women who recognized that women in America were not given the same rights as men. The organizers of the conference, Elizabeth Cady Stanton and Lucretia Mott, worked with others to create the Declaration of Sentiments, which advocated equality for all and was based on the Declaration of Independence. One of their tenets was that women should be given the right to vote, but it was years later, on August 18, 1920, that this finally passed and on August 26 became a law, just in time for women to vote for the first time in an upcoming presidential election. Other critical female figures, such as Sojourner Truth and Harriet Tubman, both born enslaved, also fought for the cause of abolition and women's rights. Truth, in her famous speech "Ain't I a Woman?" given in 1851 at the Ohio Women's Rights Convention, spoke out strongly about women's strengths and need for equal rights. Tubman worked for the cause of suffrage as well as her antislavery work with the Underground Railroad and other lasting humanitarian efforts.

Many girls now enjoy the result of what might seem like long-ago battles: the right to ownership of one's body through birth control or abortion, having equal numbers of sports teams available to girls as there are for boys through the legislation Title IX, or admission to any college or graduate school of their choice, when at one time, many were closed to female students. Because the world is constantly changing, and American culture is ever evolving, there are always new ways in which, for those who seek it, to reach for greater equality.

Girls today have options available to them that weren't "routine" for previous generations—such as the assumption that any field is open to them if they're interested, that they can have both a family and a career and, if they choose, a husband who shoulders equal responsibility in the domestic sphere. Would these girls call themselves feminists? Maybe—it's up to them. But holding the idea that all genders should be treated equally, with equal legal rights and freedom of expression to move from a stereotypical definition of gender, is part of a feminist belief system. You can wear lipstick and be a feminist—of course—and you can also eschew other female gender stereotypes and be a feminist. Boys and men can also be feminists. Growing up with these freedoms seeming ordinary is actually a great triumph for girls, and holding systems of equality firmly and working to even out other inequities as they emerge brings feminism forward to a new generation so that their daughters will know the same rights and even more freedom.

Young beauty pageant contestants at the first night of preliminary competition at the Miss America Competition in Atlantic City, New Jersey.

CHAPTER 2

GIRLS' BODIES, GIRLS' SELVES: BODY IMAGE, IDENTITY, AND SEXUALITY

THE SIGNS ARE EVERYWHERE—LITERALLY. Look up at a billboard in any major American city and what's being sold isn't just the newest soft drink or face wash. It's usually also an attractive woman, most often below the age of twenty-five, smiling or posing suggestively. Movies, television shows, music videos, magazines, video games, and ads for products varying from clothing to toothpaste to cell phones feature young women, and in American culture, a certain look for these girls and women—slender body; flawless (and more often than not white) skin; delicate, even facial features, enhanced by makeup; carefully coifed hair—is ubiquitous. This often isn't even cause for comment—but the images are absorbed and "normalized" by viewers at almost every turn.

"Children are born anthropologists," girls' historian Joan Jacobs Brumberg writes in her foreword to photojournalist Lauren Greenfield's 2002 exposé *Girl Culture,* "able to expertly deconstruct and mimic what culture offers them, especially in terms of gender roles. Before they even abandon their teddy bears, contemporary girls embrace the erotic. They also understand that their power as women will come from their beauty, and that beauty in American culture is defined, increasingly, by a certain body type displayed in particular ways." For the most part, advertising, media, and other cultural vehicles reflect certain physical "standards" for girls and women—that thinness is attractive, that clear skin and certain kinds of Caucasian features are beautiful, that heterosexuality is the norm. Endless images of alluring, flirtatious, slender, usually white, and presumptively heterosexual young women imprint as "normal" and desirable "standards" of feminine appearance into girls' (and others') minds, without those viewers necessarily realizing how these values have infiltrated.

Greenfield's images in *Girl Culture* paint an alarming portrait of how different girls respond to this cultural focus on the female body: One eighteen-year-old is shown being "blind weighed" with her back to the scale at a treatment center for eating disorders (implying that she can't face the disheartening result); a five-year-old girl picks out clothing in an upscale Beverly Hills boutique; and college girls in bikinis strut by hooting men at spring break competitions, some seeming self-confident, others seeming uncertain.

The girls in Greenfield's photos often see themselves as too thin, too fat, not stylish enough, too trendy, attractive or ugly or desirable or hideous. Comfort with one's body appears all but nonexistent. "I don't know a girl who's happy with her body," states eighteen-year-old Ashlee in text accompanying pictures of the debutante Cotton Ball in Chattanooga, Tennessee. Ashlee, a vegan who says she dislikes wearing makeup and dressing up, attended the ball and participated in its rituals, including shaving her armpits, to appease her family. "I just don't understand shaving every day," she says. "I like my armpit hair. My boyfriend likes my armpit hair, too. People just buy into the unattractiveness of unshaven armpits. My whole family cheered when I shaved."

A girl's body, almost from birth (when her first weight is taken), often reflects cultural expectations and conventions—in how she dresses, how she is allowed to use her body, how she presents it to the world, and how comfortable she feels within it. When she is younger, her body is measured against standards of health and growth, as it would be for any child. But near adolescence, a girl's growing breasts, widening hips, and changing skin become the site for many other standards. Her breasts are not just a physical aspect of her body, but a way in which others will perceive her as a teenager rather than as a child—custom will dictate that it's time to wear a bra, parents might deem her old enough to handle more privileges and responsibilities, and she might receive more sexual attention from acquaintances and strangers. Adolescent girls find themselves on the receiving end of increasingly sexualized expectations—from peers who cast a critical eye on girls' appearance and behavior, from parents who might either assume girls will date or fear that girls will date too soon, and from a culture that is often uncomfortable with women who don't embody certain sexualized stereotypes. A changing body means other changes in a girl's life—some that she might be emotionally able to meet, and some that she resists. But there is no doubt that as she moves from childhood to adolescence, an overlay of expectations—sexiness, attractiveness, availability—can blanket a girl's individual pacing of her desire to venture into womanhood.

While boys and men are increasingly presented with images that also stray far from the reality of the average male body, the use of male models to sell mundane products isn't as pervasive, and the presence of a conventionally attractive or sexualized male body isn't considered as strictly standard to sell a product or tell a story. When women are consistently objectified—that is, used as vehicles to sway public view through their sexuality or projected attractiveness—it sends girls a clear message. The onslaught of images of impossibly perfect-looking, sexually contextualized female bodies reinforces the idea that physical "perfection" and sexual attractiveness are both normal and expected of women, and by endlessly recreating scenarios that reinforce traditional gender roles, advertisers simultaneously teach girls and women a set of lessons about what it is to be female in America.

The Body as Battleground

In the 1997 book *The Body Project: An Intimate History of American Girls,* author Joan Jacobs Brumberg traces the history of how teenage girls within America have made different body parts into "projects." Examining historical views of aspects of girls' bodies—such as menstruation, body hair, skin conditions, weight—Brumberg

Looking in the Mirror

"I grew up surrounded by Barbie dolls and magazine cover girls like actresses Alicia Silverstone and Cameron Diaz; they were my main examples of beauty. . . . I also grew up with another set of standards that went hand in hand with the common stereotypes of Asian women. I discovered that, as Asian American girls, we are supposed to be short, lightweight, petite, soft-spoken, and light-skinned, with long, straight, jet-black hair."

—Julia Wong, "Mirror, Mirror," from *YELL-Oh Girls!,* ed. Vickie Nam

"Being light-skinned or having real nice hair that doesn't kink up or whatever is definitely something some girls like to boast about. I don't even think they know that it might hurt my feelings or even bother me at all. I don't think they think about anything but having the opportunity to be something other than what most people think being black is. . . .

"I think it's so foolish the way Essence *and* Ebony *talk about different makeup foundations for black women . . . they'll be having these silly names for every shade, but the emphasis is always on making your skin look lighter so you can get that 'café-au-lait complexion' or whatever. . . . It's bad enough that we only have two magazines to look at, but when*

delineates the ways that girls (and parents, doctors, and advertisers) have conceptualized those aspects as "problematic" and devised ways of addressing each one. Recollecting a discussion in which her female college-age students discuss the "necessity" of bikini-line waxes, Brumberg realizes that yet another body part has become a "project" for girls to attend to, mold to a standard, and then maintain. Asking herself why these students were adding another area to manage to the long litany of bodily concerns they already had, she recognizes that girls are now sexualized at a far younger age, and that concern with their bodies is yet more pervasive and rampant, with advertisers eager to instruct on depilation, control, and constant maintenance.

these two magazines start turning over to the way society wants to see us, then we're in trouble."

—Jo-Laine, fourteen, from Rebecca Carroll's *Sugar in the Raw: Voices of Young Black Girls in America*

"My intensive skin-care rituals, alienation from my reflection and adversarial relationship with my own face have already forged a mindset that is equally suited to an obsession with food and weight. The transfer of my critical energies from my face to my body is seamless."

—Lee Damsky, "Beauty Secrets," *Body Outlaws*, ed. Ophira Edut

"Everywhere, we see women and girls looking in mirrors, nervously checking who they are. Some grimace; others stare intently and some pose; few flash back at the mirror a smile of happy, relaxed recognition. Women understand this kind of hyperconcern because most of us have a love-hate relationship with our own full-length and magnifying mirrors. We rely on the mirror (and also the scale) to assess personal worth and establish who we are, although both devices fail us as meaningful sources of mental and spiritual nourishment while we mature and age."

—Joan Jacobs Brumberg, from introduction to Lauren Greenfield's *Girl Culture*

Examining the diaries of girls before World War I, Brumberg explains that the girls whose diaries she finds and reads (most hailing from middle-class families) were often praised for lack of attention to their bodies: Feminine virtue was found in a kind of unself-consciousness in which vanity about one's body was considered immoral or wrong. From decades later, the girlhood diaries that Brumberg collects and reads cite numerous instances of self-consciousness; by the 1950s, girls felt the need to improve their hair, skin, teeth, and weight, among other "body projects" that required honing and then maintenance in order to hew to acceptable standards.

Throughout her book, Brumberg considers how girls' bodies (and specific physical issues such as having clear skin, maintaining virginity, or hiding menstruation) have been commodified and valued as ways in which physical perfection (or the attempt at its attainment) becomes a class-based goal. As print media began to circulate more widely after the turn of the twentieth century, through magazines, newspapers, and books, advertisers also had an opportunity to sell girls (and their parents) products intended to improve overall beauty and health, contributing to anxiety about not meeting a standard of "normalcy," which, as Brumberg shows, historically has altered but has never left American cultural consciousness.

In her chapter "Sanitizing Puberty: The American Way to Menstruate," Brumberg writes, "In the effort to sell products, menstruation finally burst out of the closet in the 1920s when popular magazines, such as the *Ladies' Home Journal* and *Good Housekeeping*, began to run ads for Kotex. These advertisements constituted the first real public acknowledgement of menstruation." She writes that later, in the 1930s and 1940s, "Newly established educational divisions within the personal products industry (i.e., Kimberly-Clark . . . Tampax, Inc. . . .) began to supply mothers, teachers, parent-teacher associations and also the Girl Scouts with free, ready-made programs of instruction on 'menstrual health.'" Postwar, "marketing strategists understood that sales to the baby-boom generation—soon to be the largest cohort of adolescents in American history—could turn menstrual blood into gold." With menstruation, as with other functions and features of the female body, Brumberg shows how marketing strategists and cultural scripts intertwine until the messages girls receive are impossible to separate out and are just accepted as part of an overarching gender code.

In her chapter "Perfect Skin," Brumberg looks at the history of teenage acne, noting that as far back as 1885 a physician at New York Hospital realized that girls were three times more likely than boys to seek help for their skin. "Although boys surely suffer from the stigma of acne," Brumberg writes, "girls' pimples get more cultural attention. Because of cultural mandates that link femininity to flawless skin, the burden of maintaining a clear complexion has devolved disproportionately upon women and girls. . . . Skin care was really the first of many body projects endorsed and supported by middle-class parents for their adolescent children." In Brumberg's accounting, a girl's face was a key to her future: a good marriage (i.e., a marriage that put her into the same or an even higher social and economic position than she was in). As twentieth-century advances in dermatology also made acne treatment more available, families could "invest" in a daughter with skin issues so that her visage wasn't marred. Brumberg mentions a Victorian-era skin-care product called Kosmeo that was advertised in the Sears, Roebuck catalog with this copy: "When a man marries, nine times out of ten he chooses a girl with a pretty complexion." Brumberg's research concludes, "In order to avoid an unhappy future as a spinster, thousands of American girls ordered Kosmeo, and then rubbed earnestly with camel's hair brushes and Turkish towels in order to increase friction and improve blood circulation to the face."

Another historical shift Brumberg notes involves girls' response to makeup. She writes, "In the effort to look like the attractive women they saw in movies and magazines, American women in the 1920s put aside long-established objections to face makeup and began to purchase and use a wide range of cosmetics." Brumberg details products marketed specifically to African American girls and women to lighten their skin, and she recounts the "hierarchy of hue in the African-American community"; describing 1950s magazines' range of ads for lightening products, she elaborates, "Until recent times—probably the 1960s—the color of a girl's skin was central to her sense of self, as well as her place in the community of people of color. Although skin bleachers are still sold today, they generally are not used by the current generation to bleach the entire face, the way older generations did, before the Black Pride movement of the 1960s and 1970s." Reflecting, again, on how commerce intersects with "standards" that girls are told they must adhere to in order to be pleasing, or attractive, she writes: "The fact that skin bleachers and fade creams sold so well is a painful and compelling reminder of how much class and racial anxiety has been invested in skin in American society, particularly among groups who suffer from exclusion and bigotry."

What makes the female body such a battleground? The claims that parents, advertisers, and culture make on girls' bodies are dizzying— body odor must be banned, underarm hair removed, breasts lifted to a certain perk, skin made clear enough to touch, hair made glossy and enticing. The effect on the owners of the bodies means often feeling a disquieting angst that they are never good enough as they are, that they are forever being measured and found lacking. Contemporary "body projects" that girls today might undertake include the ones that Brumberg shows have lasted for decades in girls' awareness: weight, skin, haircut and color, among others. But consider how many other "body projects" are also undertaken in the twenty-first century: eyebrow grooming, development of fuller eyelashes, chemical peels and dermabrasion, tattooing, nail art, "bikini line" maintenance, colored contacts or Lasik surgery, tooth whitening, use of push-up bras or minimizers, contemporary "smoothers" to cover up panty lines, cellulite erasure, and skin buffing. And the list could go on.

Body weight and body shape come up consistently in Brumberg's history as factors to be controlled. In the chapter titled "Body Projects," under the subtitle "The Century of Svelte," Brumberg gives a brief history of the cult of thinness in America, and she also shows how trends in and expectations about girls' body shapes have changed, demonstrating again how subject the female figure has been to cultural trends and demands. She cites 1920 as the first time that "teenage girls made systematic efforts to lower their weight by food restriction and exercise" as adolescent girls "were motivated by a new ideal of female beauty that began to evolve around the turn of the century." New fashion trends that emphasized a trim silhouette replaced more voluptuous Victorian hourglass figures, with small waists and large hips. Instead, the American woman migrated toward the look of the "flapper"—flat chested, long limbed, and decidedly slender. Brumberg writes that girls around this period (starting around 1908 and progressing through the 1920s and 1930s) "bade farewell to corsets, stays, and petticoats, and they began to diet, or internalize control of the body."

The changing fashions of girls' breasts (whether their owners are trying to appear flat or large chested) is another point Brumberg explores by looking at the evolution of the training bra and undergarments sold to girls and women, especially around teenage anxiety about "developing" too quickly or too slowly. Different decades dictated that breasts either be disguised or enhanced, but the focus on controlling one's weight remained a constant, as it still seems to be. Another historical trend Brumberg traces is the focus on female legs: "Americans have talked about glamorous 'gams' ever since the Rockette made good legs a requirement back in the 1930s," she writes. "But American taste in legs has changed considerably in the past half-century." She notes that whereas the Rockettes had "shorter, chunkier limbs than today's long-stemmed, lean favorites," changes in fashion have accounted for an emphasis on "tight, narrow thighs." After miniskirts became popular in the 1960s, girls and women felt more emphasis put on their legs—particularly their thighs, which were meant to be as trim and cellulite free as possible. The phrase "thunder thighs," notes Brumberg, entered the American lexicon "in the early 1980s both as shorthand for female anxiety about the body and as a misogynistic slur." Discussing the cellulite avoidance industry, through use of thigh creams and liposuction, she concludes, "Our national concern about 'thunder thighs' says a lot about what Americans value. . . . Not surprisingly, there is more self-hatred [of the body] among women than men, and women tend to be especially dissatisfied about the lower body—the waist, hips, thighs, and buttocks. . . . This sad reality needs to be factored into our understanding of girls and the way in which they develop their sense of self."

Without question, being thin is widely held up in American culture today as an ideal to be achieved. Cultural differences play a large role in these perceptions; what's considered a "normal" body shape in a rural Midwestern community might look very different from what is considered "standard" in Manhattan. A Latina girl might have a fuller, larger frame presented to her as positive, as might an African American girl. But no matter a girl's cultural background, what is seen within American society at large is a narrow standard that's often in direct opposition to the bodies of most real women. And from the scores of models who advertise the "waif look" alongside whatever product they are hawking to the scores of slender television and film stars, the image of the thin woman is everywhere. And recent teen pop-culture icons varying from the Olsen twins to Destiny's Child, Lindsay Lohan, and Miley Cyrus tend to embody the same extremely slender stereotype.

Why value thinness? The concept that women's presentation matches the status they hold within a patriarchal culture—meant to be diminutive, shrinking, not taking up excessive space, and standing in contrast to a larger male form—is one possible explanation. There are many other viable responses as to why women are told through cultural code that being thinner and smaller is better, including the fact that most women do have smaller body sizes than men do. But the pervasive glorification of taking up less space with one's body, and the idealized feminine body shape being slight rather than large, is a widely accepted tenet of American culture, sometimes with drastic consequences.

The media literacy organization Mind on the Media reports, "Eighty percent of ten-year-old American girls diet. The number one magic wish for young girls age eleven to seventeen is to be thinner." The media are most often cited as the instigators of pressure to be thin. In many sources the height of the average American women is listed as five feet four inches, and her weight is listed as approximately 140 pounds. In a more recent study by the National Center for Health Statistics, the average American woman's weight is now listed as 163 pounds and her height is listed as just under five feet four inches. The height of the average fashion model, on the other hand, is approximately five feet nine inches to above six feet tall, and her average weight is approximately 117 pounds. This means that fashion models are on average significantly thinner and taller than the majority of the female American population, and yet they present an image to which most women and girls feel they ought to aspire. Seen in this light, the bloatedness of the diet industry—in which book authors, pharmaceutical companies, dieting organizations, makers of special exercise equipment, magazine publishers, and support groups feed

anxiety to women about weight while filling their own bank accounts—
becomes quietly disturbing.

According to the National Alliance on Mental Illness (NAMI),
anorexia nervosa is "a serious, often chronic, and life-threatening eating
disorder defined by a refusal to maintain minimal body weight within
15 percent of an individual's normal weight." Asserting that anorexia
most often occurs in pre- and postadolescent girls, NAMI's website
explains that "one reason younger women are particularly vulnerable
to eating disorders is their tendency to go on strict diets to achieve an
'ideal' figure. This obsessive dieting behavior reflects today's societal
pressure to be thin, which is seen in advertising and the media."

Bulimia (or bulimia nervosa), another well-known eating disorder,
occurs when girls eat excessively (or "binge") and then purge their food,
whether through vomiting, use of laxatives, or diuretics. With both bulimia
and anorexia, overexercising can be common, along with a sense of "body
dysmorphic syndrome"—the sense that one's own body is distorted,
bloated, and unacceptable, despite what a mirror or scale might reveal.
Left untreated, both disorders can be fatal, and even with treatment both
can cause lifelong damage to the body through inadequate nutrition and
through the development of a vexed relationship with food.

Estimating that between one-half to 1 percent of all females in the
United States will develop anorexia, NAMI also states that "because
more than 90 percent of all those who are affected are adolescent
and young women, the disorder has been characterized as primarily a
woman's illness." The complex motivations underlying different cases
of anorexia are many—girls might experience starving themselves as
a way to exercise control over their changing bodies, or they may see
it as a way to comply with a cultural standard of extreme thinness,
promoted to them daily and tacitly praised by parents who admire
models' or actresses' bodies.

In response to these concerns, activists and girls' advocates have
pushed in recent years for magazines aimed at adolescent girls (and
magazines geared toward women) to employ diverse models with
"real" figures that exemplify different body types. Agitating for change

with how girls and women are perceived by the public—and hence, perceive their own bodies—is nothing new, although advocating for change has taken different forms. Feminist activists of the 1960s and 1970s prominently crusaded against the sexist and racist standards of beauty pageants: The group New York Radical Women organized a protest in 1968 in which two hundred activists in Atlantic City, New Jersey, gathered to express outrage over the Miss America Pageant's objectification of girls and women, likening them to animals being judged for their physical attributes. According to Rory Dicker in her work *A History of U.S. Feminisms,* the protesters carried signs with messages such as CAN MAKEUP COVER THE WOUNDS OF OUR OPPRESSION? and THE REAL MISS AMERICA LIVES IN HARLEM. Dicker explains that the last sign made reference to the pageant's embedded racism: "Until 1940, contestants had to be white, and as of 1968, no black woman had competed in, much less won, the contest."

These campaigns of the past, and those of the present, have often been met with mixed success. In 2004 the skin- and hair-product company Dove launched a Campaign for Real Beauty, during which scouts recruited a variety of "ordinary-looking" women and asked them to pose in basic white underwear while looking naturally proud of their nonmodel-size bodies. Dove also set up the Dove Self-Esteem Fund, which sponsored a series of videos and online resources meant to promote body acceptance among women and girls, no matter their shape or size.

Dove's campaign sought to use "real women" to defy use of expected body shapes and types, as well as ages of models, and it pinpointed bolstering self-esteem in girls as a crucial starting point to having grown women appreciate their bodies as they are. In a "Girls Only" part of its website, the campaign offered interactive tools for girls to use to think about issues of body image and self-esteem, with activities designed to help girls figure out who best supports them in their lives, identify where their inner strengths lie, and determine what they need to feel good about themselves. In the site's "Girls Only Interactive Self-Esteem Zone," users could learn how to decode media messages aimed at girls and women and view "before" and "after" images of models whose bodies had been cosmetically retouched and digitally manipulated.

And yet it is critical to look more closely at what this media campaign is selling—just as Dove advises media-literate girls to do. Detractors are quick to point out that, fundamentally, Dove is still hawking products to girls and women that they probably don't fundamentally need—but with different, "affirming," packaging. And a further catch? One of the original ads for the Dove Real Beauty campaign was for a cellulite-firming cream, pointing to the disconnect between promoting women's self-acceptance and selling a product that diminishes the size of women's thighs.

Reporter Rebecca Traister critiqued the campaign—and other media campaigns that use a "feel good about yourself" tactic to fundamentally tell girls and women that they need to do (or buy) more—in a 2005 Salon.com article, citing the tagline used in the Dove marketing: "For too long/beauty has been defined by narrow, stifling sterotypes [sic]./ You've told us it's time to change all that./We agree./Because we believe real beauty comes/In many shapes, sizes and ages./It is why we started the Campaign for Real Beauty." Traister, pointing out the cellulite-firming cream conundrum, writes, "As long as you're patting yourself on the back for hiring real-life models with imperfect bodies, thereby 'challenging today's stereotypical view of beauty and inspiring women to take great care of themselves,' why ask those models to flog a cream that has zero health value and is just an expensive and temporary Band-Aid for a 'problem' that the media has told us we have with our bodies?" Traister also describes a similarly conflicted girl-focused ad campaign, colaunched by Bath and Body Works and American Girl dolls, that purportedly focuses on "Real Beauty Inside and Out" by selling young girls "personal care products 'designed to help girls ages 8 to 12 feel—and be—their best.'" The products—"body lotions, splashes, soaps and lip balms, all dressed up in girl-friendly 'hues of berry'"—arrived "with an inspirational message like 'Real beauty means no one's smile shines exactly like yours,' 'Real beauty is helping a friend,' or 'Real beauty is trusting in yourself.'"

In 2007, the Campaign for a Commercial-Free Childhood (CCFC) launched a letter-writing campaign to Unilever, Dove's owner, citing the hypocrisy in Dove's hyping its marketing campaign for girls "while simultaneously advertising Axe Body Spray by degrading them." The organization's press release cites CCFC director and cofounder Dr. Susan Linn: "Even as Unilever basks in praise for its Dove Real Beauty campaign, they are profiting from Axe marketing that blatantly objectifies and degrades young women." Unilever's Axe product line, marketed to boys, featured ads trading on the humor of over-the-top sexist, stereotypical gender roles: In one promotional online music video for Axe, the Bom Chicka Wah Wahs, a young female singing trio wearing only panties, bras, garters, and high-heeled boots, gyrate seductively atop a bus, fondle their own breasts, cuddle up to a variety of phallic objects, and sing pantingly about how the scent of Axe "attacks" and overwhelms a woman's "common sense." The singers writhe around stripper poles and along the floor while the camera repeatedly cuts to the women's crotches and bottoms. A "nerdy girl" with glasses who is first seen ironing and mentions she needs to get to work is then transformed into a sex kitten like the other singers; claiming she wants "true love like Romeo and Juliet," she is then "converted" to the other singers' hypersexual look with their implication of sexual licentiousness. "[The group's] suggestive theme song and video is all about how the Axe aroma causes women to lose control sexually," CCFC writes. "Sample lyric: 'If you have that aroma on, you can have our whole band.'" Bob McCannon, copresident of the Action Coalition for Media Education, calls the Dove campaign "marketing masquerading as media literacy." Whether it's viewed positively or negatively, it's certain that the Dove campaign for girls and women has caused a stir—and maybe one that will edge change forward by other marketers. However, if change simply means new types of marketing for products that fundamentally tell women their bodies need improvement, does it really mean true progress?

Girls and Dolls: Playing with Body Images

Even their favorite toys deliver girls messages about body image, and almost no girls' toy more so than Barbie. Her birthday is March 9, 1959, the day she officially "launched" at the American International Toy Fair in New York City. She's been a standard toy given to girls ever since and sometimes a source of scorn as girls grow up and think more about what she represents.

But what does Barbie represent? Blond, long-legged, with pointed, arched feet, she came with a range of outfits and accessories that have evolved with the decades—from airline stewardess Barbie to lab scientist. Her "dream house" has morphed into a bachelorette pad, and her accessories and accoutrements now include a cell phone, although she remains a statuesque figure with a body that, if replicated for a living adult, would be physically impossible. Barbie's boyfriend Ken, introduced in 1961, has been a permanent fixture even though Barbie has always remained a single woman. The very names "Barbie" and "Ken" have come to represent women and men who emulate or resemble the dolls' physical presentations and, correspondingly, a kind of vapid look that both dolls share.

Barbie's evolution has served as a cultural barometer of sorts. One of the most common critiques of the doll cites her unrealistic proportions. The standard doll is eleven and one-half inches tall, which correspond to a woman measuring five feet nine inches. Her breast-waist-hip measurements have been estimated to correspond to thirty-six inches (chest), eighteen inches (waist), and thirty-three inches (hips). In 1965 Slumber Party Barbie came with a book titled *How to Lose Weight,* which offered this advice: "Don't eat." The doll also came with pink bathroom scales reading 110 pounds, which would be significantly underweight for a woman of her projected height. In 1997 Barbie was given a wider waist, with Mattel saying that this "would make the doll better suited to contemporary fashion designs." It was considered a newsworthy event that the icon was remodeled to more closely resemble the proportions of the average American woman rather than serving as an impossible standard.

Within the broader culture, Barbie has made her way onto television. In 1994, the elementary school–aged *Simpsons* television character Lisa Simpson highlighted one of Barbie's most controversial moments when she acquired Malibu Stacy, a talking Stacy doll that says such things as "let's buy makeup so the boys will like us!" Lisa, disgusted by the "sexist drivel," creates an alternative, Lisa Lionheart. The episode refers to Teen Talk Barbie, released by Mattel in 1992, which offered programmed sentences including, "Will we ever have enough clothes?" "I love shopping!" and the one considered most controversial: "Math class is tough!" After receiving considerable criticism, Mattel announced that Teen Talk Barbie would no longer be programmed with the final sentence.

Barbie is a part of the American cultural landscape, whether girls are fans or have no interest. Like so much else about girls' dolls, Barbie has imprinted a stereotype of what girls are supposed to play with, emulate, and enjoy.

Until recently, Barbie was the most popular girl in the doll world. But her long-standing dominance has been challenged by the line of Bratz dolls that have recently been introduced and that have even begun to outsell the pointy-toed icon. The Bratz pack (Cloe, Dana, Jade, Sasha, Yasmin, Fianna, Nevra, and Meygan) have begun to chase Barbie from girls' bedrooms with their "stylin'," "kickin'," and "funky" selves. According to Sharon Lamb and Lyn Mikel Brown in *Packaging Girlhood: Rescuing Our Daughters from Marketers' Schemes,* "Bratz dolls don't share Barbie's 'body issues.' . . . They can stand on flat feet, for one thing, and they don't wear a double-D-cup bra. But like Barbie there is just one body type—thin—and their big heads and feet make their skinny bodies seem even more emaciated." However, like Barbie, they claim, Bratz dolls are stereotypically feminine and unapologetically focused on fashion and boys, although billed as the girls "with a passion for fashion" with a funky edginess. Brown and Lamb write that with a wide range of accessories, "Bratz sassiness may have the feel of independence, but it's the same tired message in new kickin' garb: Get a boyfriend and shop."

The American Psychological Association raised fresh concerns about the body image and lifestyle the Bratz dolls seem to promote when it established the Task Force on the Sexualization of Girls in February 2007. The report published to accompany the task force's founding cited concern over the sexuality the Bratz dolls portray, writing, "Bratz dolls come dressed in sexualized clothing such as miniskirts, fishnet stockings, and feather boas. Although these dolls may present no more sexualization of girls or women than is seen in MTV videos, it is worrisome when dolls designed specifically for 4- to 8-year-olds are associated with an objectified adult sexuality."

Of another popular doll, American Girl, Lamb and Brown write: "Let the buyer beware. As a product line there is much to celebrate about American Girl dolls and books: real-looking bodies, choices of skin and hair color, and varied stories that pull girls to the center rather than push them to the margins of history." The dolls don't have overly sexualized figures and are more girllike in their presentations than most popular dolls. But the authors exhort parents to teach their daughters to be critical of many of the familiar messages that the line also promotes: stereotyped mother figures who encourage restraint in their daughters, and "typical" boys as "troublesome, mischievous pests" who are set in "opposition to showcase the niceness of girls." Along with the American Girl dolls are accompanying books, accessories, and a myriad of other products (never mind the 2008 film). At $80 apiece, the dolls are not cheap, and the influx of marketing and available commodities to accompany the doll (as with many lines, of course) is another deterrent to thinking that this line has made a real paradigm shift.

Sexy from the Start

When Miley Cyrus, fifteen-year-old pop icon, posed in a series of provocative photos in the June 2008 issue of *Vanity Fair,* there were those who thought that she was too young to do so, and there was loud objection from Disney, one of her corporate sponsors. And then there were those who thought nothing of it, except that she was putting herself forward as girls do—attempting to look sexy, sophisticated,

Girlification: Join the Club

When VIP stands for "Very Important Princess," as it did at Club Libby Lu, it's hard to imagine what girls will think when they hear this term in other contexts. When I visited a Club Libby Lu, a glittery, overly made-up sales clerk stood near the store's front entrance offering to sprinkle glitter "fairy dust" on entering girls if they made a wish. "Every girl is a princess here," she told me.

A relative newcomer to the consumer scene, founded in 2000, Club Libby Lu sprang up in malls across America, offering girls from as young as age two to their twenties an intense baptism in girlification. "Total in-doctrination" was the phrase that quickly came to mind. Package deals offered to girls include "makeovers" that could mean nail polish, makeup, and new hairdos. The clerk mentioned that she had performed makeovers on girls as young as four, and the club was a popular destination for girls' birthday parties.

An inundation of pink, purple, and hearts and flowers, the books found in the shop covered topics such as cooking, journaling, and how to make up and accessorize oneself (and friends), and there were multiple copies and displays of the latest pop boy bands' CDs and paraphernalia. The club logo was a crown-topped heart and decals on the walls read, I Love Your Hair and Hip Chick and Spoiled written in big-sister, best-girlfriend tones. The sales clerks were called "club counselors," and according to Peggy Orenstein's article "What's Wrong with Cinderella?" new sites for stores were chosen based on what the company called its GPI or Girl Power In-dex, which predicted potential sales revenues. Although the chain's suc-cess was short-lived and it went out of business in January 2009, the mar-keting and merchandising of the "princess fairy tale" lives on, particularly in Disney's promotion of this theme—through princess makeovers at its parks and other products.

and older than her years. A question often underlies debates about issues such as the Cyrus photos (or the scantily clad Bratz dolls that are marketed to preschoolers, or toy makeup kits for kindergartners, or thong underwear sold in girls' sizes): How young is too young for girls to understand that one of their roles is to project sexiness? *

The marketing of sexuality and conformity to girls is everywhere— and often so pervasive and considered so standard that it's not really even seen at all. Parents might object to midriff-baring tops for the preschool set, or they might think it cute to dress their toddlers in clothing or Halloween costumes that emulate a much older, sexier look. Products that promote sexiness, even for little girls, are everywhere: thong underwear for elementary schoolers, padded bras for girls as young as six, T-shirts with coy or flirtatious messages for toddlers and girls. Makeup kits and nail polish can be found in the "toys" aisle of almost any store, marketed to girls who can barely talk. Tiny purses, flashy shoes, and dress-up jewelry teach girls to accessorize at an age just past when they have learned to walk. And for adolescent girls, the pressure to be sexualized is near-unavoidable, and with that pressure come presumptions of heterosexuality and an imperative to conform to a mainstream look that is often thin, white, and "all-American" in a way that harkens to previous decades in which the melting pot was thought to blend to a pale neutral color.

Young people are "sexualized at an earlier and earlier age," commented Susan N. Wilson, director of the Network for Family Life Education (now called Answer) at Rutgers University, in a 2004 Fox News article. "There's no antidote to what society and the media says." Teen stars—Britney Spears, Christina Aguilera, Destiny's Child, Lindsay Lohan, Cyrus—are made up to look years older than their chronological ages, and they are told that their "peak years" as actresses will pass before they turn twenty-five. And a cultural obsession with youth puts further pressure on girls to mimic the teen idols of their generation. "We use sex to sell everything in this country," Wilson said. "Kids must be very perplexed."

Rosalind Wiseman's book *Queen Bees and Wannabes* discusses the

Dressing the Part

There is no doubt that marketing products that sexualize girls are in evidence everywhere. In the summer of 2008, two women launched a business selling high heel shoes (pink of course) for baby girls. The heels are squishy "crib shoes" made for children up to six months old. Reporter Deborah Feldman says in her story for King 5 *Living*, "They could very well possibly be the smallest stilettos ever." Feldman reports that the company, named Heelarious, found its way into "350 stores worldwide" in just three months. Any criticism the pair has received, Feldman says, they brush off by saying the shoes are "all meant to be in good fun."

A casual look at Halloween costumes available for girls reveals that this occasion for dress-up is one in which the sexualization of girls is widely sold. In a *Los Angeles Times* article in October 2008, Monica Corcoran writes, "In the last couple of years, the Halloween costume industry has figured out a way to sexualize almost every conceivable option. Witch costumes now feature fishnet stockings and velvet miniskirts." Corcoran describes pirate costumes with "short, off-the-shoulder dresses and long gloves" and finding an $18.29 "French Maid Child Costume" available online. She sees "devil looks rang[ing] from scanty red satin short-shorts to velvet gowns with side slits and feather-trim necklines" and a "honeybee suit for teens, with thigh-high, striped stockings and an ultra miniskirt."

Diane E. Levin, coauthor with Jean Kilbourne of the book *So Sexy So Soon: The New Sexualized Childhood and What Parents Can Do to Protect Their Kids*, says in an interview in the *Los Angeles Times* on October 27, 2008, "Halloween costumes for 7- and 8-year-old girls and even younger have become downright titillating, and for tweens and teens, the vast majority of those sold in stores and on the Internet are unabashedly sexually alluring." She adds, "This is a continuation of what's been going on for quite a while: Halloween costumes are reflecting an increasingly oversexualized childhood. They often reflect the stars and starlets and popular culture role models that girls have, starting with Disney princesses or

Hannah Montana when girls are young. But even traditional favorites, like witches and pirates are sexier every year. And French maids are quite the thing for tweens and teens."

A casual trip to a local Target shows the polarized roles that boys and girls are meant to assume. The girls' aisle bursts with no fewer than ten types of princess dresses, princess accoutrements, and few other costume options. The boys' side devoted half an aisle to a vast array of plastic weaponry, including a large and menacing-looking cleaver, jumbo ninja sword, and headman's ax, as well as bulging, padded muscle suits meant to imitate a grown man's buff physique. Media tie-ins prevailed with Disney costumes available to match the latest popular films and television shows. But the lifespan for these costumes is short, as girls quickly vault into preteen or tween "dress-up" through the sexualized versions of these roles. With few other choices, how are girls to understand that they are not conscripted into these roles?

"Kids are trying to figure out from an early age, 'What does it mean to be a girl, or to be a boy'" says Levin. "They look at the most dramatic examples they can find to figure that out. Marketers are making it the most extreme they possibly can for that reason. Sexy is part of that marketing to girls—just as macho and violent has become the way to market things to boys." Sharon Lamb and Lyn Mikel Brown, in their book *Packaging Girlhood: Rescuing Our Daughters from Marketers' Schemes*, also comment on the options available to girls on Halloween and the pervasiveness of the message that no matter how young, this is a chance to flaunt sexuality. They write, "According to these costumes sold in department and drugstores, in catalogs and online, girls get their power almost solely from their looks." What they find are "dancing queens, pink cheerleaders, divas, fairies, and Barbies, Barbies, Barbies." Lamb and Brown insist, "Even the more traditional Halloween-type costumes speak to the ultrafeminine and increasingly sexy—pretty witches and gothic princesses, sexy genies and hot devils who aren't scary but plan to 'paint the town red in a stretch velvet leotard with fluffy marabou trim.'"

phenomenon Mary Pipher calls "lookism"—the concept that most girls are judged on their appearance and therefore invest mightily in how they look—and the very real feeling that girls are also judging and assessing each other on the basis of physical appearance. "Adolescence is a beauty pageant," Wiseman writes. "Even if your daughter doesn't want to be a contestant, others will look at her as if she is. In Girl World, everyone is automatically entered." Others judge girls' appearances—parents, teachers, boys who have their own prescriptions to hew to. If a girl deviates from conventional standards, her parents, for example, might not be happy. In a culture where girls and women are judged largely by how attractive they are, deviating isn't often well received, and particularly not in the microcosm of middle or high school.

And how does one "win," if such a thing could be possible? By hewing to cultural standards, by paying attention to the latest clothing and accessory trends, by watching budding starlets' fashions and obtaining the "right" brands? Feminist activism and generational changes have stamped a different look on "traditional" femininity; for example, girls are no longer widely expected to wear skirts instead of pants at school or in workplaces (though it's worth noting some of the exceptions: Female teachers in three schools in the Pomona Unified School District weren't granted the option of wearing pants in the workplace until 1997, and one Florida high school disallowed female students from wearing slacks to their graduation ceremony until the ACLU intervened in 2002). But a specific range of acceptable appearances is still prescribed for girls, differing from that of boys not only in its emphasis on sexualization (or, at the other end of the cultural spectrum, buttoned-down modesty), but in the social consequences heaped on those who flout norms. And if a girl "marks" herself in a way that breaks from whatever norms she faces—shaving her head, wearing her hair natural, avoiding makeup, wearing "boys'" clothes—that can also reveal her place, or lack thereof, within a social hierarchy.

Wiseman brings up the fact that while some schools have begun "media training" that teaches girls how images are distorted, it is still hard for them to overcome entrenched beliefs. She says that girls know that companies and advertisers are all in the business of making girls feel insecure so that girls will buy their products, yet despite this, they still get sucked into chasing the "powerful and simultaneously elusive" variety of femininity sold by advertisers and media. While many girls are often already aware that images of women in ads are airbrushed or Photoshopped, the unrealistic and hypersexualized images are still absorbed to shape girls' definitions of attractiveness. When Wiseman makes presentations to girls, she also raises the issue of racism within beauty standards—the favoring of lighter skin and more Caucasian features. Regardless, Wiseman advises parents, of your daughter's "race, class, religion, or ethnicity, it's important for her to realize the connection between cultural definitions of beauty and racism. These definitions push girls to want to be what they aren't." Describing the way momentary feelings of happiness and pride in one's body can be taken away through a quick magazine flip or negative comment, Wiseman writes, "In order to get along with other girls and deal with our culture's preoccupation with beauty, girls have a high tightrope to walk across with no net. The definition of femininity is complicated, and it's easy to make mistakes."

A study released in 2007 by the American Psychological Association Task Force on the Sexualization of Girls reveals the many long-lasting negative effects girls suffer when steeped in what Dr. Tanya Byron describes in the United Kingdom's *Times Online* as a "'pervasive culture' that focuses on the female body" and bombards girls and boys with sexualized images of women. Much of the study's research was done with college-age women, but the APA points out that its findings are likely to "generalize" to younger adolescents whose sense of self is still being formed. "Girls . . . sexualize themselves when they think of themselves in objectified terms," the study says, explaining the effects of self-objectification as meaning that girls internalize an outsider's perspective and then "learn to treat themselves as objects to be looked at and evaluated for their appearance." Under the broad categories of cognitive and emotional consequences, health, both mental and physical, sexuality, attitudes and beliefs, and impact on others, the

APA report details ramifications that start in girlhood but last through life. For example, the APA says, "Cognitively, self-objectification has been repeatedly shown to detract from the ability to concentrate and focus one's attention, thus leading to impaired performance on mental activities such as mathematical computations or logical reasoning."

Citing a 1998 study in which researchers asked college students to try on and evaluate either a bathing suit or a sweater, the APA report's executive summary says, "While they waited for 10 minutes [in a dressing room] wearing the garment, they completed a math test. The results revealed that young women in swimsuits performed significantly worse on the math problems than did those wearing sweaters. No differences were found for young men." In conclusion, the APA researchers report, "thinking about the body and comparing it to sexualized cultural ideals disrupted mental capacity. In the emotional domain, sexualization and objectification undermine confidence in and comfort with one's own body, leading to a host of negative emotional consequences, such as shame, anxiety, and even self-disgust." It reports that both adolescent girls and adult women experience this association between "self-objectification and anxiety about appearance and feelings of shame."

The APA report also points out how the oversexualization of girls negatively affects boys and society in a broader way overall: "Exposure to narrow ideals of female sexual attractiveness may make it difficult for some men to find an 'acceptable' partner or to fully enjoy intimacy with a female partner." Adult women, the researchers say, may suffer in trying to conform to unrealistic ideals and standards of female beauty; meanwhile, "more general societal effects may include an increase in sexism; fewer girls pursuing careers in science, technology, engineering, and mathematics (STEM); increased rates of sexual harassment and sexual violence; and an increased demand for child pornography." Some of these far-reaching charges have begun to be addressed—particularly in the area of supporting girls' aspirations toward STEM fields—but others remain issues that are still being played out.

Changing Bodies, Changing Lives: Girls and Sexuality

Adolescence can be a perplexing, thrilling, terrifying, and astounding experience—girls' bodies change, sometimes daily, moving them closer to womanhood, with all the expectations that American culture imposes on women's bodies. It can also be a time of exciting growth—on physical, emotional, and mental levels. For many girls, menstruation and developing breasts are markers of leaving childhood behind. In America, the average age of menarche has declined throughout the past decades; as of the early 1990s, it was determined to have dropped to twelve years and five months, a moment when girls may still not be emotionally prepared to leap from the harbor of childhood into adolescence.

But a changing body can also bring a new sense of power and of strength. While girls' bodies remain a complicated interstice between many cultural impositions and expectations, it is important to remember that they are also a site of pleasure, pride, and self-expression. Girls can feel themselves growing toward their likes and dislikes, forming a clearer sense of who they are, and reaching toward new goals and ambitions. Sports can be a place where girls feel real prowess with their bodies' capabilities and can connect them to a sense of healthy competition. Participation in student government, volunteer work, a first job, or civic involvement can also give adolescent girls a real chance to lead, form supportive peer networks, and develop independence. Strong female mentors can serve as role models for whom girls might yet become, as they too become aware of modeling, for younger girls, the challenges and the joys of inhabiting a girl's body.

The "Sexually Active" Girl, Or Not

The average age of first intercourse in America is listed as anywhere from the mid- to late teens, with demographics often shaping and casting the information in different charts according to education, race, and other factors. A girl may start having sex at any age, and her first sexual experiences can take any number of forms: She might be by herself, or she might be with a male or female partner. She might be knowledgeable about her body and how it experiences pleasure, she might be informed about safer sex and preventing STDs and pregnancy, and she might be confident in her ability to communicate her own desires and boundaries. Or she might be forced to have sex against her wishes, by an acquaintance, partner, relative, or stranger. Or she might decide to put off her first sexual experience until adulthood, or marriage.

Living in a changing body can mean many things for a girl—the chance to experience herself as sexual and desirable in positive ways, and in ways that might seem bewildering as she figures out her relationship to her own sexuality. For each girl, uncovering the experience of sexuality will be different, and for each girl, it will be an individual journey, one that begins in girlhood and continues throughout her life.

Joan Jacobs Brumberg's *The Body Project* traces the history of virginity in America from the early start of the twentieth century to the present day, touching on the fact that prizing virginity is not culturally specific to the United States. Most cultures have always kept constrictions around female sexuality through control of women's bodies. In patriarchal societies, where the practice of patrilineal descent is still practiced (as in American culture, where children are usually given their father's last name), controlling pregnancy is particularly necessary, so that the male family line is preserved. Cultures that prize virginity and "purity" discourage women from having sexual partners before the sanctioned partnership of marriage; thinking through virginity's historical significance for women helps us to understand how far a culture has moved toward egalitarian gender relationships and to also recognize what vestiges of patriarchal rules are still present. Girls are the ones who can get pregnant, but why is it that girls' sexuality is often more restricted culturally? And why is a larger onus placed on a girl retaining her virginity, when her male peer is often encouraged to lose his?

In traditional patriarchal culture, girls and women are controlled by and considered the "property" of men, in part because they can bear offspring and continue a family's line. In England, when Princess Diana married Prince Charles in 1981, the popular wisdom was that her virginity had to be confirmed by a doctor, so that the "purity" of the royal family line would be ensured. In the United States, nearly thirty years later, a bride's virginity at marriage is still important to many. Even among those who don't consider female virginity to be an issue, vestiges of gendered expectations do remain: For instance, most brides wear white, originally meant to symbolize their purity, and when a girl or woman is walked down the aisle by her father at a wedding, she is being "given away" to the groom in a ritual that represents the passing of a woman from one clan to another.

In her chapter "The Disappearance of Virginity," Brumberg writes specifically about the hymen—considered a marker of purity, marriageability, class value, moral standards, and a family's regimentation of a daughter—and discusses how the narrow membrane, physically unseen, still acts as a portal to adulthood through the act of first intercourse. Recounting the history of the gynecological exam, Brumberg reveals not only American society's general discomfort with female anatomy but also the cloak of moral opprobrium that surrounded touching a girl's genitalia, even among medical practitioners. In the early twentieth century, she explains, some doctors required a girl's mother to perform her daughter's exam herself, as it was unseemly for a male doctor to observe the private parts of a young female patient. Other times, a rectal exam substituted because it was considered so controversial to examine the vagina—never mind risky that the hymen might actually be broken during an exam. "As late as 1939," Brumberg says, "gynecologists were advised to obtain the permission of the groom, since it was still assumed that he had a custodial right to the membrane."

Through time, as girls' sexuality became more permissible, and as the idea diminished that "good girls" don't feel or express desire during and after the sexual revolution of the 1960s, the gynecological exam changed. Brumberg writes that doctors became progressively more open to performing pelvic exams on young women, and in turn, girls, as they became more comfortable with their bodies, didn't associate shame or discomfort with the experience. She contrasts the post-Victorian emphasis on keeping a girl's hymen intact until marriage—and the corresponding emphasis on a "purity" that denied female desire—with 1990s-era teenage girls going on their own for gynecological checkups and birth control in a generational shift reflecting an ease with sexuality unthinkable just a few decades before.

Brumberg, quoting several girls' diaries throughout the twentieth century, reveals how far these girls "went" sexually with their boyfriends, and the often coded language they used to reveal and also conceal admission of their own desire. She shows how the term "sexually active" came into parlance, "an important semantic innovation because it described a social state without reference to morality" in the 1970s and 1980s. "Older terms such as *ruined, wayward,* and *promiscuous* disappeared," Brumberg writes. "The concept of a 'sexually active girl' represented a sea change in American attitudes. It not only implied that sexual activity among female adolescents could be voluntary, autonomous, and guilt-free, but it also cast the hymen as irrelevant." With virginity no longer holding the central place it once did in defining a girl's sexuality (wherein "good" girls or "nice" girls were ones who kept themselves pure), a spectrum of new choices opened to girls—including the one to abstain from intercourse, whether because of religious beliefs, concern about disease, or the desire to move at one's own pace into sexual activity.

Religion and Sexuality: Purity Balls, "Silver Ring Things," and Abstinence

Girls' feelings about sexuality stem from many sources, and religious belief systems may be one place where some girls find great comfort in having guidance. Since the late 1990s there has been a rise in the number of "purity balls," which girls attend with their fathers and during which they commit to remaining "pure" until marriage. During the formal dinner and dance the girls' fathers also pledge to protect their daughters' virginity until they are married and to shepherd their own behavior to always be a model of upright and moral conduct. This tradition usually takes place within the context of an evangelical or fundamentalist

Christian setting. Girls often wear a ring to remind themselves of their own pledge to remain physically "pure" and to agree to abide by a set of mores that precludes physical intimacy until "given" in marriage by their fathers. Within this tradition, a father might even select a future husband for his daughter, or at least decide whom she might begin to date seriously, and an interested suitor would be expected to first ask permission from a father to "get to know" his daughter. Hand-holding is often the most physical a couple can get, and their dates are expected to be chaperoned. Their very first kiss will take place at their wedding altar, only after they are pronounced man and wife.

The very first purity ball was created by Randy Wilson in 1998, in Colorado Springs, and he has since become a figurehead of this movement. In an article in *The New York Times*, "Dancing the Night Away, with a Higher Purpose," reporter Neela Banerjee quotes Wilson's twenty-year-old daughter, Khrystian, as saying, "The culture says you're free to sleep with as many people as you want to. . . . What does that get you but complete chaos?" Banerjee writes that "studies have suggested that close relationships between fathers and daughters can reduce the risk of early sexual activity among girls and teenage pregnancy." However, she says, "Studies have also shown that most teenagers who say they will remain abstinent, like those at the ball, end up having sex before marriage, and they are far less likely to use condoms than their peers."

For the Wilsons and the growing number of people who have attended purity balls, premarital sex is seen as inevitably destructive, especially to girls, who they say suffer more because they are more emotional than boys. Fathers, they say, play a crucial role in helping them stay pure. Yet in an article for *Glamour* magazine, writer Jennifer Baumgardner cites counterevidence to the balls' efficacy. According to the National Longitudinal Study of Adolescent Health, more than half of virginity pledgers go on to have sex within three years of making their vows, with 88 percent still having sex before marriage. Another result the study reveals is that teens who take a pledge of virginity have higher STD rates and are less likely to use condoms, since, in part, having condoms would admit premeditation to engage in sexual activity. Baumgardner also cites critics of the purity ball movement, such as psychologist Dan Kindlon, author of *Alpha Girls*, who says, "Virginity pledges set girls up for failure," commenting that denying anyone access to something only makes him or her crave it all the more, although he lauds the focus on father-daughter bonding and his own research supports the idea that girls with high self-esteem usually enjoy strong relationships with their fathers.

Feminist activist Eve Ensler comments, "When you sign a pledge to your father to preserve your virginity, your sexuality is basically being taken away from you until you sign another contract, a marital one." One aspect of the purity ball movement to consider is the pressure it places on teen girls—not boys—to remain "pure," and its reaffirmation of a patriarchal structure in which girls are "given" from father to husband, as girls' own agency, sexual and otherwise, is subsumed beneath this priority.

Among other trends that promote abstinence—Christian rock bands that sing about this message, online sites to help pledgers keep their promise, and reports of girls being told that nonvirgins are akin to used pieces of tape that will no longer stick to their future spouse (having been "used up" by other connections)—another movement has sprung up around the "Silver Ring Thing." The Silver Ring Thing is literally a ring, but one that is put on only after participating in a training session sponsored by a youth ministry program that advocates abstinence until marriage, and after participants have pledged to do so.

Targeting teens in middle and high school, the program also offers a message of "Second Virginity" for teens who have already been sexually active. Through their pledge, they can rededicate themselves to "purity" and rejoining the path of abstinence until marriage. The group also offers a "12-Step Faith-Centered Follow Up Program" to support teens through temptation. On its website, Silver Ring Thing states that it wants "to motivate, educate, support and transform generations of young people to embrace a lifestyle of Christ-centered sexual abstinence until marriage" and lists its vision as "to create a culture shift in America where abstinence becomes the norm again rather than the exception."

Whether a girl feels strongly about abstinence until marriage through her religion or personal belief system, being taught abstinence through sex education at public schools has become a hotly debated issue, in which some see a religious message being pushed through promotion of a conservative social agenda. Allocation of public funding to teach sex education has long been a touchy subject, but using tax dollars to promote abstinence, and particularly if it carries a religious message, is yet more sensitive. When abstinence from sexual activity is the only option students are taught in public education, the line between pushing religious tenets and offering enough information for students to make a free choice becomes contested.

In 2005, the group Silver Ring Thing had a federal grant suspended because it appeared to be using tax money for religious activity. According to *The Washington Post*, "Officials at the Department of Health and Human Services ordered the group to submit a 'corrective action plan' if it hopes to receive an expected $75,000 grant this year." *The Post* reports that the American Civil Liberties Union (ACLU) had filed a lawsuit against the Department of Health and Human Services, "accusing the administration of using tax dollars to promote Christianity." The ACLU's complaint alleged that Silver Ring Thing's activities were "permeated with religion," reports *The Post,* and used "taxpayer dollars to promote religious content, instruction and indoctrination." The group, in turn, claimed that it offered both secular and religious programs that teach abstinence, and teens can choose which to attend. Yet the ACLU claimed a "partial victory" in receiving acknowledgment that the group had used public taxpayer dollars to promote religious faith. No matter which path a girl chooses to follow as she becomes sexually active, and whether her choice comes from conservative or liberal religious values or family expectation, having access to information is critical.

The authors of a 2007 press release from the Guttmacher Institute report, "Most recently, a nine-year, $8-million evaluation of federally funded abstinence-only-until-marriage programs found that these programs have no beneficial impact on young people's sexual behavior. The congressionally mandated study found that students who participated in what were thought to be the most 'promising' abstinence-only programs were no more likely than nonparticipants to delay sexual initiation, nor to have fewer partners or use condoms when they did become sexually active." By contrast, their own findings reveal that "one in three teens currently get no education about birth control at all, and of those who do, many do not get it when they need it most—before they start to have sex," and that improvements in the decline of teen pregnancy are due to improved contraceptive use and not teens abstaining from sex.

Heather Boonstra, a Guttmacher senior public policy associate, says, "Despite the fact that the bulk of the recent decline in U.S. teen pregnancy rates is the result of improved contraceptive use, the Bush administration and some members of Congress want to increase funding for abstinence-only-until-marriage programs. There is no evidence base to justify current policies—let alone the well over $1 billion that the federal government has poured into ineffective abstinence-only programs over the last decade." She advises a focus on a more comprehensive approach to sex education, which may in part include information about choosing abstinence.

The National Campaign to Prevent Teen and Unplanned Pregnancy, in its white paper "Some Thoughts on Abstinence," puts forward that it strongly favors "encouraging teens to delay sex as the best way to prevent early pregnancy and parenthood." Yet it distinguishes between abstinence as a behavior (being given the message to wait), abstinence as a message (teaching this alongside more comprehensive information about contraception), and abstinence as an intervention (secular organizations that promote and support abstinence). It notes that "millions of federal dollars are dedicated for abstinence-only programs (where the evidence of effectiveness is weak), and no dedicated funding streams support more comprehensive approaches (where the evidence is appreciably stronger)."

Birth Control and Sexual Health

Considerations of abstinence aside, access to birth control, information about sexually transmitted diseases (STDs), and choices about abortion can depend on many things—parental openness, state laws, what schools can and can't distribute to students or even inform them about, financial considerations, how comfortable a girl feels touching her body, how closely she connects risk of pregnancy with the possibility it could really happen to her, how willing she is to plan for sex.

In a 2001 article published by the American Academy of Pediatrics, author Lori O'Keefe reports on the imbalanced picture of sexuality that adolescents within the United States encounter in the media; O'Keefe cites an estimate "that the average American adolescent views nearly 14,000 sexual references per year but only 165 of these references deal with birth control, self-control, abstinence, or the risk of pregnancy or STDs." This fraction of time spent on these realities can lead teens to underestimate their impact, and the absence of clear communication with parents, mentors, or other adults, or lack of good information, can leave teens without the necessary tools to enter into sexual relationships responsibly. *Pregnant Pause,* the blog of the National Campaign to Prevent Teen and Unplanned Pregnancy, reports that a new study from the Rand Corporation "is the first to·directly link sexual content on TV to the likelihood of teens getting pregnant or causing a pregnancy" with the fact that "teens who are drowning in sex-saturated TV are twice as likely as their peers who watch little sexy stuff on TV to get pregnant or cause a pregnancy by age 16." Its National Campaign public opinion polls also "make clear that teens (76 percent) and adults (72 percent) want the media to focus more on the consequences of sex."

The Children's Defense Fund's publication *The State of America's Children, 2005* states, "Despite the fact that teen birth rates are at their lowest since the 1970s, the United States still has the highest rates of teen pregnancy and births in the western industrialized world. According to the National Campaign to Prevent Teen and Unplanned Pregnancy, the concerns about these numbers are manifold. Teen mothers are less likely than other teens to complete high school and go on to college and are more likely to require public assistance."

The Centers for Disease Control and Prevention (CDC) reports that in the United States in 2006, mothers between 15 and 19 gave 435,436 births, a birth rate of 41.9 per 1,000. Of those births, nearly two-thirds among those under 18 and more than half among mothers 18–19 were unintended. It also reports that besides teen pregnancy and birth rates, sexually transmitted disease (STD) and abortion rates are considerably higher than in most other developed countries, although, according to *Newsweek,* teen abortion rates have plummeted in the last three decades because of the success with educating teens about the consequences of sexual behavior.

Concern about STDs is also very real. The CDC reports in a study released in 2008 that "one in four (26 percent) young women between the ages of 14 and 19 in the United States—or 3.2 million teenage girls—is infected with at least one of the most common sexually transmitted diseases (human papillomavirus (HPV), chlamydia, herpes simplex virus, and trichomoniasis)." The study also found that African American teenage girls were the most affected: "Nearly half of the young African-American women (48 percent) were infected with an STD, compared to 20 percent of young white women." Based "on an analysis of the 2003–2004 National Health and Nutrition Examination Survey," the report explains that the health effects of STDs for women can be severe and encourages "prevention strategies," including the new HPV vaccine.

In *Voices of a Generation: Teenage Girls on Sex, School, and Self,* a report released by the AAUW's Educational Foundation in 1999, the authors put forward that "a 'one size fits all' approach to teen pregnancy prevention in schools is not likely to meet all girls' needs because girls' views of pregnancy and sexual risks vary according to social and cultural contexts." Rather, they suggest that sexual education and pregnancy prevention programs "may differ by race, ethnicity, or other social background variables."

Offering solid birth control and information about sexual health to teens of all sexualities is also critical. The organization Advocates for Youth states, "A recent study of GLBTQ youth who received gay-sensitive HIV prevention education in school showed they engaged

Slut!

"One of the biggest inner conflicts I have with my work," *Queen Bees and Wannabes* author Rosalind Wiseman writes, "is encouraging girls to be proud of their sexuality while making sure they understand how vulnerable they are in a world that constantly exploits their sexuality. The most frequent way girls are trapped in this conundrum is when they accuse each other of being a slut."

Wiseman puts her finger on yet another double bind girls find themselves in—wanting to exercise and explore their sexuality, yet still having to deal with the many people who are uncomfortable with female sexuality and prefer to contain or control it. Dressing sexily, showing off a budding sexuality, and being conventionally "attractive" are part of what a teenage girl is told she should do—but to a mysterious point. Cross the line and attract too much attention from boys, exercise too much enjoyment of sexual exploration, and you may be labeled a "slut." And being thus labeled, Wiseman claims, "also makes girls more vulnerable to sexual coercion and violence from boys." Addressing the deep conflicts that girls face as they enter a sexualized sense of themselves in adolescence (or even before), Wiseman writes, "Girls often feel they have to choose between being themselves and displaying a sexy costume. It's a huge conflict. If a girl opts for the costume and plays the part, she'll get the boys' attention, but she'll also incur the girls' wrath." She might also feel she's selling out, says Wiseman, and will often try to please both groups, with "two competing agendas."

Boys don't face this dilemma, although they are often railroaded by gender agendas of their own that can be equally restrictive—heterosexist and steeped in chauvinistic tradition. The currents of gender expectation can run deep, despite lip service to change, and they affect teenagers of all genders and sexual orientations. When a boy uses the term "slut" to describe a girl, he may be responding to a scripted sense of sexual mores—one that expects girls to be sexual yet punishes them for it. For a girl to lob this label (or any of its variants) at another girl, other, more complicated tensions can be at work. Girls may feel betrayed by a girlfriend who has begun turning her attention to boys, or who is competing with other girls with whom there was a bond. The sense of competing for the "prize" of male attention can be discomfiting—part of an alienating

continued

realization that this is now where girls' attention is meant to turn, that this is part of a new rubric of relationships that forces them to walk a fine line between engaging with their sexuality, but not going too far, or too fast. And meanwhile, the rules shift at every step, as girls learn that while they are meant to feel entitled by their power, they can also simultaneously be condemned for it.

"I wish that every girl who enjoys her sexuality was not considered slutty, and dirty. I wish that all the girls could walk around all schools with all the pride as guys have."

"Someone said that I was a slut. You always try to pretend that what people say about you doesn't affect you, but it does. You slowly start to believe what's being said about you."

Both quotes come from the AAUW's study *Voices of a Generation: Teenage Girls Report About Their Lives Today*, in which girls recapitulate their experiences. Most speak openly about sexual harassment at their schools, and often the lack of administrative response, as well as frustration that the onus of curtailing sexual behavior within a relationship still falls to them while boys escape this expectation, and the double bind they find themselves in, caught between wanting to express their sexuality and, in the words of another teen girl, "Women always have to worry about *accidentally looking slutty* or like she's trying to turn someone on."

Two books, *Slut! Growing Up Female with a Bad Reputation*, by Leora Tanenbaum, and *Fast Girls: Teenage Tribes and the Myth of the Slut*, by

in less risky sexual behavior than similar youth who did not receive such instruction." There is no question that teens need access to good information about sexual health, including birth control, but how much is available to them, how often they will receive it, and how trustworthy the source all remain highly variable.

Heterosexism and LBTQ Girls

With the generational change to new openness about sexuality, cultural acceptance of bisexuality, homosexuality, and transgendered girls has also developed, although the way has been, and still is, difficult for many of them. Matthew S. Robinson, writing for the

Emily White, both include personal narratives of women who were labeled sluts during their teenage years, and the long-standing, and often devastating, effects this word had. Some of the girls were called sluts arbitrarily—labeled through the mere fact of being new to a school's social infrastructure, or the first to physically develop, or they reached a point where an innocent friendship with a boy is suddenly construed through the lens of sexuality and the girl is considered the provocateur. Many of the women each author interviews recall rage at what happened to them during middle and high school, and how annihilated they felt by their peers. A sense of powerlessness is also prevalent, with some girls pushed to limits that include hurting themselves physically. Often ashamed to tell their parents, either because they don't want to reveal the label of "slut" or they are simply embarrassed by being victimized, their stories recount very difficult years, often with lasting effects.

Tanenbaum gives a history of the idea that "nice girls don't" and "bad girls do," and how the existence of this concept persists through use of the word "slut" and the reiteration of a double standard that boys still evade. "Slut-bashing shows us that sexism is still alive and that as boys and girls grow up, different sexual expectations and identities are applied to them. Slut-bashing is evidence of a sexual double standard that should have been eliminated decades ago. . . . Slut-bashing sends the message to all girls, no matter how 'pure' their reputations, that men and boys are free to express themselves sexually, but women and girls are not."

educational foundation Edutopia, tells the story of one girl's high school experience: "For Elizabeth, a bisexual teen from Maryland who wishes to remain anonymous, life at school was misery. 'My freshman year, only once did a teacher ever stop someone saying, "That's so gay!"' she recalls. 'No one ever stopped the kids.' Not knowing how or where to find help, Elizabeth became discouraged. 'I didn't talk to as many people as I might have,' she admits, 'because I didn't want to get to know somebody who wouldn't accept me if I were gay.'"

Veering from heterosexist norms is a challenge to girls (and boys) at any age. In a heterosexist culture, the assumption of heterosexuality

Not in the Right Body

Gender dysphoria—a sense of discomfort with gender norms, and a sense that one's body doesn't match one's inner consciousness of one's gender—has become more widely discussed during the past half century. Christine Jorgensen received wide public attention in the 1950s as the first well-known U.S. adult to have sex reassignment surgery (male to female). The terms "transsexual" (describing someone who wants to live as the opposite gender than the one assigned at birth, and who may alter his or her body through surgery or hormones to do so) or "transgender" (the sense that one's assigned gender identity doesn't match one's actual gender identity) are still not widely heard in mainstream American culture, but awareness is growing as further recognition is given to the idea of a spectrum of gender identities, or fluid shifts between definitions beyond the binary "female" and "male."

In 2007, Barbara Walters interviewed a range of families with transgendered children; some rejected their children's sense of being born into the wrong body, and some had adjusted their expectations to accommodate and help their child live as the opposite sex. For most families, their child's preference to live as the opposite gender was clear at an early age, and fighting their child's impulses only led to unhappiness for all. In a 2008 National Public Radio story by reporter Alix Spiegel, two different therapists prescribed radically different therapy for two young children, both born male-bodied, who had from the earliest ages asked to be

as the "norm" is privileged—the idea that men and women are sexually attracted to each other and this is the "correct" kind of relationship. Communities show their approval by treating heterosexuality as a presumed norm for everyone and by granting only heterosexual couples certain rights: to marry in a variety of religious traditions and to receive extended benefits, wherein, for instance, one heterosexual partner may receive health insurance through his or her partner's employee plan.

Varying from the script of "girl meets boy, and then they fall in love, become engaged, and get married" is difficult when other options often identified as girls and craved girls' toys, clothing, and other experiences boys were not "supposed" to want. One therapist, based in Toronto, suggested that the parents gradually diminish their child's access to "girls'" toys and experiences until the boy was resocialized into a masculine sphere; the other, based in Oakland, Califonia, counseled acceptance, and the parents agreed to let their child live as a girl. Both therapists felt strongly about their points of view, and both sets of parents believed they were choosing the best route for their children. But what is clear is that both children, while still under five years old, knew that they didn't want to be boys and were drawn to girls' toys and clothing.

One parent in Spiegel's report describes herself finally agreeing to let her biologically male child wear girls' clothes: "Before then, or since then, I don't think I have seen her so out of her mind happy as that drive to Target that day to pick out her dress." Dr. Diane Ehrensaft, the Oakland psychologist who counsels acceptance of children's transgender feelings and wishes, states, "If we allow people to unfold and give them the freedom to be who they really are, we engender health. And if we try and constrict it, or bend the twig, we engender poor mental health."

Most children experience fluidity around gender when they are very young, but for transgendered children puberty adds a new layer of dilemma when hormones will accelerate their maturation further into a gender that they eschew. Some parents are willing to use experimental hormone therapy, in which shots are given to hold off on adolescent development into puberty, to give children more time to be certain of their choices.

go unrecognized, legally or culturally. And within the fishbowl culture of middle and high school (unless the school is part of a minority of progressive programs), girls who are lesbian, bisexual, questioning, or transgendered may find it especially difficult to obtain support and acceptance from peers and teachers. According to Robinson, "In a recent national survey of more than 3,400 gay and straight students and 1,000 educators, 65 percent reported verbal abuse or physical assaults rooted in homophobia and prejudice in the last year. . . . [The survey] also indicated that 84 percent of those surveyed reported hearing derogatory remarks such as 'faggot' or 'dyke' at school, and nearly 70 percent reported hearing 'gay' used in a derogatory manner." A high percentage of students also said they had experienced harassment, in part because of sexual identity, and the survey found gay, lesbian, bisexual, and transgender students more likely to skip school if they were in an environment that felt inhospitable or unsafe.

According to the Washington, DC–based organization Advocates for Youth, "Research shows that homophobia and heterosexism greatly contribute to LGBTQ youth's high rates of attempted and completed suicide, violence victimization, substance abuse, teenage pregnancy, and HIV-associated risky behaviors." And last, Advocates for Youth also puts forward information about the additional challenges that LGBTQ teens of color may face: "Up to 46 percent of LGBTQ youth of color report experiencing physical violence related to their sexual orientation. Nearly 45 percent of youth in one survey were verbally harassed in school regarding sexual orientation and race/ethnicity."

Reporter Carrie Kilman explains that LGBTQ students, "as well as students perceived by peers to be gay, are the most common targets of harassment at school. That harassment can reach its most fevered pitch in middle school." According to the 2005 National Campus Climate Survey by the Gay, Lesbian and Straight Education Network (GLSEN), "64 percent of middle school students reported anti-gay bullying and name-calling as major problems in their schools—18 percentage points higher than what was reported by high school students." Kilman cites Eliza Byard, GLSEN's deputy director (now executive director), as saying, "There is something about the name-calling environment in junior high and middle school that is particularly prevalent, and it makes middle school an important focus for behavioral change."

LGBTQ advocacy groups are springing up in schools and a cultural shift from heterosexism is under way, if uneven in its progress throughout the United States. As Robinson reports, a number of U.S. states have school antibullying policies that specifically mention sexual orientation, and organizations such as the Michigan-based Triangle Foundation are working to enact legislation that specifically protects LGBTQ students.

Gay-straight alliances (or GSAs) are groups that students and advisers form to help students forge connections across lines of sexual orientation and lessen bullying through awareness. According to Kilman, "At the end of the 2005–2006 school year, more than 3,000 GSAs were listed on GLSEN's high school roster. . . . Three years ago, there were fewer than two dozen middle school GSAs. Today, at least 500 exist—serving one out of every 20 middle and junior high schools nationwide. The growth can be attributed, in part, to younger students learning about GSAs from high school siblings, the prevalence of the Internet, and the fact that in general, students feel more comfortable discussing issues of sexual orientation at an earlier age." The rise of gay-straight alliances has created more safe spaces, and the organization of events such as No Name-Calling Week and a National Day of Silence has helped to promote tolerance and awareness.

In middle school, where girls shape their identities through interactions with friends, sports, clubs, and cliques, knowing that there's a group they can belong to if they are lesbian, bisexual, transgendered, or questioning can feel like a lifeline. At a middle school in Madison, Wisconsin, Kilman observes a weekly GSA meeting (started in 2002) during which students discuss the issue of questioning their own sexuality. She reports one girl's response to the idea that middle schoolers are too young to know their own sexual orientation: "We're not too young to know how we feel. . . . It doesn't take a certain age to know yourself." Another girl, writing "LGBTQ" on a chalkboard, says, "The 'Q' stands for 'questioning.' . . . I think Q is a safe place to be at our age."

While a growing number of school programs enable LBTQ girls to express themselves, in many communities, particularly those in more rural areas, girls lack the support they need, making the process of uncovering their own sexuality even harder. When girls come out as lesbian, or bisexual, they may not enjoy familial acceptance. Parents might object to their daughter's choices based on religion or on disappointment that she's not going to follow an expected cultural script. Girls who take the step of coming out to their families, and coming out at school to their teachers, peers, and administrators, in a culture that doesn't yet legally endorse same-sex marriage and rights, risk estrangement, abuse, or outright rejection.

GSAs and other school-based LGBTQ support groups may face other obstacles. Matthew Robinson cites examples of more rural school communities where it may be particularly difficult for students to find teachers who will sponsor groups and also have enough students willing to attend. And opposition can find its way to the highest levels: Robinson refers to an effort in Virginia to pass "commonwealth-wide legislation that would require students to obtain parental permission to join any extracurricular groups, including LGBT organizations." But the push to protect all students is seeing results: In states such as California, New Jersey, Washington, and Wisconsin, Robinson reports, where "antibullying policies have been established that specifically mention sexual orientation . . . rates of bullying, including acts of harassment based on sexual orientation, are 25 percent lower."

If girls can't feel safe coming out or discussing sexuality and sexual orientation within their communities, they can turn to the vast resource of the Internet. But a quick search using terms such as "lesbian girls" brings up, more often than not, pornography sites offering the polar opposite of what girl advocacy groups want to promote. While not the same as having a supportive parent or peer to turn to with questions about sexual identity or sexual activity, the Internet can still serve as a useful tool, particularly for girls whose immediate communities are hostile to GLBTQ people or simply unwilling or unable to provide teenagers with comprehensive sexual information. Girls who are questioning or learning about their sexuality can look to positive educational Internet resources and communities such as the website Scarleteen.com; online support groups can provide much-needed information and community.

Dangerous Relationships: Violence and Abuse

Having resources is essential for any girl, and if she is facing violence, of any kind, for any reason, it's important for her to know she has the right to get help. If a boyfriend, family member, or girlfriend turns violent or abusive, girls may not know where to turn or feel empowered enough to know that they have the right to stop abuse. When a parent, sibling, or partner is abusive, a girl who feels powerless may think there is no way out of her situation. One commonly heard reaction to abuse, for teenage girls, is that they fear further exposure to their peers by making their situation further known; caught between suffering through an abusive situation at the hands of a partner or a parent and the potential exposure that going to a teacher or counselor could bring, teen girls often think they have no viable choices.

Teen girls can also face difficulty defining, recognizing, or reporting abuse, especially if they are in an untenable situation that makes it impossible to get themselves out, such as reporting a parent when there isn't anywhere else to go, or protecting a partner they feel deep affection and attachment for—a partner who may be affectionate and loving most times, but then abusive. Removing oneself from a social clique or a "bad boyfriend" who is popular can make a girl feel as if she is in the wrong for extricating herself from an unhealthy situation. The Alabama Coalition Against Domestic Violence (ACADV) offers other scenarios that can make recognizing violence difficult for teen girls, such as the mere fact that teens are often "inexperienced with dating relationships," or they may want "independence from parents" and act out by remaining in an abusive relationship as a way to defy parents or to have their own space, even if it's unhealthy. According to ACADV, teen girls may think that they are responsible for solving problems within a relationship or think a partner's jealousy, possessiveness, or even abuse is "romantic"—or they may simply have no one to ask for help.

"Dating violence crosses all racial, economic and social lines," ACADV's site states. "Most victims are young women, who are also at greater risk for serious injury." A 2000 Bureau of Justice report on intimate partner violence supports the statement: "Women ages 16 to 24 experience the highest per capita rates of intimate violence—nearly 20 per 1000 women." ACADV reports that roughly "one in three high school students have been or will be involved in an abusive relationship" and "Forty percent of teenage girls ages 14 to 17 say they

No Place to Call Home

Girls who leave home, voluntarily or involuntarily, often face great health risks. There are many reasons girls might need to escape family or home situations that are harmful—sexual exploitation or abuse, substance abuse issues within a home setting, or an unstable environment that holds the threat of violence. Or a girl might be disowned by her family because of her sexual orientation, a belief system that differs from her parents', or her family's intolerance of her different lifestyle. According to the National Center for Exploited and Missing Children, "The sexual victimization of children is overwhelming in magnitude yet largely unrecognized and underreported. Research indicates that 1 in 5 girls and 1 in 10 boys will be sexually victimized before adulthood." If a girl is being abused at home and has no one to turn to or advocate for her, simply leaving her home might seem the best move to make, but it's one fraught with other perils.

Girls who become homeless are at significantly greater risk for sexual exploitation, disease and illness, and a spiral into other harmful activities. Entering prostitution or sexual trafficking is one such risk. According to the website Medscape Today (www.medscape.com/medscapetoday), "STIs [sexually transmitted infections] are common among homeless girls and women, a function of limited access to reproductive health services, prostitution, and survival sex (ie, sex in exchange for food, drugs, or temporary shelter)." Additionally, the site reports, "Homeless women have a pregnancy rate about twice the national rate. HIV rates are higher than in the general population, which has been attributed to higher prevalence of intravenous drug use, STIs, prostitution, survival sex, and limited access to condoms."

know someone their age who has been hit or beaten by a boyfriend." It also offers, "In one study, from 30 to 50 percent of female high school students reported having already experienced teen dating violence." Sites such as www.loveisrespect.org, sponsored by the National Teen Dating Abuse Helpline, offer resources to girls (and boys) that include a national hotline to call for help and a "Teen Dating Bill of Rights" intended to help teens better understand what they are entitled to in a relationship, and what they should never put up with.

Barrie Levy's book *In Love and in Danger: A Teen's Guide to Breaking Free of Abusive Relationships* offers vivid portrayals of teenage girls who are caught in abusive relationships and how to parse both the subtleties and overwhelming realities of their situations. In one section, Levy lists reasons why girls stayed in a violent relationship and didn't leave right away, and the reasons reflect some of the realities of teens' lives. One girl says, "My friends think he's great and, ashamed to admit we had problems, I kept trying to make things work." Another states, "I felt lucky to have him and believed that no one else would want to be with me; I was convinced that I was ugly, stupid." Still another girl explains, "We go to the same school. I was pressured by his friends, like I was doing something terrible to him when I told him I wanted to break up." Levy also highlights statements from teens in healthy relationships, modeling how positive connections are possible. One teenage girl, Selma, says, "You know what I like best about Tony? He's on my team. It's going to be hard to get through all the years of college I have ahead of me. He cheers me on every step of the way! We do that for each other."

Sexual harassment, fear of rape, and understanding oneself in relationship to safety and danger are complex issues for all girls. Girls receive a complicated mixture of messages about how to navigate nighttime streets, darkened party corners, uncomfortable car rides, and a myriad of other situations that may be inhospitable to their safety and comfort. Abuse and harassment can be much more than physical harm. It can mean being called names that are demeaning or cruel, a partner who demands to always know where a girlfriend is, controls whom she can see, disallows a girl from seeing her friends, limits contact with family, or treats a girl like a sexual object. In and of itself, anxiety about being harassed can irrevocably tilt a girl's understanding of her power in the world, her right to be in a room, and her ownership of the place where she belongs.

Educational programs that teach children to identify the difference between "good touching" and "bad touching"—and to object to the latter—can help young girls (and boys) understand the impact of unwanted contact and feel in control of their bodies. Role playing with dolls or stuffed animals, and offering girls books that address the issue of how touch feels, can build girls' body awareness and reiterate that it's not only okay, but expected, that girls raise their voices against unwanted contact and break with the stereotype of submissiveness, even to a relative's unwelcome embrace. Self-defense programs for girls are another important source of empowerment, but a larger, societywide response is also called for, in which boys and men are held responsible for changing their behavior.

Yet for girls to feel safe from sexual assault requires a constellation of factors to align. Can a girl trust that the male date she's at a party with doesn't feel "entitled" to sexual contact through his own gender conditioning, and if refused, doesn't think that he has the right to physically demand contact? Does a girl believe that she is in control of her sexuality and can act out of true desire, rather than hitting a mark of experience that she thinks, at her age, she should meet? If she suffers a sexual assault, can a girl turn to her parents, or is home not necessarily a safe place—or is it even the place in which she was assaulted?

Reconditioning boys' attitudes toward sexuality is critical so that they are not stuck in a mind-set of "machismo" that privileges their desires and leads them to treat girls as objects, rather than as subjects for whom they show respect. Opening discussion about sexuality to all teens can break down patterns of gender stereotyping that lead boys to equate aggressiveness with sexual prowess and girls to think they ought to deny desire and withhold sexuality from boys as a play of power. Reconsidering the idea that boys are sexual predators who are lauded for their "conquests" while girls must control their sexual agency and deny desire or risk harm or being labeled negatively for acting on their desire is crucial to reconditioning social expectations.

Sexual abuse is a serious issue—with life-changing consequences for girls who experience it. If a girl is sexually assaulted, it is imperative that she seek not only physical aid, but also emotional support. And living with the threat of assault can be damaging in circumstances in which emotional abuse accompanies physical or sexual abuse. Gender expectations—boys may learn they are expected to control a situation and the people within it, and girls may learn that they "should" abnegate their own feelings or soothe others' tempers, blaming themselves for others' actions—can shape a dynamic of coercion, set the stage for relationship abuse, and make it harder for girls to leave an abusive relationship. An abusive teen relationship is also known to be a precursor to an abusive adult relationship.

The statistics around sexual assault and rape for girls and women are alarming. RAINN (Rape, Abuse, and Incest National Network, which uses the subtitle "The nation's largest anti-sexual assault organization") claims that "one in six women will be sexually assaulted in her lifetime," and that "college women are four times more likely to be sexually assaulted." The Bureau of Justice's May 2000 *Special Report: Intimate Partner Violence* offers that a survey of 500 young women, "ages 15 to 24, found that 60 percent were currently involved in an ongoing abusive relationship and all participants had experienced violence in a dating relationship." Its statistics on rape reveal that "38 percent of date rape victims were young women from 14 to 17," and "a survey of adolescent and college students revealed that date rape accounted for 67 percent of sexual assaults. More than half [of] young women raped (68 percent) knew their rapist either as a boyfriend, friend or casual acquaintance" and the site reports, "Six out of 10 rapes of young women occur in their own home or a friend or relative's home, not in a dark alley."

In cases of sexual assault and harassment, hostility toward women and girls is often a factor. In the AAUW's 2000 report *Voices of a Generation: Teenage Girls Report About Their Lives Today,* 17 percent of participants identified "some form of sexual coercion, such as sexual harassment, teasing, or date rape" as a major issue in their lives. In the AAUW's report *Hostile Hallways: The AAUW Survey on Sexual Harrassment in America's Schools,* published in 1993, "fully four out of five 8th to 11th graders surveyed (81 percent) report that they have been the target of sexual harassment." The girls surveyed often reported nonchalance from administrators or school officials, which underscores the idea that harassment is acceptable, and girls' efforts for change are invalidated. Of course, there are rules against this—legal ones—but their enforcement can be less simple than it ought to be, and a culture of shame that prevents girls and women from coming forward about rape or abuse, in tandem with a culture that lauds male aggression, contributes to a difficult dynamic.

Deborah L. Tolman, author of *Dilemmas of Desire: Teenage Girls Talk About Sexuality*, writes that "being a girl, living comfortably in a girl's body, is neither easy nor especially safe." She describes girls experiencing "the socially manufactured dilemma of desire" that "pits girls' embodied knowledge and feelings, their sexual pleasure and connection to their own bodies and to others through their desire, against physical, social, material, and psychological dangers associated with their sexuality." The "dilemma of desire" girls experience, she explains, is a direct result of "social constructions that produce privilege and oppression." Supportive, trustworthy relationships throughout a girl's adolescence are vital, Tolman says.

Freedom and Choices

In the final chapter of *The Body Project*, Brumberg writes, "At the end of the twentieth century, living in a girl's body is more complicated than it was a century ago." She lays out a late-twentieth-century dilemma that still resonates in the twenty-first, in what some still consider a "postfeminist" era: Girls, she explains, are told "on the one hand . . . that being female was no bar to accomplishment. Yet girls of [this] generation learned from a very early age that the power of their gender was tied to what they looked like—and how 'sexy' they were—rather than to character or achievement." Absent the Victorian-era "protective umbrella" that once shielded girls (and restricted them) from sexuality, girls have more freedom than ever, but, according to Brumberg, "their freedom is laced with peril."

Yet openness about sexuality in a post–sexual revolution era also gives girls options they would never before experience: the choice to explore their sexuality before marriage or committed partnership, to understand their own desires and needs, to discover whether or not they are heterosexual, bisexual, lesbian, or want to move between definitions.

"Knowledge is power" is a popular saying, and it is remarkable how much more informed girls can now be—through Internet resources if there isn't open discussion within their own families or good information given through school or other community resources. Knowing more about their bodies and about sex leads girls toward making their own choices, although careful media education is still needed to decode options that are "normalized," such as being sexualized at early ages or at a moment when a girl feels she "should" be, but might not be, ready.

Artist Barbara Kruger's famous statement "Your body is a battleground" is often heard within circles where women examine issues pertaining to bodies, gender, and cultural expectations. Girls' more recently won freedoms—to participate in sports, to envision and plan for careers previously limited to (often privileged) men, to access accurate information about sexuality and sexual health—intersect with a consumer culture that sees girls and women as both bait and targets, and a society that has not come as far in abolishing limiting and harmful stereotypes of gender and sexuality as it likes to think. The site of a complex locus of cultural issues surrounding power, identity, and sexuality—often converging at uncomfortable angles—a girl's body is hardly peaceful to inhabit.

A popular seventh-grade clique in a middle school cafeteria.

CHAPTER 3

"MEAN" GIRLS AND "GOOD" GIRLS: SOCIALIZATION, FRIENDSHIP, AND AGGRESSION

"If you don't have anything nice to say, don't say anything at all."
"Boys will just tell you when they're mad, but girls are sneaky."
"Girls are catty."

These are just some of the statements girls often grow up hearing (and then repeating) as they are socialized to assume the traits of traditional femininity. As they grow older girls learn—from their families, teachers, friends, and communities, and from portrayals of femininity in the media—that they should repress their anger, avoid physical fights, use words instead of fists, and avoid conflict and confrontation; they are even, sometimes, counseled to avoid being too assertive. Boys, by contrast, often learn from those same sources that a certain level of aggression and outspokenness is not only "normal" but expected of them within the culture of masculinity.

"Being nice" for a girl can take many forms—smiling, being welcoming, available, open, nurturing, kind, nonconfrontational. And girls are repeatedly told, both explicitly and subtly, that this is how they're meant to be: Parents often encourage sharing and cooperative activities, or discourage "rough" play and overt competition, praise friendliness and games or habits that socialize girls into the feminine sphere, such as having tea parties, playing dress-up, or practicing for motherhood with baby dolls.

Sharon Lamb writes in her book *The Secret Lives of Girls: What Good Girls Really Do—Sex Play, Aggression, and Their Guilt* that "research shows that mothers increasingly punish girls between the ages of four and six for aggression and decreasingly punish boys." Girls are also trained, covertly and overtly, to learn that between girls friendship and cooperation are expected, anger and rejection are not. In her chapter "Dear Diary, I Hate Her! Secret Anger in Girls," Lamb mentions an African American middle-class woman who remembers tolerating playing with a girl she never liked because the girl was her mother's best friend's daughter. To relieve her displeasure in being forced to play with the girl she would do "little" mean things to her, a theme that echoes within other studies about girls' friendships and the complicated ways in which girls act out when they can't voice their frustration or anger. In her chapter, Lamb details how many girls found that their diaries—meant to be secret, silent receptacles that no one is supposed to read—were the only place girls felt they could legitimately unleash their rage.

Lamb's research explores the many ways in which girls' anger is disallowed and the often excruciating pressures girls experience as these feelings are suppressed with few acceptable outlets. She writes, "Much research has shown, however, that for middle-class girls it is not okay to feel angry and that adults teach girls from a very young age to mask their anger so that, after time, it is even unrecognizable to themselves." Rachel Simmons, another researcher who has studied this subject extensively, writes in her book *Odd Girl Out* about how girls are taught from a young age that a range of aggressive behaviors and angry emotions are unacceptable. She says, "Research confirms that parents and teachers discourage the emergence of physical and indirect aggression in girls early on while the skirmishing of boys is either encouraged or shrugged off. In one example, a 1999 University of Michigan study found that girls were told to be quiet, speak softly, or use a 'nicer' voice about three times more often than boys, even though the boys were louder."

The concept of the "good girl" who hews to a standard of feminized behavior has been long-standing. Girls, when young, are socialized to conform to this rubric with variations often marked by race, class, and ethnic and cultural expectations. Yet tenets that define feminine behavior for girls (being more cooperative, being agreeable, having domestic interests) often have a broad stranglehold. In *The Secret Lives of Girls* Lamb explores the stereotypical definition of the "good girl" that most girls are trained from birth onward to believe they must be. How this is defined, however, can move along a spectrum of "feminized" behaviors, although some expectations always apply, such as cultivating "niceness," being nurturing, quiet, compliant, and agreeable.

Lamb writes, "Most girls measure themselves against this ideal of the good girl, though ultimately it hurts them. Because ideals of goodness often are confused with real or possible behavior, living, breathing girls cannot live up to the image and find themselves demoralized from trying. Not only does the ideal shut out girls from low-income neighborhoods whose lives don't match up, it rejects middle-class girls who know in their hearts that they are not as good as they should be." She says that girls feel tremendous blame and shame when they cannot fulfill the standard of the good girl and anger and aggressive acts escape them, despite their attempts at control. It is also critical to consider the overarching conundrum of systemic denial of girls' anger, how this is broadly sanctioned within mainstream American culture, and the resulting impossibility girls then experience trying to erase this emotion from their lives.

To make the point of how children's behavior is stratified by gender, Lamb traces the figure of the tomboy. Inhabiting this label allows a girl to venture into stereotypically male terrain—acting aggressively, not caring about appearance, valuing rough-and-tumble play, while at the same time reinforcing the concept of separate spheres for boys and girls' behaviors. Most girls who hold this role when young are nudged from it as they enter adolescence and are then told that they are meant to inhabit a more feminized role. The mere label of "tomboy" (with its lack of positive counterpart for boys) reveals how stratified gender expectations are and that this label is a way in which a girl can "pass" into "boy" traits or habits, until she's told that a world of action and aggressive activity is no longer hers to share.

Differences Among Girls

"Part of being an acceptable girl in a culture so deeply infused with white middle-class values, is to be, or at least appear to be, 'nice,'" writes Lyn Mikel Brown in her book *Girlfighting*. "So girls who buy into prevailing views of femininity are likely to hide the 'bad' or 'shameful' parts of their relationships when they can. Girls who, because of race, ethnicity, sexual identity, or class define femininity differently or who experience being female as something more active and direct and physical are put in their place and soon learn about the advantages offered to those who assimilate or pass. Those who resist, who refuse to map onto any simple notion of girlhood, risk being labeled troublemakers, stupid, or worse." It sounds like a large burden—and it is—for girls who want to deviate from conventionally "acceptable" norms of femininity or whose backgrounds exclude them from these standards. In her book, Brown writes of learning to "gender pass" as a young woman so that she would be taken seriously by male colleagues. How girls of color or of working-class backgrounds also navigate gender to "pass" is worth considering.

Through her research Lamb finds that "the African-American girls I spoke to seemed to be not as burdened by the idea of perfection in their judgments of what makes a good girl." One reason as to why this is, Lamb suggests, is the idea that since African American girls less frequently see mainstream ideals of beauty and goodness that represent them, they may think these standards are less relevant, perhaps shielded from "the media's deleterious influence."

In a later chapter on loudness (a quality girls are stereotypically expected to reject), Lamb points out the cultural and racial implications of valuing this trait. She writes that many white middle-class girls "have mastered the quiet of the good girl." When girls are willing to be loud in school, this may reflect speaking out against a "historical and institutional silencing," says Lamb, although she is quick to point out that for a girl, refusing to be silenced by being loud often has other consequences. She writes, "The idea of loudness is associated with badness, but for African-American girls who are loud, it means presence. The paradox for African-American girls is that the louder they are, the more visible, yet the more they risk being seen as bad, wild, unruly, or simply unacceptable."

Being loud, speaking out, affirming oneself are all ways to command attention, and girls tread a fine line between asserting themselves and suffering repercussions for doing so. "But when women and girls take up space," writes Lamb, citing Dana Crowley Jack in *Behind the Mask*, "they are considered male and stigmatized as pushy and unfair. In fact, middle-class girls' goodness often has been defined against boys' messiness and loudness in schools." Further, Lamb writes, "Loud girls make themselves more 'masculine' in the eyes of their teachers and the culture when they are loud, and this may make them more vulnerable later to proving their femininity in stereotypical ways." Lamb also points out that when girls choose loudness as a strategy for attention in school, they defy an expectation of the "good girl student" and risk punishment and disconnection from teachers who might provide mentoring by not complying with an educational model that reinforces quiet cooperation. And yet they also defy invisibility and silencing, which may be indicative of positive self-esteem.

To further complicate understanding of girls' aggression, Lamb suggests that when stereotypically "good girls" turn aggressive, they often claim that this behavior came out of nowhere, and they see it as alien or "othered" or borrowed from an ethnic or racial category in which they don't see themselves as fitting. When aggressive behavior is ascribed to African American or Latina girls, says Lamb, "It fits the stereotypes and allows white girls to feel superior in comparison." More frustrating, although perhaps also liberating, is the idea that it is harder for girls of color to see themselves fitting into society's standard of the "good girl" (the example she uses is of a girl with high grades and leadership awards), and yet there are potential pitfalls if they overly "embrace sexuality and aggression." As she finds in her research, African

American girls are more willing to be confrontational and direct, unlike middle-class white girls, and yet their avoidance of this pattern may only set them up for other criticism.

In Simmons's exploration of race and class within girls' friendships she found that girls whose lives were marked by oppression were often those for whom "assertiveness and anger were tools of spiritual strength." Simmons writes, "Where economic struggle and disenfranchisement prevail, self-assertion and aggression become . . . part of the social landscape. . . . In this world silence can mean invisibility and danger." Simmons references the 1990 AAUW study that found that adolescent black girls scored highest when their self-esteem was measured, and that these girls were often most able to handle conflict well. Citing Carol Gilligan and Lyn Mikel Brown, Simmons asserts that girls on the margins of their school communities, whether they were there because of race or class, "were more likely to stay in touch with their thoughts and feelings and to have close, confiding relationships."

Brown reports through her research in *Girlfighting* that girls of color are, on the whole, more likely to have families that support them while they "publicly claim their realities," as well as their "critique of white femininity." "Their struggle is not necessarily with the seamless collusion of their families, communities, and the wider culture," Brown writes, "but how to move through disparate worlds with a sense of integrity and hope." She states that black and working-class girls were often more able to be clear about their feelings, that "being their loud complicated selves could get them in trouble, but it was better than being victims or invisible."

Girls who are comfortable with conflict or who won't deny their own emotions reflect a stronger sense of self-worth, and as Simmons points out, if their survival depends on raising their voices, they are also more prone to feel entitled to do so. Simmons quotes scholar bell hooks, who warns not to romanticize the "truth telling of African-American girls." Paraphrasing hooks, she says that "truth telling and assertiveness" are not necessarily the same as building high self-esteem. She writes, "An outspoken girl might still feel worthless because her skin was not light enough or the right texture." Simmons emphasizes how difficult it is to make broad assumptions about a girl's behavior based on her race or class alone; it is important to reject the notion of a "universal minority female experience" and to remember that "dominant middle-class notions of femininity are foreign to the experience of many white girls," particularly those from working-class backgrounds, where children might be socialized "to use physical aggression to protect themselves from their peers." Yet she writes that many working-class girls she interviewed were "unwilling to bring anger into their close relationships," not because they think that anger is culturally inappropriate, but rather because they need the support of their friends in their lives.

Speaking out, being loud, making demands, and asserting oneself are still complicated actions for most women. The risk of being labeled "difficult" or even called "angry" or "bossy" as an insult remains, while a man who engages in similar behavior is likely to be rewarded for the same choices. Differing influences, such as class-based pressure to assume a job, or care for younger siblings, or ethnic expectations, such as those around dating or respecting elders, will clearly affect a girl's socialization and sense of herself. But the thread of traditional femininity weaves its way through girls' socialization and the ways in which their behavior will be measured by society at large. It's a fabric that is most often supposed to blot out anger, or cover it up, leaving girls caught between denying their natural inclination to, at times, be angry, and feeling transgressive or punished for doing so.

Friendship and Anger

So where do girls find space to express the anger, frustration, and even fury that all human beings experience? How do girls learn to deal with this set of emotions when owning anger outright often earns them the label "bitch" or other negative names? What happens when they are, as everyone is at times, just plain mad?

As more light has been shed on girls' experiences of being gendered, what's revealed (and then, often as not, hotly debated) are some of the powerful ways many girls find to express anger and aggression—

sometimes in the only way they have, covertly, through subterfuge and below the radar. Journalist Margaret Talbot's 2002 *New York Times* article "Girls Just Want to Be Mean" contextualizes the genesis of attention to girlhood aggression and anger. "For years," she writes, "psychologists who studied aggression among school children looked only at its physical and overt manifestations and concluded that girls were less aggressive than boys." But in the early 1990s, Talbot continues, a team of researchers interviewed a group of middle school–aged girls about their behavior and concluded that the girls were just as aggressive as boys—but in different, and usually overlooked, ways. Barred from physical fighting and discouraged from direct, forthright confrontation, the girls in the study turned to other methods: being emotionally hurtful through rejection, sending rumors around, gossiping strategically, and withholding or denying friendship in order to reinforce or foster a social pecking order that left certain girls out. Talbot adds that later researchers "noted that up to the age of four girls tend to be aggressive at the same rates and in the same ways as boys—grabbing toys, pushing, hitting." However, she says, as many girls grow older and are told this is unacceptable behavior (and while boys are often told this too, they are often covertly still allowed to act in these ways), girls' aggression is forced underground. They learn that they can't use physical force to act out their angers, so they turn to subtle and less visible ways to express this emotion, often labeled acts of "relational aggression."

Relational aggression has been defined by a small group of psychologists at the University of Minnesota, writes Simmons in *Odd Girl Out*, as acts that "harm others through damage (or the threat of damage) to relationships or feelings of acceptance, friendship, or group inclusion." According to Simmons, "relationally aggressive behavior is ignoring someone to punish them or get one's own way, excluding someone socially for revenge, using negative body language or facial expressions, sabotaging someone else's relationships, or threatening to end a relationship unless the friend agrees to a request. In these acts, the perpetrator uses her relationship with the victim as a weapon."

Simmons writes that close relatives of this include "indirect aggression," which includes covert acts in which the perpetrator makes it seem as though there never was any intent to be hurtful (such as spreading rumors). Simmons also discusses "social aggression," which she defines as behavior intended to damage others' self-esteem and social status within a group by indirectly aggressive acts such as rumor spreading or social exclusion. Giving harsh looks or staring with intentional disapproval are other acts, as are bumping other girls in a school hall in a way that is supposed to be an "accident" or "innocently" asking hurtful questions or wounding through innuendo. The Internet, with the cover of writing under an assumed name and the lightning speed with which information or a picture can be widely broadcast, has also become a powerful way in which aggression can be channeled.

Because girls are generally assumed to have more empathetic natures than boys and are socialized to be nurturing and to value friendship, their emotional intimacy with other girls is often highly prized and a source not only of personal fulfillment but social strength. Considered to have stronger "emotional" intelligence, girls are thought to be more skilled at navigating and negotiating the treacherous waters of school hierarchies.

Simmons is explicit about how integral friendship is to girls, and thereby, when they use friendship as a weapon, how wounding it is. She writes, "To understand girls' conflicts, one must also know girls' intimacy, because intimacy and anger are often inextricable. The intensity of girls' relationships belongs at the center of any analysis of girls' aggression. For long before they love boys, girls love each other, and with great passion." Simmons emphasizes that girls are "urged to identify with nurturing" when young, and with their best friends they discover "the joys of intimacy and human connection." Yet, she says, "ours is a culture that has ignored the closeness of girlfriends. Many people believe that girls should . . . channel their caretaking toward husbands and children. Anything up to that life stage is assumed to be practice, if not insignificant."

The complex ways in which girls value friendship, yet use relationships as a means through which to undermine or invert these connections, are complex and often devastating. It is important to see acts of relational aggression within a cultural context that often devalues girls and denies them a place for conflict and anger. Forced to move their anger underground, since it is disallowed in the open, girls turn to other ways of expression that are more invisible and often socially sanctioned.

"In fact, it is the deep knowledge that girls have of relationship and the passion they lavish on their closest friends," writes Simmons, "which characterizes much of their aggression. The most painful attacks are usually fashioned from deep inside a close friendship and are fueled by secrets and once-shared weakness." Since girls are so routinely steered away from experiencing conflict, says Simmons, even as adult women many don't understand that a relationship can sustain this, rather believing that any form of conflict means a termination of their relationships. She insists, "Since relationship is precisely what good, 'perfect' girls are expected to be in, its loss, and the prospect of solitude, can be the most pointed weapons in the hidden culture of girls' aggression."

In her book *Girlfighting*, Lyn Mikel Brown writes explicitly about the value of girls' friendships when they are young. Making close friends, or even having a "best friend" as a preadolescent, can be akin to a first romance, she says, as a girl experiences for the first time validation through a peer's eyes. Understanding the pull of having close friends during childhood leads, around age nine or ten, she says, to new anxieties about inclusion or exclusion, particularly at a time in which feelings of loneliness can emerge, as well as a preoccupation with being seen as "normal," however that is defined. Girls' friendships, says Brown, begin to undergo a "sea change" in preadolescence as fears of exclusion or the threat of withdrawal of friendship becomes very real to them as they survey the landscape ahead, realizing they are meant to move into a more structured, gender-specific social sphere.

As Brown writes, "Normal can now mean fitting a predefined standard" and the irony "is that reasserting the normal . . . makes so many girls feel unsafe, sad, and defensive." Brown also points out how "normal" often rules out difference, which can in white contexts mean girls of color become outsiders. As "normal" becomes more narrowly defined, girls begin to compete over who fits in and who doesn't. For most girls, Brown writes, "normal" will mean being the ever-present "nice" and "not causing a ruckus," which again teaches girls that their anger is not permissible. The signs of "normal" and "nice girl" behavior for girls means they have to get along, says Brown, and have to be friends, and as they "mask their strong feelings," she writes, "they hone their creative tendencies to express what they want indirectly and communicate their desires and anger in more subtle relational ways."

Both Simmons and Brown reveal that girls' friendships are considered integral to their development and to their emotional lives. Yet girls' friendships, while recognized for their importance, have not historically been valorized. The possibility of threat to boys or the patriarchal order is often cast around the edges of female closeness and the turn from orientation toward boys and men. It is not unusual to hear a rejected man call two women who won't flirt with men at a bar or refuse to entertain male attention "lesbians" in a derogatory way. Alongside this name-calling comes the insinuation of anger that two women would choose to prioritize their time alone together rather than participate in a hetero-normative social ritual in which men are expected to prevail or at least have their right as suitors be entertained.

Carroll Smith-Rosenberg's well-known article, "The Female World of Love and Ritual: Relations Between Women in Nineteenth-Century America," explains how common closeness was between female friends in the nineteenth century, with girls openly using expressions of great affection to one another in letters and in person, and gladly sharing a bed during overnight visits. "It was a world in which men made but a shadowy appearance," she writes. Smith-Rosenberg describes how girls' close friendships, often expressed in diaries and letters, were sanctioned and not pathologized; rather, they were considered healthy, supportive, and nurturing. Girls' emotional ties to each other were considered a powerful bond and there was an unabashed expression of affection and love between friends. While girls today might feel the same, the expression of same-sex closeness and homosocial bonds is not allowed in the same way. Within a significantly more sexualized culture that reiterates a heterosexist script, with variation still considered "deviant," girls learn, often at very young ages, that they are meant to turn their attention from other girls and to boys, and that bonds with other girls can be sacrificed along the way. They also learn that their own role within a patriarchal culture is to be of value to boys, and later men, and participating in this assigned part can mean breaking close ties to girls in ways that are painful for both parties.

"Not surprisingly, in a culture that obsessively promotes heterosexual romance and values male independence, assertiveness, and protection, the disintegration of girls' groups and the tensions and fighting between close friends are most often associated with finding and keeping boyfriends," writes Brown in *Girlfighting*. It is a general cultural assumption, she says, "one that white girls in particular tend to internalize, that girls will and should privilege romantic relationships with boys over girlfriends, even the closest, long-term friendships on which they've come to rely for emotional and psychological support." When this happens, girls feel a deep sense of loss, often jealousy, and also anger. The sense of "passionate friendship" that Smith-Rosenberg describes is echoed by Brown, who says that many girls experience connection with a "best friend" in childhood in a way akin to falling in love for the very first time, as one first feels validated through another's eyes. Yet Brown points out how girls may feel "hampered" by the threat of crossing a line into the appearance of lesbianism and transgressing "codes of sexual and gender 'normalcy.'" As girls move from elementary school to middle, middle to high, and move through stages of adolescent development, so do their friendships often shift and change, and within an increasingly strict gender coding for behavior, close childhood friendships often break apart.

Girl Bullying

In writing *Odd Girl Out*, Simmons draws on her own experience of a painful year of bullying when young; for her research she studies girls' social networks by visiting ten schools, public and private with different socioeconomic composition, within three different regions of the country. Simmons begins to identify the types of bullying that occur between girls and how deeply destructive this pattern of behavior is. In a process that's often unobservable to outsiders, she explains, girls keep silent about what they endure because they are ashamed of being ostracized or think that the intervention of parents, teachers, or counselors will only make things worse.

One of the first hurdles Simmons discovers is the assumption by many parents, teachers, and administrators that girl bullying is "just business as usual." She frequently heard the comments "It's typical girl behavior" or "It will pass" and the assumption that "girl bullying is just a rite of passage" of sorts and there's nothing to be done about it. But she disagrees this is behavior that everyone should just accept: "Yet the rite-of-passage argument paralyzes our thinking about how the culture shapes girls' behavior. Most importantly, it stunts the development of antibullying strategies." She also states that this thinking makes several other "disturbing assumptions," such as that girls "must be predisposed to this behavior" and that "meanness" is simply part of their social structure to be tolerated, as if "it's not really abuse at all." She is quick to point out, as other researchers do, how hard it is to catch girls' relational aggressions, since often nothing looks wrong, while in fact, much is.

As the AAUW reports have shown, it is boys who often reap more attention in the classroom, even if for more rambunctious behavior than girls'. Girls' campaigns of relational aggression are likely to be far less disruptive and, in a harried classroom, to go unnoticed, making calling girls out on this behavior harder. Another pitfall, both Simmons and Brown point out, is that girls often don't want parents to know about the bullying they experience because they are ashamed that they've been singled out and isolated. Most often, they concur, girls blame themselves for their own victimization and feel helpless with no resources to turn to, most poignantly especially if it is a close friend or group of friends who have deliberately turned away. Since girls have such little experience with overt conflict and anger, how to cope in this situation is utterly unknown to them, and they fear that telling a parent, teacher, or counselor might only make their ostracization worse.

Yet Brown is also emphatic about dispelling the perception that girls are just "mean" to one another and that this behavior is part of their natures. Until recently, she claims, bullying and aggression have been seen largely as boys' issues, and by contrast, "there has also been a prevailing view that complaining and bickering, deceit and back-stabbing are normal aspects of growing up female and thus not worthy of serious scholarly attention. Girls are simply, by nature, catty and mean to one another but compared to, say, shooting their classmates, this is nothing. When it came to really serious bullying behavior, girls were the victims, not the perpetrators. This cultural conception has enormous power." The more recent attention given to girls' meanness can be a two-edged sword: On the one hand it raises awareness of a problem often allowed to simmer below public consciousness (yet that is all too real for those girls who experience it), and on the other, when presented as another example of girls' "catty" natures, and not as part of a larger context that considers gendered bias around anger, the attention only reinforces negative stereotypes about girls.

In Talbot's article "Girls Just Want to Be Mean," *Queen Bees and Wannabees* author Rosalind Wiseman details the ways in which girls manipulate each other or vie for power within a social hierarchy: She describes girls using subtle but destructive methods such as leaving messages on a home answering machine that a parent might hear ("Are the results of your pregnancy test back yet?"); organizing three-way calls in which one girl remains silent while one entices the other girl to gossip about the girl listening in and then is ostracized for her act of "betrayal"; and denying a girl a spot at their lunchroom table. In both Wiseman's work and in Simmons's, the authors detail the complicated punishments and difficulties inflicted on girls through what Wiseman calls "Queen Bees" and Simmons will simply call "bullies." Both authors now run girl-empowerment programs that seek to change these dynamics at the root, or cut them off before they take hold in

Mean Girls

In 2004, Rosalind Wiseman's hallmark book *Queen Bees and Wannabes* served as a springboard for the popular mainstream film *Mean Girls*. Catching the post-*Reviving Ophelia* wave of interest in the emotional lives of girls, Wiseman's book shifted from seeing girls as mainly victimized, or buoyed about in a sea of "girl-hating" culture, to seeing girls as the ones doing the hating—toward each other. She explores the dynamics of girl bullying and the circles and cycles of what has been called "relational anger" between and among girls. The film centers around the experiences of fifteen-year-old Cady Heron, who is starting high school in the Midwest after being raised in Africa by her zoologist parents. As an outsider, she quickly learns to map the cliques of her new high school: the "plastics" ruled by a queen bee figure, the "Asian nerds," the "cool Asians," the "burnouts," the "varsity jocks," and the "art freaks." Initially befriended by two of the "art freaks," Cady is swept up into the "plastics" circle, where she is stunned to learn the many rules imposed about dressing, hair style, association, and how to act. As she works through her friendship with them, particularly Regina, as well as with Damian and Janis (the "art freaks"), she comes to realize where her values lie.

The film deftly touches on many of the rituals and rules of "Girl World": dressing sexily for Halloween, the imperative to remain thin, and bonding with female friends through shopping and body scrutiny. Cady deliberately does poorly on a math test to try to impress a boy she likes, and in a triumphant move at the film's end, answers a key question for the math team, which she later becomes unabashed to join. Relational anger among girls is in evidence through the film: three-way calls in which one party is silent but listening for betrayal, "accidental" bumping in the hall, hostile looks, deliberate messages returned from a cell phone to avoid showing caller ID, a "burn book" that circulates with aggressive and hurtful messages about many students not deemed "cool" by the in crowd. In one scene, Regina's significantly younger sister is seen mimicking the sexy moves of dancers on MTV, showing how girls at her age are already socialized into thinking this is how they must be.

Toward the film's end Tina Fey, who plays a teacher at the school, assembles all the girls to address the hostility and competition among

continued

them, and it seems, at least momentarily, that she gets the girls to realize the ways in which they destroy relationships with each other is not worthwhile. "You have *got* to stop calling each other sluts and whores," Fey insists. "It's just bad for business." In one of the film's closing scenes, it is clear that the cliques have been disbanded and the hostility between groups has eased as there seems to be new movement between the previously exclusive groups.

During commentary in the "special features" section, both Fey and Wiseman speak to the necessity of making this film. Fey, who read Wiseman's book and then constructed a narrative to encapsulate the struggles and themes within "Girl World," felt strongly about bringing attention to the difficulties that girls experience. Producer Lorne Michaels mentions that interest in this topic was "in the air." The attention the film received rode the wave of interest in girls' relational aggressions and smartly showed how destructive they can be. Within the humor of the film, there is an intelligent through-line that looks through the lens of Cady's outsider perspective to ask what purpose the anger and infighting of the school serves.

On one hand parodying the supremacy of Regina, the school's "queen bee," and on the other showing how hurtful her imperious power is, the film was largely well received as another wake-up call to the insidiousness, and realness, of aggression within "Girl World." One danger with the film was the possibility of again trivializing girls' anger and the social restrictions that they often believe they must bow to—with Lindsay Lohan

younger girls, and point out to teachers and parents, and the culture at large, how covert and how damaging these behaviors can be.

Some researchers have likened girls' jockeying for power within social cliques as a way to fulfill an otherwise unfulfillable desire for power—they act through the limited channels available to them, knowing that while American society is still highly conflicted about accepting female leaders, society does value popularity and social success in girls.

Girls form alliances, cliques, trios, or pairings of alliances in many ways and school hierarchies reflect many social factors. They might find commonality through religion or youth group affiliation. Sports, after-school activities, band, or other mutual interests might draw as the film's star and miniskirts on the other lead girls, the film offers a sexualized view of high school girls. And yet, this is its point—to show the social pressures girls feel, and the punishment or estrangement that comes if they transgress. Ultimately, most reviewers and viewers commented on the film's accuracy in exposing rifts between high school factions and the pressures girls face in navigating between groups.

"Meanness" among girls reached a peak of public interest with the film, largely bringing positive attention to a phenomenon long ignored, in the context of showing how harsh girls' interactions can be. In Wiseman's commentary on the film she mentions how her program, Empower, designed to teach how to curb violence for both boys and girls, is reflected in the film's relationships. Wiseman describes how she tries to teach that treating others badly, no matter at how small a level, plants a seed toward making poor choices and potentially violence. She says that she wants outsiders to realize how the girls in the clique treat each other badly, even though from the outside they look as if they all get along, and that this kind of treatment can lead individuals to lose a sense of who they are, which can lead them to make bad choices just to conform. "Girls get messages from the culture," she says, "and then they are the enforcers." "It *is* a big deal," she says emphatically of the interpersonal relationships portrayed in the film, and not a rite of passage, she insists, as girls navigate the halls and worlds of high school, figuring out who they are and who they yet want to be.

girls together. But within the hierarchy of high school, girls also band together through other social labels—the "nerds" or the "popular" girls, the "outcasts" or the "in" crowd. How these social lines divide a school's population differs from place to place, but it's likely that groups will fall out according to similar structures no matter the school, often with class and race as dominant factors. When girls cross dividing lines at school through friendship, or through aggression, often the effect is noticed. Transgressing from one social group to another can be seen as an act of defiance (for example, by befriending a girl from another race or higher or lower tier in the perceived hierarchy), and it can also be an act of deliberate manipulation, inviting the girl in only to show the power of inclusion and then later exclusion. The demands of social relationships at school for girls (and boys) can be a minefield of intricate maneuvering, with shifting alliances and loyalties. In many schools, whether public or private, chances are that groups will form along ethnic and racial lines, with classism also an element as girls group along socioeconomic lines, sometimes with material objects (clothes, purses, backpacks, accessories) as visible commodities of status. In the fishbowl of school politics and pecking order, these can be powerful dividing forces and another social tool through which girls express anger, aggression, and power.

The ways in which girls sublimate their angers into covert actions that twist acceptable behavior into destructive patterns reveals how complicated the contradictions are within girls' social lives. Because girls are often rewarded for harboring close friendships, exclusion from within a tight circle of friends is often the hardest punishment a girl can suffer. Because this exclusion and silencing might not be visible to teachers or parents, the dynamics of this practice can be hard for adults to see when observing from the outside. When girls use friendship and its denial as weapons—during the vulnerable middle school years in particular, when girls cope with changing bodies and identities and cultural expectations, arguably needing the support of friends the most—the resulting damage can linger into adulthood. The consequences of girlhood bullying can be devastating in the moment, and the lingering effects can be long-ranging.

At the end of her book, Simmons quotes Marcie, who was one of the first women she interviewed. In her late twenties at the time of her interview, Marcie says of other women, "I know it's internal, and that there's a little part of me that will never quite trust them. There's a little part of me that believes they will turn on me at any moment." Simmons writes that Marcie's words echo the voices of many girls and women she met, who, "injured in childhood by their peers . . . [still] feel a raw hurt and bewilderment. These women are asking why the people around them, sometimes their closest friends, expressed anger indirectly and at times without warning, leaving them disoriented, alone, and full of self-blame." Earlier in her book, Simmons presents the example of Vanessa, a woman who as a girl turned away from other girls to befriend guys. When Simmons asks why, she again hears the echo of other women's voices in Vanessa's answer: "I think in a way it's because I don't trust women." She adds that the feeling that "they're going to get you again. And you've got your defenses up at all times" is something that she can't shake. The effects are long-lasting and another way in which distrust between women perpetuates division and impedes uniting for change.

A Tear in the Larger Fabric

In her book *Girlfighting,* Lyn Mikel Brown describes the context in which the complicated strands of girls' friendships intertwine. "Two seemingly contradictory themes emerge over and over again," she writes. "First, girls depend on close, intimate friendships to get them through life. . . . Second, girls can be excruciatingly tough on other girls. They can talk behind each others' backs, tease and torture one another, police each other's clothing and body size . . . and can promote a strict conformity to the norms and rules of idealized femininity, threaten rejection and exclusion, and reinforce gender and racial stereotypes." In doing so, she argues, they participate in and maintain "our society's largely negative views of girls' and women's relationships as untrustworthy, deceitful, and manipulative."

Brown describes girl-to-girl aggression as a reflection of a sexist culture in which girls internalize and continue their own oppression: "Girlfighting is not a biological necessity, a developmental stage, a rite of passage. It is a protective strategy and an avenue to power learned and nurtured in early childhood and perfected over time." She continues, "Undermining other girls for attention or boys' favor is qualitatively no different from jealously protecting one's small piece of patriarchal pie from other women. The bigger question, too infrequently asked, is who cut the pie this way in the first place?"

Working through the internalization of a patriarchal society's stance toward girls, Lamb writes in *The Secret Lives of Girls,* "Girls who struggle to exist within a male-dominated culture align themselves with dominant voices. For example, while dominant society might use the term 'slut' to keep women in their place and allow greater freedom to men, girls adopt this name-calling of other girls in order to set themselves apart from other girls and to presumably be seen in a more favorable light to boys, men or some monolithic, imaginary (male-controlled) other called culture." Lamb also cites Paulo Freire and the example of "horizontal violence" that he gives in his book *Pedagogy of the Oppressed* as a way in which to understand girls' acting out toward other girls. She also mentions Brown's use of the term "ventriloquation"—girls channeling white male patriarchal authority when they talk about other girls. Lamb explains that Brown borrows the term from Mikhail Bakhtin to represent the ways in which girls appropriate the white male authority figure in judging other girls and replicating the standards and tenets of a patriarchal society.

Lamb points out that girl-to-girl solidarity does exist, especially with girl groups, girls' athletic teams, and girl gangs. She says that society wants girls to be nicer to one another, more inclusive, and to rid themselves of the practice of exclusive cliques, but these appeals will never be met without other acceptable means to channel girls' competitiveness and to "honor girls' anger and self-righteousness as well as their very human feelings of competition, rather than covering them over with 'good girl' values of caring and sympathy." Unless this happens, she writes, enforcing "the girl-to-girl solidarity will have a falseness to it.

The pressures on girls to ascribe to conventional understandings of femininity are well documented, and the contradictions that girls experience as they move into adolescence can be dizzying. On one hand, they often hear "you can be anything," "there are no more shut doors because of gender," and "boys and girls are equal now." And yet for many girls, this is hardly the reality they experience. Within a largely still patriarchal culture, girls learn how they are meant to orient themselves around boys, and later men, and to ascribe to a mostly still traditional definition of feminine behavior. Brown writes,

"As girls become visibly like women—as their bodies begin to change, as their faces mature, and as boys begin to enter the picture to confirm their emerging sexuality—they confront a fresh wave of pressure to be 'good' and desirable women in the conventional sense." She continues, "Girls this age are moving into a culture that takes women less seriously and values them most for their physical beauty and their compliance. . . . This is a precarious time precisely because there are so many contradictory messages."

Brown writes, "For white middle-class girls this is an especially confusing time, since their families, school, and the media often collude in a construction of white femininity that is very different from the way girls have experienced and known the relational world of childhood. They are expected to modulate their voices and narrow their possibilities in order to fit in or not make waves." She continues that "white middle-class girls . . . describe their voices as 'muffled'" and that it is "dangerous to speak their knowledge publicly." She says that girls comment that they know when they are "pretending, performing, or impersonating the right kind of girl in order to keep their relationships with boys or satisfy others' views of appropriate behavior." As girls look out and see that they must subscribe to a narrower range of behavior than in childhood and that they will be judged for their adherence to this standard, and possibly ostracized if they do not comply, they begin to watch each other and to police behavior that deviates from the expected norm, even if its rules also restrict them. Girls experience, says Brown, the pressure of trying to meet the new ideals they are expected to live up to and learn, she writes, "to see themselves as others want them to be, rather than to experience and feel and think as they are. To be objectified as a girl is not a new thing for them, but to own it—to actually experience oneself as an object—is new. And part of experiencing it, owning it, is generalizing it to other girls—that is, learning to police others, to judge others on the same terms." She gives the example of staring down other girls with a look that is aggressive, controlling, and even shaming. It's a silent act, and one that is not likely to be seen by a teacher or parent, but the girl on the receiving end will feel its wrath. Girls move toward secretive methods of expressing anger, domination, and control because these emotions are publicly disallowed. "[Girls] use culturally relevant forms of control to bring other girls in line," Brown writes, citing "teasing, joking and criticism" to teach each other how important it is to be "normal," even though "normal" might be a media construction that does not reflect the reality of girls' lives. Brown points out that girls, constricted by the rules of "heterosexual normalcy, about white racial constructions of beauty, about appropriate ways to be a girl in any given context, about the reality of scarce resources and limited chances for visibility and power," enter this context using what tools they can to survive. "Girls are acting just as people in subordinate or less powerful positions are 'supposed' to act with each other," she writes. "They are becoming card-carrying members of a sexist ideology that stereotypes and judges girls and women and denigrates qualities associated with femininity." The grip of the status quo and pressure to fit in and be perceived as "normal" damages girls' freedoms and binds their individuality.

Cultural messages about what it means to be a "good girl," says Brown, invite "constant comparison and competition" and girls take out their own failures to meet this definition on other girls. "No one wins," she writes, "because jealousy directed toward those close to perfection is as divisive and damaging as the rejection of those who don't have a chance." Brown is clear, however, that "the line between good girls and bad, nice and mean, popular and unpopular is not a line girls created, but one they've absorbed from the wider culture in which they live and one they're expected to maintain and anticipate wherever they go." Girls gain power through boyfriends, or social means through school, with transgressions from "normalcy" met with anxiety on every side. For white, middle-class girls, the competition is over meeting the feminine ideal, according to Brown, but if she attains it, a girl opens herself to envy and attacks from others who collectively scrutinize flaws to reassure themselves of their own status. Girls also walk a fine line between being proud of themselves and then critiqued because they think they are "all that," revealing again the intricate line to be negotiated at all times.

Teaching Anger

In the 1990s girls were often painted as suffering from lack of self-esteem, shrinking back, and losing a sense of themselves. Learning that some girls feel powerful and act out, even if in vengeful or destructive ways, can almost be heartening; it shows girls are capable of a fuller spectrum of emotions than those grouped on the "pink" end of the behavioral spectrum. But the fact that girls' anger is so often turned against other girls, reflecting girls' internalization of the belief that girls are worthy of derision, targeting, and bad treatment, argues for a cultural change larger than merely acknowledging girls' anger and attributing it to individual psychosocial processes.

Lamb, writing in *The Secret Lives of Girls,* suggests that "if girls learn to accept their anger and their feelings of aggression, they can tap into this potential and transform it, sometimes in creative and positive ways." She says that girls' aggression will come out in other forms when it is physically reined in and that "girls turn it against themselves: through eating disorders, self-mutilation, hypercriticism about their talents and bodies, and depression." She says that even if girls in these circumstances are given treatment, "girls who own their aggression—even feel entitled to it—have a source of energy and creativity that will do them well in the lives ahead of them." She emphasizes that empathy is, of course, a worthwhile quality to cultivate, but that parents and society have often already done this for girls. "But it's not a zero sum equation," she writes. "Being a full human being means having the capacity for both compassion and anger and frustration. Along with the former comes the ability to care; with the latter the ability to act aggressively and be angry."

In *Odd Girl Out* Simmons addresses the inherently conflicted positions that both perpetrator and victim are in. "Silence is deeply woven into the fabric of the female experience," she writes, referring to a range of potential moments in women's lives; among the topics that have come to public attention, such as rape, incest, domestic violence, and women's health, she sees the issue of bullying among girls also coming forward. Toward the end of her book, she describes an experiment in which she asks girls to define what constitutes a good leader, and many girls realize that qualities such as "taking charge, saying no, and engaging in conflict" are in opposition to the limiting "good girl" qualities they have learned. Teaching girls how to assert themselves, she urges, is not only necessary for their psychological survival, but for their future careers. She reiterates other prominent researchers' conclusions about the sense of restraint girls encounter as they enter adolescence and how the disconnection they feel from their true selves serves no one, least of all the women they will one day become. As they adopt "facades of the 'nice and polite,'" she writes, and "lose the ability to 'name relational violations,' or assert feelings of hurt or anger towards another person," they lose the fullness of who they can become. She concludes, "We might work harder to prohibit girls from engaging in alternative aggressions and instead guide them into more assertive acts of truth telling and direct aggression." Simmons offers structured suggestions how to teach girls assertiveness, comfort with conflict, and a variety of strong feelings. Change will come, she says. "When we can agree that nice girls can get really angry, and that good girls are sometimes quite bad, we will have plowed the social desert between 'nice' and 'bitch.' When we have built a positive vocabulary for girls to tell each other their truths, more girls will raise their voices."

Through the work of Wiseman and different girl-empowerment programs, such as Simmons's Girls Leadership Institute and Brown's Hardy Girls, Healthy Women, much of the silence around girls' behavior has been lifted, although how to eradicate these behaviors, and the social expectations that support them, is still not entirely clear. "Resiliency" is a concept that shows promise in helping girls create positive, supportive communities for themselves. Brown writes that Hardy Girls, Healthy Women strives to create "hardiness zones" for girls in which they can learn how to find support and be resourceful and emotionally strong. The group's website claims, "The programs we create move away from focusing on single issues such as disordered eating or self-esteem. Instead we focus on the social and political landscape that girls grow in, and women live through. Girls' and women's positions will not improve until those social and political landscapes are improved." The foundation also challenges everyone to refocus attention "from the individual to their environment—families, schools, and community organizations—as the key agents of change in girls' lives," stating on its website, "We believe that it is not the girls, but rather the culture in which they live that is in need of repair."

By thinking about girls as the product of a nexus of oppressive social systems—still shaped, in subtle and unsubtle ways, by corrosive influences of racism, classism, heterosexism, and ableism—mentors, parents, and educators can find useful tools to increase girls' awareness of these systemic issues, give girls increased control over their lives, and help girls thrive. As Hardy Girls, Healthy Women states, girls are not "the sum of any particular pathology (self-cutting, disordered eating, drug use) or struggle (body image, self-esteem, early sexual activity), but . . . whole beings living within and affected by a variety of social systems."

It is important to note that cultural messages can be very different depending on influences within girls' individual lives or within their cultures of origin; the emphasis on quietness, niceness, and passivity as positive markers of femininity is a value most often ascribed to middle-class white girls. Resilience might take shape very differently for a girl of color—or for a girl from a working-class background who finds that self-reliance or working is a given in her life. Oftentimes, girls who participate in sports are better able to resist cultural imperatives to shrink their body's size or adhere to the latest fashion trends, as athletic girls' relationships to their bodies often allow them to appreciate what they can do in terms of power and strength. There's no simple—or single—answer to the question, "What makes some girls more resistant to the cliques and hooks of social interaction?" The ability to "bounce back" from rejection or bullying depends on a variety of interactive personal and cultural factors. But when girls can eschew the tangle of social hierarchies at school, tap sources of self-esteem that don't depend on popularity or conformity, or achieve immunity to the influence of institutionalized femininity, they often escape some of the pitfalls of adolescence, such as self-loathing of one's body as it changes shape and size, or the need to "dumb down" intelligence to be less competitive or to avoid being seen by peers as an unfeminine "all that." Looking at the individual girl and the gender-defining messages she receives from her family, community, and the social network and culture she lives within, and then working to change pieces of the overall system that negatively affect her, are often good places to start when cultivating healthy resilience and strong inner reserves for girls.

The reductive assertion that "girls are just mean" still frequently echoes in media reports that address girlhood. Still further evidence of cultural disapproval of feminine anger is the fact that girls' and women's physical fights are often eroticized or trivialized as pornographic fodder for stereotypical male fantasies. As an example, Brown's *Girlfighting* references an episode of the long-running twentysomething-focused television sitcom *Friends* in which a physical fight breaks out between one character, Rachel, and her sister. "Shouldn't we stop them?" asks Rachel's friend Phoebe. Joey, a male friend, responds, "Are you out of your mind? Let's throw some Jell-O on them!" After the fight ends, another male friend, Chandler, leans over and whispers, "By the way, that fight was totally arousing." "Who benefits from assumptions that girls and women are, by nature, back-stabbing, manipulative, and deceitful?" asks Brown, "The problem is not that girls are angry . . . the problem is that girls' legitimate anger has been co-opted as either erotic, trivial, or pathological, and separated from its real source."

Girls can take martial arts or kickboxing classes and be active in physically competitive sports, but they are still not allowed to duke it out on the playground as boys are; they risk being called names or shamed if they show strong emotion that isn't pleasant or pleasing to others. Simmons does an exercise in which she asks girls to define the "ideal girl" and the "anti-girl," who has traits that are considered undesirable. The responses demonstrate the fine and often contradictory line the respondents expect themselves to walk to conform to a feminine ideal: The ideal girl is dependent and helpless, yet she knows how to manipulate others; she is fit but not overly athletic or strong; she

Gamma Girls

A 2002 *Newsweek* article explored the presence of the "gamma girl," as journalist Susannah Meadows called her: a teen girl who was seemingly immune to the effects of cliques, popularity contests, or a pecking order based on values she didn't share. The gamma girl, according to Meadows, is "emotionally healthy, socially secure, independent-minded and just plain nice." Writes Meadows, the prototypical gamma girls aren't worried about being invited to parties or the cool lunchroom tables; they're too busy writing op-ed pieces for the school paper or out surfing. She takes the name for this well-adjusted girl (the "gamma") after an article written by Laura Sessions Stepp, who divided girls into "alphas" and "betas" respectively—those who were the equivalent of what Rosalind Wiseman calls "Queen Bees" and "Wannabes."

No matter the nomenclature, chances are girls will cycle through different groups throughout their adolescence, and existing comfortably with self-esteem intact in whichever group they find themselves within seems to be the challenge. Dan Kindlon's book *Alpha Girls* profiles strong-minded, high-achieving high school girls who feel unstoppable and often appear so. Kindlon finds that many girls are not only shining, but starring, within their high school careers and espouse an unstoppable drive. But other viewpoints to consider alongside these seemingly well-adjusted portraits are: How pressured do these girls feel to succeed, even if the pressure is self-inflicted? And if just a minority of girls are high-achieving "alphas," what can be said for the majority? Kindlon's sample is also narrow, and despite the sure success of the "alpha" girls he finds, extrapolating outward to suggest that all barriers are now down for girls' achievement, and that gender disparities have evened out if some girls never even see the hurdle that they're clearing, doesn't account for still-significant challenges faced by girls who live in poverty, for example, or those without access to good schools.

Without doubt, girls' studies scholars and the media have moved away from focusing on the generic description of Mary Pipher's Ophelia figure: the girl whose self-esteem plummets in preadolescence and who becomes a passive victim to social forces. But how to put into context the strong, shining figures on whom the media have more recently focused?

continued

Without question, the restrictions of gender have loosened from where they once were—but that doesn't mean there isn't further to go. Both Kindlon and Meadows mention girls' involvement in sports when they find self-confident girls who draw strength from their bodies, and they discuss the huge impact of Title IX as a way to allow girls to explore their athleticism, never mind win scholarships, demonstrate leadership, and gain team experience. Both also mention girls who have close and nurturing relationships with their fathers—a change in child-rearing that is generational. And in Meadows's article, one girl refers to the close ties she has to her church youth group and the moral strength she derives from bonding with a group of peers who support her values. When girls feel nonjudgmental acceptance by a peer group, this is usually a significant source of strength that can enable them to take more chances. None of these examples is part of a simple formula that brings girls beyond adolescent angst, but all do show evidence of changing societal mores that affect girls' lives.

Yet slotting girls into categories ("alpha," "beta," and "gamma") often only emphasizes differences and ways to measure if a girl is fitting in, or if she is fulfilling a new group's expectations of her. And while focusing on girls' successes is cheering, more negative articles about the high pressure girls put on themselves, or that they feel heaped upon them to still fit the image of the "perfect girlfriend," "dutiful daughter," and now "shining student," only describe the addition of another layer of expectations as girls are once again molded into preset definitions and types.

In *Girlfighting* Lyn Mikel Brown warns against believing that the twenty-first-century girl who is presented as free from gender restriction really is. As girls enter adolescence, she writes, they hear the contradictory messages of you "can be anything" within a culture that still does not value women. Parsing out how the contradictions apply, when the overt message is that there is no difference (yet girls feel there is), can only make a girl's passage through adolescence and uncovering self-identity all the more confusing. "The girl at the top—adored by teachers, loved by peers—must have everything in just the right amounts and must please the right people," insists Brown, who writes that girls in this case are not rising above the definitions of gender, but rather racing to meet even more standards. "It looks like a new image of girlhood—more girl power—but it isn't really," says Brown of the new image of the bold, athletic "girl as fighter" who can be "bold and dominant in some circumstances, as long as they are demure, discreet, and subordinate to men in others. This is not a new type of girl, just the old stereotype with a 'tough guise' twist."

According to Brown, "The girlfighter is now just as likely to be the girl who does well in school, who plays sports, the girl teachers like, the girl next door." Yet she continues, "But there's something suspicious about this shift." Brown cites changes in media images, such as Buffy the Vampire Slayer, for example, who is, on one hand, strong and aggressive, but who always still knows when to pull back and "redeems herself through her beauty, occasional vulnerability, and her romantic relationships" with men. The suggestion that girls now have endless choices sounds appealing, but Brown suggests, "On closer scrutiny, however, the choices seem more like the refracted colors of a prism, capable of spinning a brilliant but dizzying array of options, beautiful but illusory." Brown also points out how often girls are still punished by other girls for coming off as thinking they're "all that," meaning too proud of themselves, too boastful, or too full of themselves, which can keep girls from achieving, as the trait of success is still seen as distinctly unfeminine. Most girls don't want to see themselves as victims, and most reject the idea that they don't have free will to exercise and choices to make. Yet pulling back to a larger picture of what guides what they claim they want can reveal that "free will" isn't as open a process as most girls thought. While media focus on the successful, high-achieving girl who is impervious to peer social pressures, body angst, and other previously assumed rites of teenage angst is a welcome change, it is worthwhile to think through how representative the sample presented is, who is served by this presentation, and whether or not this only adds another prescription for girls.

is happy but not too cheerful. Simmons writes honestly of her own confusion: How are girls to embody opposing qualities at the same time? And she concludes—as notable feminist thinkers varying from transgender author/playwright/artist Kate Bornstein to scholar and sociologist Barrie Thorne have also concluded—that acknowledging and honoring a wider, more realistic spectrum of gender behaviors opens up more possibilities for what is considered "acceptable" and more freedom for girls (and boys) to define themselves and who they want to become.

Another difficult conundrum is for girls to accept the mantle of being labeled "victim" of social forces that keep them back or hold them down. Looking at the bigger picture of social forces that interact to keep girls conflicted about how aggressive they can be, how loud, how "difficult," puts together the pieces of a puzzle that still invests in girls' subjugation or reinforcement of traditional roles.

At the end of *Reviving Ophelia*, Mary Pipher offers several examples of girls who are internally strong, balanced, and able to weather the inevitable storms that life brings. Sometimes they were particularly bolstered, if not by their immediate families, by an alliance with a friend, an aunt, or other role model who acknowledged their personal strengths and who affirmed faith in their ability to survive and thrive. Pipher suggests that it's not just the individually lucky girl who should find herself in this position; larger cultural scripts must be reshaped to offer all girls a place to grow rather than places to try to fit in. Pipher, for example, advocates more "androgyny" in parents—that is, for parents to defy stereotypical models with nurturing fathers and mothers who model self-sufficiency and self-love. She proffers a quote by the nineteenth-century French author Stendhal: "All geniuses born women are lost to the public good." While this statement would be widely and hotly refuted today, it still holds a grain of truth. Pipher argues, ultimately, "Let's work toward a culture in which there is a place for every human gift" and argues for "wholeness" that supports a range of behavioral acceptance. Hoping that girls—regardless of their race, cultural background, socioeconomic status, sexual orientation, and dis/ability status—never experience truncation of their sense of potential means working toward the kind of societywide change that allows everyone this room to maneuver.

Brown, too, argues for a broader contextualization of girls' emotions. She writes of overturning the dichotomy between "nice girls" and "mean girls" as if these are the only two positions for girls to inhabit. Making room for the "in-between" rids girls of the polarization between "nice and mean, good and bad, virgin and slut," says Brown, and makes space "for girls who don't map onto or who actively question white-middle class ideals to have status and visibility and power on their own terms." Taking the judgment out of these terms (and labels such as "girly girl" and "slut"), Brown emphasizes, means they lose their power, and the expectations that girls are meant to meet can be reframed.

"When rooting out girl meanness becomes a goal in and of itself, we risk losing the bigger picture," Brown writes. "Let's catch it, label, and fix 'it' and then what? We'll have our girls back? And which girls are we talking about?" She continues, "Neither the literature on relational aggression nor the popular accounts of the ways girls enact it on each other seem to address the larger issue of power. Little consideration has been given to the fact that a girl's social context, the options available to her, and the culture in which she lives will affect how she aggresses. No substantive consideration has been given to the fact that girlfighting might have something to do with the range of injustices and indignities girls experience in their daily lives."

"The culture sets girls up for girlfighting," writes Brown directly, citing a pervasive heterosexist environment that normalizes the bombardment of gender-specific behavior from birth onward. Brown urges teaching media literacy so that girls can deconstruct the plethora of cartoons, films, ads, billboards, and so on that infiltrate girls' minds with messages about gender. "Built into the ideal of white femininity, perfect for getting and keeping a prince, are messages about girls' place in boys' life cycle: girls are objects to own or cheerleaders to boys' adventures; they explain and protect the emotional lives of boys." As these images accrete, she insists, their collective power takes hold.

Brown is clear about how girlfighting is symptomatic of a culture in which girls and women are devalued. She writes, "Simply put, girls' treatment of other girls is too often a reflection of and a reaction to the way society sees and treats them." It's not something society is willing to admit, but girls and women "have less power and garner less respect in our culture. . . . Because the power they do have so often arises from qualities they either have little control over, don't earn, or openly disdain—their looks, their vulnerability, their accommodation to others' wants and needs, their feminine wiles—they too often take out their frustration and anger on each other." By "policing" each other's behavior for not matching up to feminine ideals, writes Brown, girls perpetuate the same standards that plague them and this struggle reflects their way to hold power in a world that fundamentally disallows this for them. "It may look good for those girls who easily map onto white middle-class notions of nice girlness. . . . But growing evidence suggests that conventional femininity is bad for these girls too," she writes, given that "it is associated with loss of voice, lowered self-confidence, depression, body image disturbances, and eating disorders."

In her call for a "wide-screen view of girlfighting," Brown insists that the flip side of relational anger is the deep desire for close female friendships. With the support of close friends, she finds in her research, girls feel supported and valued. She writes, "In all this work, two seemingly contradictory themes emerge over and over again. First, girls depend on close intimate friendships to get them through life. The trust and support of these relationships provide girls with emotional and psychological safety nets; with their friends behind them, they can do and say things that are remarkably creative and brave and 'out of character.'" Brown and other primary researchers in this field have many suggestions in their work for how to reframe and take the anomie that pervades girls' connections in order to build on the closeness and support girls both feel and need. But it is not a simple process. They also have ample suggestions for parents, particularly mothers, who must reject perpetuating cycles of girlfighting into their adult years. By shifting the focus from the ways girls hurt one another to a broader understanding of how society sets girls up to repress their anger, compete in games in which no one can win, and inhabit multiple inherently conflicted positions, change can slowly come, girl by girl, friendship by friendship, when supported by families, schools, and the community at large.

A teenage girl reading at a magazine stand.

CHAPTER 4

GETTING AND MAKING THE MESSAGE: GIRLS AND MEDIA

True speaking is not solely an expression of creative power;
it is an act of resistance, a political gesture that challenges
politics of domination that would render us nameless and
voiceless. . . . It is that act of speech, of "talking back" that is
no mere gesture of empty words, that is the expression of our
movement from object to subject—the liberated voice.
—bell hooks, *Talking Back: Thinking Feminist, Thinking*
Black

Where do girls' voices arise in the media, and what do they sound like? When are they liberated from the scripts of commercialism or cultural expectation? There's no question that girls, growing up today and for the past several generations, live in a media-saturated world: A hypothetical American girl might wake up in the morning to a clock radio blaring Top 40 songs, dress herself in clothes bearing Nike logos or Disney characters, watch some TV, put on a Mulan backpack, and walk to school or the bus stop past billboards, cars, taxis, and buses printed with ads; after school she may come home and watch more TV, listen to music, and, if her household has a computer and Internet access, go online to play games or spend time on a social networking site such as MySpace. In her channel-surfing seconds she might glimpse a woman serving dinner to her family, a sexy teenage girl giggling at a boyfriend, and a variety of media images that more often than not perpetuate gender and other stereotypes. The numbers are impressive; according to a 2000 report in the *Journal of Adolescent Health,* children ages eight to thirteen spend a total of more than eight hours daily exposed to various media: television, movies, video games, print, radio, recorded music, computer, and Internet; girls spend about twenty minutes less a day than boys do.

How does this media saturation affect girls? How do the media steer or reinforce these stereotypes? And what happens when girls take charge of media, whether through printing their own stories rather than reading conventional teen magazines for girls (see also Chapter 5), writing their own lyrics, or starring in and directing their own films? As the world of media becomes increasingly vast and girls take in media at ever younger ages, what effects do the messages of mainstream media have? And how do girls, as bell hooks writes, "talk back"?

Looking at Girls

This chapter considers the historical and present-day implications of how girls have been represented in the media, touching on advertising, and beginning in the 1930s, tracing the concept of "narrative cycles" as they applied to teenage girls. Later, in the mid-1950s, when television first became ubiquitous throughout living rooms within the United States, the presence of the teenage girl also became a barometer of how girls were perceived. Despite the changing images presented to girls and the newly developed variations within types of media, educators and critics all agree that the stereotypes presented are crucial, if not crushing, in forming understandings of gender and cultural expectation.

The mavens of Madison Avenue have long been invested in convincing consumers that they need commodities to be socially acceptable and existentially fulfilled. And American girls and women have long faced contradictory expectations, such as be smart but not too conceited, or assertive but not too bossy. But the advances of technology, particularly after World War II, intensified the outpouring of these messages through the presence of more media channels. Advertising—whether through television commercials or print—increased and the general population was urged to consume at levels never known before. Advertisers also became more sophisticated in marketing to set segments of the population, packaging messages that were "sold" alongside the products espoused, all classified to appeal specifically to age group, gender, stage of life; advertisers structured and crafted messages to address these specific categories. For girls and women, this has meant constructions of femininity that circle and define scripted roles: the princess-wannabe younger girl, the sparkles-and-pink tween, and fill-in-the-blank high school accessories and cool clothes that tweens and twixters need. Variations such as the athletic girl, the "urban" girl, the artsy type, and the budding dweeb exist, but investment in media-made cultural stereotypes is strong. Today, students will often argue that they decide which products to buy, which consumer choices to make—that they're not forced or strong-armed into a "look" or product's appeal. But when they realize how pervasive advertising is (and are educated to understand what advertising really is and where to find it), they begin to "see" on levels they didn't before and to understand how coercion of choice can be as subtle as it is insidious, and that choices are rarely made in a void—but rather reflect a constellation of desires, some original and some superimposed.

The Face of Advertising: Not the Girl Next Door

When a girl opens a magazine—whether one specifically targeted to her age group or one she finds in a waiting room, what is she most likely to see? In all likelihood, hyperskinny models, rarely of color, whose proportions are a far cry from those of the average American teen girl or woman. Despite Tyra Banks's popularity, particularly around her model-search reality television show, models of color are often represented in a token way, seen in advertisements and fashion spreads that are a far cry from the realities of America's demographic makeup. Yet because these images are so pervasive, girls come to see these body types as "normal" and an example to which they ought to aspire. Why must models be thin, when so many in the U.S. population are not? Why are so few models of color evident?

In an October 2007 *New York Times* article, "Ignoring Diversity, Runways Fade to White," Guy Trebay focused on the exclusion of models of color from fashion shows, mentioning that the fashion industry is a rare one in which people are still allowed to refer to others by their skin tone or type. Trebay reports how, after a burst of interest in the 1970s in having models of different races, the decrease in opportunities for African American models and models of other non-Caucasian backgrounds became very real. Trebay quotes J. Alexander, judge for Banks's *America's Next Top Model,* as saying, "Now some people are not interested in the vision of the black girl unless they're doing a jungle theme and they can put her in a grass skirt and diamonds and hand her a spear." Trebay concludes, "It is not just a handful of genetically gifted young women who are hurt by this exclusion. Vast numbers of consumers draw their information about fashion and identity from runways, along with cues about what, at any given moment, the culture decrees are the new contours of beauty and style." In September 2007, journalist Ed Pilkington reported in the *Guardian* that "several of the world's top black supermodels, including Naomi Campbell, Iman, Liya Kebede and Tyson Beckford, yesterday launched a campaign against race discrimination in the fashion industry—which they say is at its worst since the 1960s." A series of gatherings in New York were arranged to raise awareness of racism and rally support against it after several top designers used only white models in their recent shows.

There are some signs of change, but they are in the minority. Some in the U.S. fashion industry have agreed to follow the lead of progressive leaders and reconsider the use of "ultrathin" models on the fashion catwalks. In 2002, the editor in chief of *YM* magazine banished stories about dieting and mandated that *YM* use models of all shapes and sizes. Awareness has been slow to develop, and change yet slower, but there has been steady resistance to the dominant "standards" for beauty that girls are presented with by the fashion and advertising industries, and before they have the knowledge to critique these images, that they will absorb and assume are the shapes they, too, are meant to be.

Sharon Jayson reports in *USA Today* on recent studies by the

American Psychological Association (APA) that show the connection between what girls see in advertisements and their sense of their own bodies, with the conclusion that "advertising and media images that encourage girls to focus on looks and sexuality are harmful to their emotional and physical health." Jayson writes that the APA report "analyzed some 300 studies over the past 18 months. It included a variety of media, from television and movies to song lyrics, and looked at advertising showing body-baring doll clothes for pre-schoolers, tweens posing in suggestive ways in magazines and the sexual antics of young celebrity role models" with the result that "the researchers found such images may make girls think of and treat their own bodies as sexual objects." Task force member and professor Tomi-Ann Roberts comments, "The preponderance of evidence suggests a cause for concern in these sexualized images and the mental health outcomes for girls." Although Roberts acknowledges that individual studies have "found problems related to eating disorders, low self-esteem and depression," she says more study needs to be done to show that these issues are "directly linked" to sexualized ads.

The Canadian nonprofit Media Awareness Network offers a history of stereotypes within the media, with a focus on advertising. The network offers an answer to why certain beauty standards are imposed: "The roots, some analysts say, are economic. By presenting an ideal difficult to achieve and maintain, the cosmetic and diet product industries are assured of growth and profits. And it's no accident that youth is increasingly promoted, along with thinness, as an essential criterion of beauty. If not all women need to lose weight, for sure they're all aging . . . and, according to the industry, age is a disaster that needs to be dealt with." By making women feel insecure about their bodies, the industry forges the link that just the right product will help reduce this anxiety and bring newfound confidence and satisfaction.

Weight loss is frequently promoted in women's magazines. According to the Media Awareness Network, women's magazines have ten and one-half times more ads promoting weight loss than men's magazines. It also cites television and movies as responsible for reinforcing the cult of thinness. Girls and women are constantly told by American culture that their bodies need improvement and change—and that this can be solved through treatments, creams, and body management plans—which of course means more consumerism, which in turn feeds the advertising industry. More plainly put, the industry has nothing to gain by telling women and girls that they are just fine the way they are.

The network also cites Jean Kilbourne, a media expert who studies advertising. Kilbourne argues that "the overwhelming presence of media images of painfully thin women means that real women's bodies have become invisible in the mass media." The real tragedy, Kilbourne concludes, is that many women internalize these stereotypes and judge themselves by the beauty industry's standards. Women learn to compare themselves to other women and to compete with them for male attention. This focus on beauty and desirability "effectively destroys any awareness and action that might help to change that climate."

Kilbourne describes through her research how insidious advertisers' work is to convince girls and women—and boys and men—that they are imperfect as they are and must have products—whether a hair-care smoother or a certain kind of bathroom cleaner—to fix themselves and retain value in American society. She discusses how media images of beauty and feminine "standards" influence how girls and women feel about themselves—and what boys and men come to view as an ideal against which to measure girls and women. She also puts forward the idea that advertising is not solely responsible for creating strict gender roles—but it is so pervasive within our lives and so embedded within American culture that the roles and images portrayed become assumed as "normal."

Advertising has been around for as long as there have been products to sell, and the use of an attractive model using the product being sold is nothing new. But the blatant sexualization of the product, the model, and often the act of using the product (no matter what it is) was a fixture of the twentieth century, with advertisers now in the twenty-first pushing the limits on titillation and exploitation to even greater extremes.

In a visual web essay, "Sex in Advertising," the marketing research company Gallup and Robinson offers a brief history of the advertising industry's use of sexuality, from innuendo and double entendre to outright come-on. In the earlier half of the twentieth century, according to the piece, the use of sexuality was more closely monitored because of strict turn-of-the-century Victorian concepts of morality, the Hays Office (the organization that monitored U.S. media for "objectionable" content), and America's lingering Puritan ethic. The historic advertising images the site offers from the 1920s and '30s mostly include illustrations that convey romantic story lines with attractive women as the featured character. It cites a turning point as World War II, when the concept of the "pinup girl" (an attractive, shapely young woman whose image was pinned up on calendars or advertisements) became prevalent in popular culture. Photos of more scantily clad models became widely used, although they are almost modestly dressed by today's standards. The photo pinup became a standard for advertising during this post-war period, with the models chosen reflecting America's racial divide at the time—virtually all were Caucasian, wholesome, "American girl next door" types, with a figure that, proportionally, was larger than what is considered fashionable now.

Gallup and Robinson attributes the largest shift toward use of blatant sexuality in advertising to the arrival of *Playboy* magazine in 1953: "What was once considered pornography became an acceptable art form for the mass culture. It was truly intoxicating and advertisers eagerly embraced it." Permissive cultural changes in sexual and social mores in the 1960s further exacerbated a move toward the use of sexuality within advertising, until the association between sexiness and selling products became cemented as a concept that is taken for granted now.

It's useful to remember that the purpose of advertising is fundamentally to make money for a company whose product is being touted—and to plant the idea that this product—whether for a vacuum cleaner or hair gel—has the potential to bring to the viewer the same allure (or success or achievement) it brings to the person seen in the ad.

Girlhood Becomes a Story

When the figure of the teenage girl popped up on the big screen of the cinema, her presence reflected messages about American cultural mores and understandings of that time. Ilana Nash, in *American Sweethearts: Teenage Girls in Twentieth-Century Popular Culture,* studies a series of what she terms "narrative cycles" about girls. A narrative cycle, as she defines it, is "a collection of stories about a single character across several media." By looking at cycles about the character Nancy Drew, the "Junior Miss" cycle, and others, Nash examines the figure of the teenage girl up until the mid-1960s as a way to interrogate "America's traditional attitudes toward its daughters."

First she describes how the figure of the teenage girl, from the 1930s forward, was often polarized into one of two stereotypes: She was a "quasi-angelic creature, praised for her bubbly charm, her obedience to authority, and her chastity, or else she was an exasperating agent of chaos who challenged the boundaries and hierarchies of a patriarchally organized society." In both roles, Nash says, the teenage girl was "more or less than human, never simply a whole person with her own three-dimensional subjectivity." Rather, she had to be boxed into a "type." As these projected "types," she writes, girls served as Other to adult men, a foil for other characters' motivations. "American news media, political rhetoric, entertainment industries, advertising, and other modes of public address have historically viewed the world through the eyeglasses of the mature male, a perspective that casts non-males, and non-adults as Other. Consequently, both women and youth figured in mainstream culture throughout the twentieth century as objects of intense pleasure, curiosity, and anxiety."

The teenage girl, between girlhood and womanhood, says Nash, is consistently "put back in her place" by mass-media narratives, with her femininity meant to serve her sexual objectification and her youth rendering her more "ignorant and diminished than grown women." By looking at how teenage girls are defined, says Nash, the role of the "average man" is defined in contradiction to how opposed identities surround him. Nash notes the commentary on an installment of a newsreel produced by Time-Life in 1945, *The March of Time*, which airs this comment about teenage girls: "Of all the phenomena of wartime life in the United States, one of the most fascinating and mysterious, and one of the most completely irrelevant, has been the emergence of the teenage girl as an American institution in her own right." Encoding the "paradox of desire and disgust" that underlined the view of youth at that time, the presentation of girls as "irrelevant" is, in part, meant to serve as a way to bolster the superiority of men who are "unremarkable, comprehensible, and relevant," Nash says. The dismissive attitude toward girlhood that she finds is widely prevalent within the wider culture during that time. Her work looks closely at this narrative and how its perpetuation serves different sources.

Nash mentions that her study begins in 1930 because that is "roughly the moment at which mass culture began to take systematic notice of teenagers as a distinct category." And it ends in the mid-1960s because, she says, that is when the teenage girl "ended," too. After the 1960s, she writes, "Changes in women's and girls' roles in American culture caused images of girls to splinter into numerous kinds of representations," which are predicated on the stereotypes studied in her work but which no longer fit into unified categories. Other images, such as the physicality of the "kick-ass" girl (the example Nash gives is Buffy the Vampire Slayer), or new interest in the older "college girl," reveal different understandings of the place of American girlhood. But, by the 1970s, "the discourse of adolescence was firmly established and popular entertainments no longer had to 'explain' the teen girl to baffled adults."

Nash concludes that, despite feminism and its advances, "the dominant discourses of American teen narratives have yet to represent a girlhood that truly serves girls." Such a girlhood would demand respect from adults and from girls themselves, seeing them as competent and capable of self-determination. "Instead we continue to train girls to accept and even request their own subordination, encouraging them, through a well-established system of rewards, to fashion their identities with signifiers of a romance plot that conflates paternal(ist) interests with sexual commodification. This is the girlhood we call normal, the one that populates the 'wholesome' family comedies that comfort and reassure us with their fables of averageness."

As she ends her book, she writes of how things have changed (or not). "In the millennium, our most widely available and recycled stories about female youth still trick us with the old bait-and-switch, selling empty slogans of a 'girl power' that only means what it meant all along: the power to shop and to excite men; the power to serve capital and patriarchy. If we are to change our culture's construction of girls as non-persons, we must alter the old myths instead of recycling them; we must fundamentally revise the bedtime stories we tell ourselves—and our daughters."

Susan Douglas is another scholar who has worked extensively on how television, advertising, and film have portrayed teenage girls. In her 1995 book *Where the Girls Are: Growing Up Female with the Mass Media*, Douglas, a pop culture expert and professor of communications, intersperses cultural history with her own experience of growing up in the 1950s and 1960s. Tracing the rise of media influence in America post–World War II to nearly the present day, she examines female figures on television (mainly) and within music and film (to a lesser extent) and also through commercial advertising as she tracks their influence.

Douglas points out something that remains true today—the media often encourage girls and women to hold themselves to an impossible set of often-conflicting standards, unattainable by mere mortals, and often erase or tokenize girls of color, girls with disabilities, or queer girls. Yet this doesn't stop advertisers from raising the bar yet higher, telling consumers that with the right products they can achieve an impossible, stereotyped perfection. She writes, "American women today are a bundle of contradictions because much of the media imagery we grew up with was itself filled with mixed messages about what women should and should not do, what women could and could not be. This was true in the 1960s and it is true today." The media want girls and women to be cute, sexual, "poreless, wrinkle-free and deferential to men," but also assertive, independent, and enterprising, Douglas contends, often leaving women both buying in (literally) and only sometimes rebelling against the media messages presented. Yet particular to her argument is the historical development of how the disassembled shards of female identity left by mass consumption of culture also caused many women to embrace feminism. She writes, "But it is easy to forget that the media also suggested we could be rebellious, tough, enterprising, and shrewd. And much of what we watched was porous, allowing us to accept *and* rebel against what we saw and how it was presented." Douglas describes how girls' and women's representation in the media often forced a dichotomizing of gender roles: "For throughout this process, we have found ourselves pinioned between two voices, one insisting we were equal, and the other insisting we were subordinate. After a while the tension became unbearable, and millions of women found they were no longer willing to tolerate the gap between the promises of equality and the reality of inequality." Within her argument, it is striking once again to realize how often mixed messages are presented to girls—and they find themselves vacillating between two polarized choices, with neither thoroughly attractive and the frustrating sense that neither choice will be deemed "correct."

When the roles the media present to girls and women are deeply contradictory (sexy/wholesome, mother/working woman, girlfriend/ independent and okay with it), where does that leave each individual? Often cobbling together a series of tenuous compromises among class, race, and other connections, with the added confusion of trying to separate individual wants with the media's received, or rather imposed, messages, particularly that girls are always being judged by how they look and act.

One part of the media's message to women and girls is often that they are available to be looked at, scrutinized, to add "background scenery" to complement a male actor, or to see themselves watched by others. Much has been written about the "gaze of the camera" and, both implicitly and explicitly, the objectifying gaze of the viewer. Virtually every teenage girl understands being looked at and she learns through visual media how she should look at women and assess them. The term "the male gaze," coined by film theorist Laura Mulvey in 1975, refers to using the camera to treat women typically as objects rather than subjects within the frame. The use of the camera's angles implicitly conveys that the film's assumed audience likely are heterosexual men and the shots the camera takes reveal a male point of view. Her essay "Visual Pleasure and Narrative Cinema" considers how issues of representation and spectatorship are evident within film, and while she says the camera is technically neutral, it is inherently voyeuristic, usually held by a man and peered at through the lens of a male director. Mulvey looks at how Hollywood's traditional forms of editing narrative and cinematography relate to and reproduce traditional ideologies of gender. Complementing her theory is the more commonplace masculinization of the camera—within the home, its place is often one of patriarchal privilege as technology within the domestic sphere is often male held.

Without doubt, television, film, music, literature, and advertising create a shared, generational history and set of common references that carry a long distance into adulthood. When girls rewrite "looking" and being "looked at," they can create a powerfully enriching moment as they realize that the media, in whatever form, are a crucial source of struggle with gender self-definition.

Television

In 2001 the American Academy of Pediatrics reported that by the time adolescents graduate from high school, they will have spent about fifteen thousand hours watching television—while having spent only twelve thousand hours in school. The stereotypes that children see reinforced on TV and in other media feature "standards" that perpetuate an idealized life with particular kinds of beauty as acceptable; critics note that ethnic diversity is either rare or limited to stereotypes, and television rarely shows characters who have disabilities. Rarely is a less-than-slim female character the star on a television show.

Douglas, in *Where the Girls Are*, catalogs media representation

Airbrushed and Glossy (Or Not): Teen Magazines

The "teen magazine"—primarily, if not exclusively, marketed to girls—has long been a staple for both introduction to and indoctrination into "traditional girlhood." *YM*, published for seventy-two years, once stood for *Young Miss*, changed its acronym to mean *Young & Modern* in the 1980s and later still to *Your Magazine*, and then went to an online incarnation in 2004, although it is now defunct. *Seventeen* magazine, in print since 1944, is another staple. These magazines, some now read by the daughters of a former generation of subscribers, often tout expected story lines: how to improve one's looks, handle romantic, heterosexual relationships, how to succeed socially. Thick with advertisements, these publications offer girls advice that often combines lip service to empowerment with ad-driven imperatives to conform to a consumerist beauty culture. A study by Girls Inc. reports that "21 popular young women's magazine covers showed that 78 percent contained a message about bodily appearance. None (0%) of young men's magazines contained such messages. Also, 26 percent of women's magazine covers contained conflicting messages (e.g., a message about losing weight next to a cookie recipe) regarding weight loss and dietary habits."

Yet things have changed, if slowly, in what girls can expect from the glossy "bibles" that are marketed to them. In 2002, the editor in chief of *YM* magazine, Christina Kelly, banished stories about dieting from the magazine and also mandated that models of all shapes and sizes would be used in photo shoots. According to an article by Carol Lee on Women's eNews, in doing so the magazine took a radical step. Kelly mentions reading *Seventeen* magazine as a teen herself and learning how to count calories, and she no longer wanted to make dieting consciousness part of the magazine's mission of serving teen girls.

And now *Seventeen*'s website offers a range of articles under the heading "College and Career" and sponsors a "Body Peace Treaty," with the goal of having a million signers agree to statements such as "Remember that the sun will still rise tomorrow even if I had one too many slices of pizza or an extra scoop of ice cream tonight" and "Stop joining in when my friends compare and trash their own bodies" as well as "Quiet that negative little voice in my head when it starts to say mean things about my body

continued

that I'd never tolerate anyone else saying about me," "Remind myself that what you see isn't always what you get on TV and in ads—it takes a lot of airbrushing, dieting, money, and work to look like that," and "Know that I'm already beautiful just the way I am."

But while the topics explored within "traditional" girls' magazines may be changing, with a more proactive stance toward girls' empowerment rather than a focus on passive pleasing, critics suggest that merely looking at the advertisements embedded within for makeup or clothing and most often featuring "traditional" models, refutes any progressive message the editorial board may offer and spins girls around again between mixed messages.

A few magazines written for girls embody both the awareness of the need for nonstereotypical values and the chance to show girls empowering stories and articles that reflect their real lives. Yet more radical magazines for teen girls haven't had the notoriously long shelf lives of *Seventeen* and *YM*. *Sassy* magazine, founded in 1988 and published until 1996 under the editorial vision of Jane Pratt (who later went on to her namesake, *Jane* magazine, also now defunct), explored sexuality, political issues, alternative pop culture, and offered a fresh and feminist voice to its readers, which for those who connected with the magazine, left a lasting impression. In 2007, authors Kara Jesella and Marisa Meltzer published the book *How Sassy Changed My Life: A Love Letter to the Greatest Teen Magazine of All Time*, which detailed the magazine's cult following. An NPR interview with the authors calls *Sassy* "the antithesis of the homecoming queen, please-your-boyfriend culture. It published articles about suicide and STDs while *Seventeen* was still teaching girls how to get a boy to notice you." According to NPR, Meltzer and Jesella argue that the magazine "was less a teenage moment than an early feminist movement."

Other alternative magazines geared toward girls, such as *HUES*, founded in 1992 (and also no longer in print), also offered alternative visions. Former managing editor Tali Edut has said, "We got tired of magazines that advertised 7-foot-tall, 90-pound drug-addicted models" and "We wanted a magazine that promoted a positive view of womanhood."

Blue Jean magazine, in a similar model, was published in the United States from 1996 through 1998 and was dubbed the "Thinking Girls Magazine" by *USA Today*. According to its website, it offered new insights on body image and confidence, ethnicity and racism, and other environmental and social issues. An anthology of its best work has been published as *Blue Jean: What Young Women Are Thinking, Saying, and Doing*; an overview of the book states, "*Blue Jean* allows teenage girls to read about significant issues, not just what shade is in for the season. This anthology influences readers to get out and actually do something. *Blue Jean* goes beyond simply telling, it encourages activism—not just dreaming—doing."

The magazine *Muslim Girl,* published from 2007 to 2008 with a circulation of 30,000 (and with hopes to resume publication), was another example of a magazine that sought to reflect the realities of girls' lives, in this case North American girls of diverse inheritance who wanted to honor their cultural backgrounds. The magazine offered features about how to navigate this identity with the goal of diminishing "the impact of negative stereotypes by sharing the positive contribution Muslim Girls make to the communities they live in." Under its "Ask a Girl" section online, Muslim girls from around the world responded to topics such as "How is faith part of your daily life?" and "Are you judgmental about what other girls are wearing? How so?" among other questions.

An exception to the short-lived trend is *New Moon Girls,* which is still going strong. *New Moon: The Magazine for Girls and Their Dreams* was started in 1992 by Nancy Gruver, who thought her eleven-year-old twin daughters, on the cusp of adolescence, had no media available to them that reflected their lives. Gruver and her husband, Joe Kelly, "envisioned a magazine for all girls who want their voices heard and their dreams taken seriously." Their daughters recruited peers to join the first Girls Editorial Board, and the magazine, written entirely by girls ages eight to twelve, was born. Absent of "diet advice or popularity contests," the magazine emphasizes what makes a girl beautiful—her inner self—with creative writing and artwork, book reviews, and a "sister to sister" section that offers mentorship from one girl to another. Its mission statement states the need to "bring girls' voices to the world in ways that matter" and its editorial model gives girls real editorial power. Its online component, New Moon Girl Media, offers interactive web communities to girls, including a section for girls from ages 13 and up, and a site for parents and community leaders to help girls "build healthy resistance to gender stereotypes and inequities."

of girls and women in the 1950s, '60s, and '70s, as she was growing up and growing into her own awareness as a feminist. Her chapters about television serve to convince us what stereotypes of the time looked like, and which stereotypes have (and haven't) changed within the media. Television roles offered (or deemed acceptable) for women and girls in those decades were often strictly categorized into housewife (for women), girlfriend (for teens), or a vampy/siren role (sometimes for both), with little diversity that moved beyond racial or ethnic stereotypes, and excluding lesbian or bisexual and disabled girls and women.

Girls often seemed absent or to matter very little to the media in the 1950s and '60s, when ideas were imprinted about gender, racial, and class roles and patriarchal importance; these ideas had long-lasting effects on several generations' psyches. Douglas gives an example of the young Sally Field, playing the ever-perky yet shrewd Gidget, who demonstrated how to toe the line between "acceptable" femininity and its crafty subversion. Citing *Gidget* and the *Patty Duke Show*, which aired back-to-back, Douglas writes that the teenage girl stars had become important to advertisers and producers who then created shows around their "zany antics." She writes, "While perkiness seems so nauseating now, it was then an absolutely critical mask for girls who wanted to take an active role in the world yet still be thought of as appealing." By claiming "perkiness" as "assertiveness masquerading as cuteness," says Douglas, these teenage girl characters could claim a certain power. Using Gidget as an example, Douglas outlines how spunkiness is constrained to reveal a feminine streak as she manipulates her boyfriend, giving lip service to his male brawn and privilege while getting him to do what she wants.

Later television shows such as *Free to Be . . . You and Me* or *Sesame Street* helped to promote a shift to more equitable gender values, particularly as the songs on the Marlo Thomas special specifically challenged gender stereotypes with titles such as "William's Doll" and the ironic "Ladies First." But for the most part, television served to promote gender stereotyping that reflected the decades in which it launched, with conflicted female characters assuming power only in covert ways. Understanding how the outline of pop culture circumscribed cultural mores and represented (or failed to represent) girls is to understand part of a cultural legacy.

As televisions entered the American living room, unleashing a parade of sitcoms, talk shows, and jingly commercials, so did this medium present stereotypes that reinforced roles for women and girls as passive, decorative, and given secondary billing to male stars. Douglas outlines how 1960s pop culture contributed to an ideology that many later rejected. She says that we must "rewatch" and "relearn where the girls are" because they often seemed absent or mattered so little during this period in which media influence was widely felt.

But what does it mean to be steeped in a media culture that marginalizes you or even erases you completely? The physical presence of the television made its way into most Americans' living rooms, but its waves of influence—whether this meant rarely showing an actress of color, or if so only as a maid—were far-reaching. The prejudices and limitations of the era in which television was born reflected often-dichotomized roles for girls and women—sweet, nonstressed domestic goddess Moms and blond, cheerful, helpful daughters. Douglas's work explores what it means to deeply feel the influence of pop culture, yet to know that this was part of the "remnants of a collective female past not usually thought of as making serious history," as she puts it. The messages the media gave about the body and how gender roles have played out in the media contribute to the making of a social consciousness that distinct generations shared—and still do.

Douglas points out how in the 1960s generational contradictions grew wider as the media reflected shifting gender codes—"women's liberation" was gradually making its way into the national consciousness. Television shows, while still most often portraying girls and women in stereotypical roles, also began to show women who were powerful in supernatural roles or in the role of witch (as in *I Dream of Jeannie* or *Bewitched*). She writes that it was as if the national consciousness couldn't yet accept a powerful female character full out—rather, she had to be part of the paranormal. Characters such as the three "angels" on *Charlie's Angels* were physically strong and wielded weapons but all the while retaining a hypersexual femininity and obeying orders from their disembodied male boss. Douglas writes of how these contradictions are still present as the mass media offer the public "whopping rationalizations" to help "make sense" of the roles that tie in to family, workplace, and society.

One more contemporary standout against this backdrop is the popular show *Ugly Betty,* based on the Colombian telenovela *Betty la fea (Betty the ugly),* in which the lead character, played by actress America Ferrera, is Betty Suárez, a young Latina woman from Queens, who sports braces, unfashionable glasses, and unstylish clothes. The plot of the show revolves around the way she infiltrates and specifically stands outside the expectations of the fashion magazine where she works. In this case, her outsider status becomes a central part of the plot in order to create story lines around the ways in which she doesn't fit into a world in which everyone else is thin and polished. Or consider Oprah Winfrey, who in 1986 became the first African American woman to host her own television show; Winfrey has gone on to build a media empire with her own magazine and film production company, but she still stands out as one of a handful of African American talk show hosts. What do girls take away from television when they don't see themselves represented with plotlines that reflect the real challenges and joys of their lives, or lead characters who look like them? Or when the plotlines they see reinforce "mean girl" behavior of aggressional anger, hypersexuality, and high school drama that revolves around social cliques and financial status?

Girls often must learn how the media are constructed and that they are not natural reflections of the world but rather are backed by agendas, controls, and sources that reflect specific values. Douglas cites the media specialist Todd Gitlin, mentioning that sitcoms and advertisements are not, in fact, reflections of the world but rather deliberate constructions. Borrowing Gitlin's metaphor, Douglas writes that the media are "more like fun-house mirrors that distort and warp 'reality' by exaggerating and magnifying some features of American life and values while collapsing, ignoring and demonizing others."

Relying on the media, whether in a love or hate relationship, or some combination thereof, is part of contemporary life—it's not really possible to opt out or ignore its influence upon us. Douglas shows, through various media, how the values introduced and reinforced, "socialized us, entertained us, comforted us, deceived us, disciplined us, told us what we could do and told us what we couldn't," she writes. "And they played a key role in turning each of us into not one woman but many women—a pastiche of all the good women and bad women that came to us through the printing presses, projectors, and airwaves of America." Television has become an intrinsic part of American cultural life, and the messages it sends, whether embedded within commercials or a show's contents or a carefully edited "reality show's" plotlines, deeply reflect and influence contemporary understandings of gender. Each generation will remember its best-loved shows and favorite characters, which shape cultural references and common understandings. Yet how far-reaching their impact is can be tempered by becoming more media savvy and by analyzing the distance between a crafted sitcom that reflects a cultural zeitgest—or creates it—and the individual realities of each girl's life.

Film

In the early 1960s, as the sexual revolution began to come to the fore, stories began to emerge in print and on screen about girls and sexuality. The availability of penicillin and contraceptives made having sex before marriage available in a way that earlier hadn't seemed possible. Douglas describes a spate of movies that explored the newly allowed sexuality of teens with a frankness that hadn't been seen on the screen before.

Earlier, the 1950s films *Rebel Without a Cause* (1955) and *I Was a Teenage Werewolf* (1957) were meant to have larger appeal to teenage audiences through themes of sexual and romantic dilemmas: Should the couple sleep together? Sex began to enter the popular culture's

Free to Be ... You and Me

Rosey Grier strummed a guitar and sang about how "crying gets the sad out of you," highlighting the value of honestly expressing feelings in the song "It's All Right to Cry." What was strange or unexpected about this in 1972? Everything. Grier, an African American football star, minister, actor, and author of *Rosey Grier's Needlepoint for Men,* defied traditional gender stereotypes by presenting himself as not archetypically shut off from his feelings and subscribing to a "tough men don't shed tears" attitude; instead he expressed just the opposite, letting children know—especially boys—that crying was not only just fine for everyone (boys, girls, men, and women), but a valuable, healthy way of relating to the world. In another song, "William's Doll," Marlo Thomas and actor Alan Alda sang about a boy whose family is perplexed by his desire for a doll. "Boy Meets Girl," performed by Marlo Thomas and director/writer/comedian Mel Brooks, explored cultural gender stereotypes through a dialogue between two infants—a girl and a boy—as listeners tried to figure out which was a girl and which was a boy based on what was said about them and realized they were making judgments about "what girls do" and "what boys do" as well.

When the album and songbook *Free to Be . . . You and Me* was first released in 1972 it offered a range of surprising and new messages, asserting that girls and boys didn't have to hew to traditional gender stereo-

vernacular in ways that are today taken for granted. But it is important to realize how bold these shifts were and how much they changed the cultural landscape for girls.

Douglas writes that during the cultural shifts of the 1960s sexual revolution, a new kind of film emerged that again revealed the changing status of women and girls. She writes that the "pregnancy melodrama" was "a cross between the women's film and the youth film." As such, "its often preposterous narrative" revolved around premarital sex. The young women in these films expressed both the sexual tensions of the time and the contradictory messages they were receiving. Douglas types but could explore other ranges of behavior. And it did so in a non-preachy, entertaining, and humorous way. Through its songs' messages, the album sought to celebrate individuality, tolerance, and happiness with one's identity and the idea that all children could achieve whatever they aspired to, widening the range of possibilities from restriction or classification by gender. First released as an album in 1972, it was later made into a television special aired in 1974 and won an Emmy award. The album was the idea of singer and songwriter Marlo Thomas, who said that she wanted her young niece to learn that it was okay to eschew traditional gender stereotypes. The album was produced by Carole Hart, with music produced by Stephen J. Lawrence and Bruce Hart, and with stories and poems written and directed by Alan Alda. Proceeds went to the Ms. Foundation for Women. A sequel, *Free to Be . . . A Family,* was produced in 1988.

On the television special, the song "Sisters and Brothers" was performed by the Voices of East Harlem; "When We Grow Up" was performed by Diana Ross on the album and performed by Roberta Flack and Michael Jackson on the television special. Each song held a message about broadening the restrictions of stereotypes: for example, putting forth the idea that mothers could perform a range of jobs beyond just parenting or working within traditionally "feminine" fields such as teaching. The message given through the album's songs and the television show celebrated each child's possibilities and dreams, and the idea of being truthful to one's desires, and feeling free to express them—a radical act not just in the early 1970s, but arguably today.

mentions films such as *Splendor in the Grass* and *Where the Boys Are* as examples of cultural phenomena that worked out contradictory messages about sexuality and women's roles.

In *Splendor in the Grass* (1961), the main female character, Deanie, is described as going "crazy as a result of her abstinence" after her mother tells her that "nice girls" don't go all the way—if they do, they won't be the kind of girl a boy wants to marry—and is institutionalized, while Bud gives in to his desires with someone else and is then shown as a farmer in clearly working-class circumstances. Yet Deanie's refusal leaves her, at the film's end, "impeccably dressed, complete with hat and gloves," in contrast to Bud's wife, who appears dingy and "an ever-pregnant, slatternly wife," Douglas writes. She asks, however, if Bud is defeated, as he wanted to be a farmer (as he ends up), whereas Deanie is portrayed as living out her mother's dream. "Like most of the girls in the audience in 1961," Douglas writes, "Deanie has no place to stand. Torn between her overwhelming physical desires and a moral code that pretends they don't—and shouldn't—exist, Deanie is divided against herself. . . . Because she feels the costs of restraint and the costs of passion in the same moment, Deanie provides a powerful point of identification for the girl in the audience reacting against the moral strictures of the 1950s."

Douglas writes that by contrast, *Where the Boys Are* (1960) "sought to resolve the prevailing questions about premarital sex through a melodramatic ending that showed the horrible costs for girls of going all the way." During a spring break trip to Florida for four female friends, "three remain virgins and end up with steady boyfriends," and the fourth, who goes all the way with "the first guy she meets, then takes up with his best friend," is by the film's end a victim of date rape and is ultimately hit by a car. According to Douglas, the film served as an example of changing sexual mores, in which girls could take initiative in courtship and pursue boys, but this was restricted to "positioning themselves in the right place at the right time so as to be spotted by the right boy." The film offers a range of attitudes toward premarital sex, from the "confirmed virgin" to the "tomboy" to the "fallen angel," as it explores with contradictory effects whether or not "nice girls" do or don't desire premarital sex.

These images of the teenage girl have evolved within contemporary film and television, but one of the largest differences is how girls have moved from being the subject of these media to their producers—and when they do become producers, the media they put forward have most dramatically changed the portrayal of girls to the public.

Mary Celeste Kearney's book *Girls Make Media* cites Andrea Richards, author of the book *Girl Director,* who writes, "Yeah, you ought to be in pictures—making them, that is. . . . So are you going to be a couch potato your whole life, watching other people's stories, or are you ready to take charge and put something of your own on the screen? By making a movie you can show your perspective on a story, a song, an idea, the world, whatever. So, girl director, why not take your place on the set? We're all waiting."

Kearney researches ways girls are using media to tell their own stories and how certain media fields have been gendered (in the past, producing texts, such as diary writing, was considered "acceptable" for young ladies, along with home crafts or "handicrafts," while more active, visible roles such as directing or using technical equipment was considered the domain of males). Her work looks at girls' media production and the sometimes subtle, but more often overt, ways in which girls are encouraged or discouraged from certain roles as creators of media, and what happens when, with support, they forge ahead into these fields, particularly those that have historically marginalized female involvement, such as filmmaking.

Taking as her starting point the important work of Angela McRobbie and Jenny Garber, who in the late 1970s first recognized the need for study of girls by insisting on inclusion of gender within study of youth culture, Kearney examines girls' media production by looking not at what media are produced for girls or girls' consumerist behavior, but rather what they produce themselves. According to Kearney, when "girls invest in the role of media producer, stereotypical notions of girlhood and girls' culture are altered radically, and so is the popular understanding of media production, an activity historically constructed as adult- and male-dominated." As girls begin to create their own images and generate narratives that truly reflect their lives and concerns, they have the opportunity to take hold of the stereotypes of girlhood that they learn, disrupt or deliberately deconstruct them, and offer something else instead.

It is important to understand why girls haven't been drawn to filmmaking and the systems that have kept them out. As Kearney explores in *Girls Make Media,* the "masculinizing of filmmaking roles, technology, spaces, discourse and training" is largely still intact, and access to media equipment (cameras, computers, video editing machinery) can be a function of class, although initiatives through various educational groups and government support have enabled increased access to video technology and more media-education programs, offering more distribution of resources and offering girls more connection to filmmaking. "Because media technologies have been developed and dominated by men for decades and thus are typically gendered masculine," she writes, "boys do not question their entitlement to participate in media production." When girls do produce media, she writes, then the boost in self-esteem and the impact their participation has are all the greater.

Kearney again cites Andrea Richards, author of *Girl Director*, who writes, "I think it honestly doesn't occur to girls that they can be a film director—the possibility has never even been planted in their heads, because it's so off limits through cultural and gender stereotypes." Men far outnumber women in virtually all sectors of contemporary film production, says Kearney, and such strong male dominance puts interested females at a severe disadvantage when the primary roles within production, especially those of director and cinematographer, have been "naturalized" as male. Girls have to overcome the perception that this is a sphere in which they don't belong—no small hurdle to jump. Kearney also points out that doing the work of a director, characterized as "leading a small army" by filmmaker Michelle Citron, is the type of work women are often socialized to believe they cannot ably do, and even if they know they can, challenging others' perceptions that they aren't able can be equally hard.

Independent filmmaker Kara Herold, whose documentary *Grrlyshow*, screened at Sundance, explores girls zinesters, comments that in her training as a filmmaker, she often saw boys being taken more closely under the wing of (traditionally) male directors, an example of what Kearney describes as a "patriarchal apprentice system" historically associated with filmmaking. When Herold teaches aspiring college filmmakers today, her classes are still largely composed of male students, although she says they are no longer condescending to female students. And now that more women have succeeded in the film industry, there are more opportunities for female mentorship, especially with the rise of film-training programs exclusively for girls, although Herold reminds us that it is still a small percentage of all girls who benefit from participation in media-training programs. Yet she recalls that when she was starting out, people often wanted to either "take care of her or flirt with her" and being taken seriously could still be a challenge. The rise of women's film festivals, where her work has often been shown, has also been an important change, she notes, as mainstream distributors and filmplexes haven't traditionally embraced the viewpoints that many female filmmakers want to explore within their work.

Another obstacle often cited is the globalization of the film business in which a big-picture action film that can play well worldwide is what drives studios to produce it. Films of less wide appeal, potentially those that focus on the nuances of women's lives and that don't fall into the genres of action/adventure, have been deprivileged because they bring in less revenue. According to Kearney, films with a feminist point of view or those that treat women in a way that's not voyeuristic don't make as much money. All of this adds up to a field in which it is difficult for girls to break in and for women to succeed.

Kearney also comments that camera equipment is heavy, and the need to lift and carry it around can serve as another strike against girls. She suggests that this gendering of camera equipment (too weighty for female arms) is another way in which this industry edges girls out. Journalistic coverage of girls' films has also been sparse, with female journalists often being the ones to cover works by girls and women, reinforcing a traditional gender dynamic.

Until there are copious models, examples, and mentors who want girls to have a place in filmmaking it will be hard for them to make their way into this industry. Kearney cites examples of girl-centered programs such as Reel Grrls, It's a She Shoot, and Girls Making Headlines as places that cultivate single-sex environments to teach skills and provide mentorship to girls whose talents might not emerge in mixed-gender classroom programs. Many of the girls interviewed comment on how empowering it is to them to take hold of the means of media production and conquer their fears specifically in the absence of boys. She cites a participant in GirlsFilmSchool as saying, "I think if boys were here, boys would tend to show off more and jump in front of the camera. [We girls] don't have to hold back at all. [We're] not hiding behind them." Kearney relates how moving girls from media analysis to production often uses the same girl-centered materials (teen magazines, etc.) to engage girls but then helps them realize alternative narratives for girls' bodies and concerns. Single-sex programs create places for girls to reflect critically on culture and their place within it. Another important change in infrastructure has been the development of girl-centered film festivals, which offer a showcase to girl directors. Kearney also cites a graduate of the program Reel Grrls who says, "I want to change the world, and media is the best way to do it because media controls society. If I'm behind the camera, I can control it."

Girls are now making films, varying from YouTube videos to digital productions, in higher numbers than ever before as the equipment becomes more and more available to a wider population. Yet there are still gender-specific challenges girls experience. In a media-saturated world, when girls turn to television and film they often see a dearth of female characters and a lack of ethnic and racial diversity. Kearney cites Euzhan Palcy, the first Afro-Caribbean woman to direct a Hollywood feature film, as saying, "When I was ten years old, I decided to become a filmmaker because on the TV, and in theaters too, every time I had a chance to see a black actor in the movies . . . they had black parts, very stupid parts. I made a kind of wish. I said, I have to be a filmmaker. I have to talk about my people. I have to show what black actors can play, and to give the real image of us, not stereotype us like that. The idea worked in my mind for many years."

Kearney also writes about many of the issues and themes that girls explore in their film work—sexual identity, appearance and body image, female friendship, and competitiveness. Many girl directors use film to critically assess what it means to be female, while others seek to challenge and explore gender identity.

In one chapter on girls and film, Kearney mentions a range of girls' films that reveal understanding of girls' commercial exploitation, as in Ryan Davis's short film *Girls,* which comments on traditional feminine behavior in commercial television. Kearney writes that the film juxtaposes images of women's behavior in the 1950s with contemporary television commercials showing women shopping, cleaning, and caring for children, through which Davis makes a statement about how advertising continues to assert women's domesticity above all other identities.

Kearney also cites Tricia Grashaw's film *The Ultimate Guide to Flirting* as an exploration of heterosexual relationships and how girls are socialized to undertake these roles. The film parodies social displays girls adopt during "heterosexual dating rituals." Kearney references a range of girl filmmakers to exemplify the reach of their concerns. She mentions that "a considerable number of PSAs [public service announcements] produced by girls are about date rape and sexual abuse," such as *Love Shouldn't Hurt* by Tamara Garcia and *It's Never OK* by Arielle Davis, among many other examples.

Taizet Hernandez explores gender identity and sexuality in films such as *Are You a Boy or a Girl?,* a documentary in which Hernandez discusses the sex-specific social spaces in which her sex is questioned, such as "women's restrooms and locker rooms." Another film by Hernandez, *We Love Our Lesbian Daughters,* explores lesbians' coming-out experiences. In this documentary several parents speak about how they felt when their daughters came out to them and features interviews with the girls themselves. According to Kearney, this affords "a rare glimpse into the lives of queer young Latinas" although the film still foregrounds "sexual identity over ethnic identity."

Kearney insists that movies "made by African, Latina, Asian, Arab, and Native American female youth often focus explicitly on the intersections between sex, gender, race, and ethnicity by featuring girls of color and exploring their multiple identities." Other examples include films such as *Looks Like a Girl,* which explores "lesbian representation beyond white, Anglo culture." She also cites the film *First Impressions from Seven Friends,* which "refocuses girls' friendship narratives through an African American lens." A documentary, *Baking Bread at Santa Clara Pueblo,* "focuses on a group of Native American girls who learn bread-baking from their older female relatives," writes Kearney, as the girls are seen "learning and embracing their ethnic heritage" and challenging other "white-dominated mainstream depictions of girlhood."

Foregrounding race and ethnicity as significant modes of identity that affect girls' private and public lives diversifies girls' film culture. Yet, writes Kearney, some films take "a far less celebratory approach to race and ethnicity, typically exploring the conflicts girls of color and non-Anglo female youth experience," especially when trying to merge multiracial or multiethnic identities. She cites Miyo Ann Tubridy's film *Name,* which explores coming to terms with her "Japanese mother's assimilationist perspective," played out through spellings and usage of her name. Similarly, Indian American Komal Herkishnami's film *Seventeen* explores identity and feeling at home neither in India nor in the United States, where she was raised. Kearney quotes Herkishnami: "I never saw anyone like me in a *Seventeen* magazine." Kearney also cites the film *Latinas Proving Themselves* as revealing the conflicts Latina Americans feel as they "try to balance traditional Latino values with American ideals of achievement and individualism" by talking about "leaving home, entering college, and attempting to balance work and family life."

Representing girls with disabilities, Kearney cites the film *My Name is Ruth,* directed by Ruth Smith, as an example of someone otherwise ignored by commercial media industries. Smith explores her identity and appearance and how she has been affected by disease as she turns the camera on herself. By using her own story and narrative, Kearney writes, Smith insists that viewers look at her, her abilities, and also how she contributes as a media producer.

Kearney writes that developing a "girl's gaze" in young women allows them to challenge "ideologies of gender, generation, sexuality, race, ethnicity, and disability prevalent in US society and commercial film culture." These girl directors expand public representation, says Kearney, and they complicate stories and challenge stereotypes. Rather than mimicking the "representational practices of the film industry," using film allows girls to develop their own points of view and to believe that their stories are worth telling as they counter the stereotypes expected from commercial film culture.

Among the major themes that girls explore and for which they rewrite the rules are physical image and appearance, beauty standards, and pressures targeting female youth. Kearney cites Lillian Ripley's film *What If Barbie Had a Voice?* as one in which Ripley uses the doll icon "to foreground these issues." In another Barbie film simply titled *Barbie*, Anna Bully and Katie McCord use multiple images to subvert the doll's conventional image, turning her into Butch Barbie, Greenpeace Barbie, Gothic Barbie, Rave Rat Barbie, and more. Kearney describes other films that try to connect girls' negative opinions about themselves in relationship to dominant beauty standards and reject idealized images in "commercial pop culture." Another example, *Barbie Resized* by Kat Bauman, uses "animated images cut from teen magazines to demonstrate the inhuman body dimensions of Barbie dolls and fashion models."

Another girl filmmakers' theme that Kearney mentions is realizing that they can reject commercial, prescripted messages about unhealthy body and beauty standards, as filmmakers use the space of their media work to critique other aspects of the media. In the film *Listen to Your Angel,* made by Leah Ruthrauff and Miquela Suazo, two white adolescent girls peruse a teen magazine and discuss whether or not they need to diet, while an angel and devil inserted into the frames deliver opposing messages. Kearney writes, "By foregrounding the relationship between girlfriends 'Listen to Your Angel' suggests that female youth should turn to people, specifically other females, rather than media texts for support and affirmation."

Finally, Kearney also offers examples of films in which girl filmmakers play out the cacophony of voices that shout edicts about how a girl's body ought to be. She describes the film *Girl Power,* made by students in Project Chysalis, as a "compilation of short animations, many of which address girls' troubled body image and rejection of commercial beauty culture." In the film *Body Image,* director Mieko Krell "uses the conventions of documentary filmmaking to raise awareness about girls' different relationships to and strategies for negotiating dominant beauty standards." Kearney describes segments in which a thin white girl talks about being involved with ballet and her investment in being skinny, juxtaposed with an interview of an African American girl "who comments on how the commercial media reproduce the female ideal as white, blonde, and thin and how girls like her are virtually invisible because of race and body shape." Kearney writes that by focusing on "female youth of different races and sizes," the film "refuses to generalize girls and their difficulties, foregrounding instead the relationship of identity and culture to girls' self-esteem and cultural visibility."

Music—Girls on the Mic

"Girls wantonly jettisoned social conventions about female decorum by screaming, jumping up and down, even fainting in public," writes Douglas in *Where the Girls Are.* In writing about the Beatles, she describes how the group's presence unleashed a mid-1960s wave of "anarchy" among teenage girls that perplexed adults as their daughters surged into an embrace of not only the Beatles' image and music, but of a representation of female fandom that meant open sexual tension, fanatic devotion, and sheer longing to transcend the strictures of femininity. She writes, "The established authority of the state was totally irrelevant to dedicated Beatles fans: they crawled under, climbed over, and simply burst through police barricades, demonstrating that arbitrary boundaries and the laws of old men, meant nothing to them."

In her book *Maiden USA,* Kathleen Sweeney mentions Douglas's characterization of the exuberance of adolescent fans in the early 1960s as "a sound wave that burst through boundaries, sowing seeds for the Women's Movement." And while screaming "may seem like the girliest of activities," Sweeney writes, "it's actually a sonic release of female power." Both authors concur that the power of female fans' devotion to the Beatles unleashed a surge of energy within the field of music that crossed over to breaking other social boundaries. Douglas goes on to characterize how girl groups, just emergent at the tail end of the 1950s and early 1960s, were deeply influential. After rock and roll burst onto the music scene in the mid-'50s, there were "weeks, even months, when no woman or female group had a hit among the top fifteen records," she writes.

Then, with the 1960 hit "Will You Love Me Tomorrow," the Shirelles, a group of four African American teenagers, "cracked the number one slot." Their song was powerful, Douglas writes, because they broke with the topics female singers were expected to sing about: wanting to get married, having a dreamboat boyfriend, and innocent longings. Instead, the song spoke openly of desire, and even more significantly, of choice.

Girl group music, says Douglas, had been largely ignored by male critics. When other hits followed the Shirelles' success, "from the pouf-skirted Angels . . . to the cute and innocent Dixie Cups to the eat-my-dirt, in-your-face, badass Shangri-Las," the lyrics and themes they introduced had a riveting effect on girls. Douglas writes, "The reason it spoke to us so powerfully, was that it gave voice to all the warring selves inside us struggling, blindly and with a crushing sense of insecurity, to forge something resembling a coherent identity." Girl group songs explored boys and sex, backed by a great beat. The songs, and anthems such as Martha Reeves's "Heat Wave," which was about being swept up in a sexual fervor, were like lightning rods to girls' confusions and longings. Douglas also points out how dancing served as another form of release for teenage girls—and one in which girls usually excelled over boys. By dancing the latest fad to these lyrics, girls constrained by the decorum of the era were able to cut loose. About the Reeves hit "Nowhere to Run," Douglas writes, "While we were gyrating and bouncing around to a single about a no-good boy . . . we were as happy as we could be." Although some of the girl groups were white, most were African American, and with the rise of the civil rights movement in the early 1960s, these voices conveyed hope for the future that had yet to come. Girl group music presented to teenagers an alternate path that they hadn't seen before—one in which they could own their sexual desire, band together with other girls, and sing about boys and men as they tried to figure them out.

"Few symbols," writes Douglas, "more dramatically capture the way young women in the early 1960s were pinioned between entrapment and freedom than one of the most bizarre icons of the period, the go-go girl dancing in a cage." Starting to shake loose of the bars of social convention, but also dancing most freely while constrained behind them, the music of the 1960s girl groups served as a turning point to not only bring more women into the field of music, but to cathartically let other women experience desire, freedom, and sexuality through their songs.

In the 1980s, girls could groove to Madonna's "Material Girl," dance to quasi-empowering tunes such as Prince's "Kiss," chime along to Cyndi Lauper's feminist anthem "Girls Just Want to Have Fun," and learn all the lyrics to Salt-N-Pepa's "Push It," but no matter the song, how do female singers and the role models they present show themselves (or serve) girls today? Are female singers still stereotyped as either "sexy" or "earthy" or "folksy," with few options other than these categories?

In the early 1990s, girl music experienced a revolution. A group of bands with female members, primarily around Seattle, opened the International Pop Underground convention in 1991 and collectively called themselves "Riot Grrrls." The phrase caught on and came to also represent girls who made zines, who supported a progressive lifestyle, and who contributed to other forms of independent media. At the same moment that focus on girls and their needs came forward within popular culture, so the Riot Grrrls began to rise within the music scene. The Riot Grrrls centered their message around female solidarity and, simultaneously playful and serious about instituting change, challenged status quo constructions about the music scene and fostered a do-it yourself culture of grassroots activism. Their songs (collectively) repudiated traditional constructions of girlhood and encouraged new subjects to be sung about, new understandings of female life to be heard.

The Riot Grrrls represented many things: the return of a sense of political activism for youth (in part due to awareness of the first Gulf War), a third wave feminist awareness, and an attention to creating spaces and opportunities for girls. Bands such as Bikini Kill, Sleater-Kinney, Hole, Bratmobile, and Babes in Toyland came to represent a kind of raw energy that signaled a shift in the music world, as these bands often highlighted the contradictions girls and women were expected to perform as part of stereotypical feminine identity, and they weren't afraid to openly bring attention to their conflicting feelings about this.

According to Kathleen Sweeney in *Maiden USA*, "Despite their anti-pop stance, the Riot Grrrl revolution had an energetic impact on mid-1990s music that coincided with several other alternative approaches." Artists such as Ani DiFranco, who formed her own label, Righteous Babe records, and later Alanis Morissette, Fiona Apple, and Missy Elliott all met with success before they were twenty years old and presented a new wave of women's voices singing about issues pertinent to their lives. Young women in the music industry provided alternatives to more mainstream music and lyrics that marginalized women. The rise of women's music festivals also created a space to focus exclusively on women artists and bring attention to their voices that had been lacking. According to Sweeney, "The Lilith Fair, a consortium of more than 100 multicultural female recording artists, joined forces in cities across the country from 1997 to 1999." Named after the biblical Adam's first wife, Lilith, the idea came from Canadian singer-songwriter Sarah McLachlan "in response to concert promoters' refusal to allow two female artists to play back-to-back." Wildly successful, the fair proved there was a desire for billings of female performers, and with artists such as Queen Latifah, Missy Elliot, and teenage singers Mya and Monica on the roster, the fair raised millions of dollars for many organizations that serve women.

As Mary Sheridan-Rabideau writes in *Girls, Feminism, and Grassroots Literacies,* the Riot Grrrls albums' graphics often showed nostalgic, if ironic, images of youth, yet their songs were often about the difficulties girls and young women still faced. These musicians openly wrote and sang about the institutional limits that girls and women encountered, and through their music and personas represented the idea that women can overcome these limits and serve as agents of change. As Sheridan-Rabideau writes, "Key to RiotGrrrl was the Do-It-Yourself (DIY) mentality. DIY indicates a desire to take care of one's own needs without relying on corporate intermediaries. As the author of the grrrl zine *Bikini Kill #2* states, girls and young women 'Must take over the means of production in order to create our own meanings.'" She continues, "Sharing punk's aversion to the commercialism of rock music, RiotGrrrl bands reacted to the increasing commercialization of alternative music within the DIY framework: most RiotGrrrl bands stuck with independent labels, used new modes of production such as zines for publicity, and encouraged alternative consumption of media messages."

Although issues of race and class were a focal point in their music, the Riot Grrrl movement was largely represented by white and middle-class women who largely knew each other through college networks. Yet even with these limitations, the message went out that women and girls could make a place for themselves in a predominantly male world. The Riot Grrrls challenged traditional expectations for girls, exploring issues of sexuality and, according to Sheridan-Rabideau, "Even with these significant limitations [of class privilege], the initial wave of RiotGrrrl music inspired girls and women across the country to come together as grrrls who could participate in this largely male music world and control their own message. Popularizing the mantra 'Revolution Girl-Style Now!,' the RiotGrrrls ushered in a grrrl-centered decade and are credited with fostering a new generation of feminist activism."

Riot Grrrls fostered local feminist networks that critiqued consumerist networks, in part by writing and producing their own texts, with zines such as *Girl Germs, Satan Wears a Bra,* and *Quit Whining*. Although energizing to the participants, the counterculture media production values espoused had little impact on mainstream consumerist practices. By decade's end the original Riot Grrrls ethos seemed precisely the opposite of the later consumerist "girl power"

Girls Rock

Is music training still gendered by shuttling girls off to piano and violin practice while boys are told to pick up the guitar and pound the drums? Who gets the message about front-running rather than singing backup? And can a girl or woman be a lead singer without flaunting her sexuality in a conventional way? How comfortable are girls with being at the front of a stage and leading a band? What skills do they need that accompany performance—the confidence to lead a group, entertain an audience, compose original music, and put ideas forward? How have things changed in the music scene and what opportunities are now available for girls? Things are changing in regard to teaching girls that they can be the lead singer in a band, and not just by flaunting their sexuality. One example is Rock'N'Roll Camp for Girls, which includes in its mission statement that it believes that "Girls can play any kind of music they want," "Creative voices of girls and women need to be amplified to create social change," and "'Girls Rock' is more than just a slogan." The organization states that it wants to "eradicate all the limiting myths about music and gender that make girls afraid to speak up, sing out, and make noise." When girls are taught how to play instruments and offered mentorship and positive role models, girls learn that they can play any type of music, and that, as the mission statement says, "Every technical job and creative endeavor in the music industry, is available to any girl or woman who wants to explore it."

products to come. The original Riot Grrrl participants saw their values shunned as most often girls were encouraged to be consumers, rather than producers, of a different message about the power of girls. The cultural climate had shifted and the spirit of the Riot Grrrl movement, although it did bring valuable attention to the situation of the teenage girl, now was portrayed on very different terms. Different understandings of "girl power" and what this meant had come to the fore of the public's consciousness and became more mainstream. Corporations such as Nike, newly realizing that girls were a target market with money to spend, worked the idea into T-shirts, accessories, and a host of other products that were packaged under the rubric of "girl power" and its easy commodification. In the early 1990s the phrase represented a feminist project for musicians who were working to change the commercialization of art and its gendered stereotypes. Within a decade, representations of girl power became linked with consumer culture with the phrase imprinted on almost every sort of saleable item. As Sheridan-Rabideau writes, "The edge of the early message—where RiotGrrrls wrote SLUT across their belly, sang about child abuse, and campaigned against commodified images of girls—changed into perky songs played in shopping malls and into doe-eyed superheroes that girls and parents alike could embrace." The British girl group the Spice Girls also popularized slogans around "girl power" with spin-off marketing, although feminists were quick to realize that printing this phrase on a baby-doll pink T-shirt did nothing to further the cause of girls and women.

In contrast to the Riot Grrrls, the Spice Girls seemed to thrive on media attention and repetition of media stereotypes that they gladly perpetuated. Wildly successful, they sold out concerts globally and manufactured movies, videos, and products to a young audience. Unlike the Riot Grrrls, they espoused stereotypes of sexiness, yet they brought attention to the phrase "girl power" and to a more mainstream audience. They promoted valuing female friendship and awareness of a "girl universe," although a conventional one that often replicated patriarchal values. While widespread consumerism helped this phrase to become mainstream, feminist critics questioned, if not condemned, the facile co-opting of the phrase without real investment in social change to support girls' agency. Rachel Fudge writes in her essay, "Girl, Unreconstructed: Why Girl Power Is Bad for Feminism": "Girl power tricks us all into believing that girls are naturally powerful and therefore ignores the many ways their power is contingent on adhering to cultural expectations of female behavior." Easy adoption of the phrase allowed many to feel that girls were being promoted without questioning what types of girls, for what types of behaviors, and without questioning the systems that reinforced these stereotypes. Fudge notes it was a very different message from the "grrr" in "grrrl," which sought social, political change that questioned gender stereotypes and advocated for real change. Yet there is common agreement that the phrase's popularity within popular culture shows a receptivity to giving attention to girls, although again, in a way that reinforces traditional stereotypes.

Media Literacy and Real Girl Power

One challenge girls have in attuning themselves to the media's pervasive presence and far-reaching influence is understanding how to look critically at a force that seems as commonly part of their lives as air. Multiple programs have sprung up around the country, primarily within the last decade, to train girls to think more critically about assumptions and gender stereotypes that are presented as "natural."

A number of girl advocacy organizations, such as Mind on the Media, focus on promoting "media literacy": teaching girls to decode, understand, and ultimately better resist harmful messages in ads and other media. Showing images of models before and after heavy makeup is applied, and photos before and after professional retouching and airbrushing, can reveal to girls that what is presented within a magazine's pages is simply unattainable through nature—and can also help girls to make the connection that they should stop striving for something that is impossible to have without heavy intervention. Girls Inc.'s Media Literacy program includes a program called Girls Re-Cast TV, in which girls analyze television shows and characters and then rewrite scenes in order to have them better represent their own points of view. Its Girls Get the Message program brings together media industry leaders with girls so that they can talk about how they would like to see girls and women portrayed. On the website AdiosBarbie.com, an interactive game called Feed the Model lets players disrupt the assumption that a superskinny model shouldn't eat by giving her food.

Even for girls who realize that they are presented with contradictory images and messages, and who may come to harbor a love/hate relationship with the media, things are not necessarily easy. Susan

YA Fiction: Is It for Real?

Almost every reader remembers from her youth one book or author who made a strong impression, whether it was a Judy Blume book that explained menstruation or a contemporary rendering of a fairy tale; young adult fiction has the power to leave strong impressions. YA fiction can be a reflection of contemporary teenhood today—with the subjects portrayed and characters created serving as a mirror—or books for this population of readers can also serve a different purpose. In a 2006 article in *The New York Times Book Review* ("Young Adult Fiction: Wild Things"), Naomi Wolf lambastes YA tie-ins to popular TV shows such as *Gossip Girl* and the book series A-List and Clique, in which the protagonists mimic the worst of "mean girl" behavior through their concern with fitting in, popularity, sexuality, and looks. Wolf wonders how these books serve girls as they turn to reading for both pleasure and to learn about the world.

In a more recent post on *Racialicious* in 2007 ("Oops, Where'd We Go? The Disappearing Black Girls in Young Adult Literature"), blogger and librarian Latoya Peterson draws attention to another unreality often portrayed: the absence of young women of color within the majority of these teen-directed series. After reviewing the most popular YA series, Peterson writes, "I can see where we have an issue. In the new YA lit arena, people of color are non-existent." She continues, "Now, I am sure that there have to be books written by and for young women of color circulating around the library." She, however, checked only "the top requested books in the YA category. Nary a person of color to be found. (Do not be fooled by Gossip Girl's multi-culti covers—people of color are passing references and side characters, if they appear at all.)"

Peterson does concede that some new series are "challenging the chokehold that white girl reality has on teen fiction." In a 2008 *Bitch* magazine article, "Why Not?: It's a New Golden Age of Young-Adult Fiction," Anastasia Masurat interviews five new YA authors who specifically seek to challenge the boundaries of YA fiction, in part by including subjects that were before considered "inappropriate" (and stand in contrast to series such as Sweet Valley High or the Baby-sitters' Club) but that the authors think authentically reflect contemporary teens' lives. No topic seems taboo anymore, one author says, although there still is sensitivity to how some topics are rendered for teens. One author, Justina Chen Headley, mentions banding together with nine other Asian American authors to create Fusion Stories, a website to introduce readers to YA novels written by Asian Americans.

Yet the importance of books to girls has also been measured in positive ways, as Tara Parker-Pope reports in "Healthful Messages, Wrapped in Fiction," a 2008 story in *The New York Times* Health section. Parker-Pope highlights a new series of books published by B*tween Productions, aimed at nine- to thirteen-year-old girls and standing in contrast to much of the other "teen or preteen" fare that features popular television shows such as *Gossip Girl*, in which characters worry about fashion, sex, and popularity.

Rather, in this series, the story lines revolve around five middle-school girls in Brookline, Massachusetts, and were developed "with the goal of helping girls build self-esteem and coping skills" and focusing on topics such as weight and cyberbullying. Parker-Pope reports that at the annual meeting of the Obesity Society, Duke medical school researchers presented "remarkable" findings on *Lake Rescue*, "a Beacon Street book that focuses on the struggles of an overweight girl named Chelsea Briggs." The girls in the study who received a copy of *Lake Rescue* "posted a decline in average body mass index scores of 0.71; those who didn't read the book had an average increase of 0.05." While the difference is minor, the researchers were encouraged to believe that reading the positive message within the fictional text had an impact. Parker-Pope quotes Sarah C. Armstrong, a pediatrician who directs Duke's Healthy Lifestyles program, "The results of the study are not striking in how big they were but that it worked at all," she says. "It's such a positive, easy intervention."

The series was created by Addie Swartz, the founder of B*tween Productions, when, she says, she had an "aha" moment while shopping with her eight-year-old daughter and her friends and one objected to a scantily clad model. In a second article, Parker-Pope quotes Swartz as saying, "It felt like there were so many messages out there that were bombarding her and her friends and girls her age." As an antidote, Swartz created the series, which receives input from childhood health experts. Swartz says that parents have offered anecdotal evidence that the books have helped their daughters ("Parents would say, 'Your books have helped my daughter deal with this issue.'"). "There's no risk to giving a girl a book," says researcher Alexandra Russell, a fourth-year medical student who led the study. "If she doesn't lose weight as a consequence, at least it's promoting literacy. It's risk free and easy to implement."

Douglas comments that most women assume "they are the only ones who love and hate *Vogue* at the same time" and that they are the only ones who are "riddled with internal contradictions" and that these feelings are "unusual." Not at all, she responds—this ambivalence and sense of contradiction are "also at the heart of what it means to be a feminist." So it can be for girls who are often given conflicting messages and may experience a range of desires for themselves in response to media images.

Media saturation, of course, doesn't mean that the media control girls' actions or self-esteem entirely. Yet, as Douglas will say, "They have the cameras, . . . and we don't." In part, programs that teach resistance have been so powerful because wresting control of the tools of media production has felt so rewarding to girls, and because these programs teach that the messages produced are just that—contrived and deliberate. Redressing or rebalancing the distance between the realities of girls' lives with the sitcom situations they view on TV can be empowering on multiple levels, from teaching technological skills to deconstruction of previously unrealized subtexts.

Organizations such as Girls Write Now, New Moon Girls, or Reel Grrls show what happens when girls control media production instead of being objectified by it, or write magazine articles addressing issues that are really important to them, rather than reading those that tell them what they should care about. Traditionally given diaries in which they are told to record their thoughts or hopes and dreams—all with the catch that they keep these literarily under lock and key—for girls, going public with their writing, or being the lead rather than the backup singer, or the director rather than the femme fatale star or accompaniment to the male lead, is a significant shift. It is one that can signal for girls new relationships with the media that correspond to greater understanding of their own potential.

When girls step forward into media making, they have the opportunity to rupture what has historically been an adult and male-dominated field, and they have the chance to radically alter notions of girlhood and its representation as well as reconstruct their own identities into new shapes. While girls are still operating within networks of race, class, sexuality, and ethnicity and ability, often revealed within their work, they can also use the creative practices of media production to work through conflicts and control their representation.

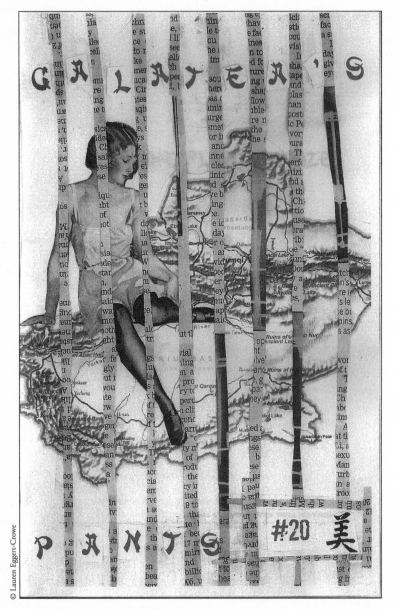

Galatea's Pants #20, March 2007. Galatea's Pants is a print zine that began in 2000.

CHAPTER 5

GIRLS FINDING THEIR FUTURES

As the concept of "girl power" has come forward into popular culture, the phrase has come to stand for the idea that girls can be strong agents of their own wills, not secondary actors to boys. Academic writing has intermingled with and informed the work of activists who want to promote girls' development, to change the way girls understand themselves and how girls' power is understood; activist groups, academics, and girls' advocates within popular culture often work specifically with cohorts of girls and young women who are charting their own visions for gender equality. Creating political foundations and writing zines, forming online activist communities, organizing national music tours, and enacting local grassroots action, girls and young women are increasingly visible and powerful within popular culture. Without necessarily calling themselves feminists, they are creating new images of powerful girls who align with feminist identities by creating a society in which all genders are treated equally.

As technology has become more widely accessible and the computer and Internet have become commonly available tools, girls have found new ways to forge community with each other, locally, across the country, and even the world. Girls are learning at younger and younger ages that to speak out and work toward change is something they can do. One milestone is the First National Girls' Conference, held in 1997, which more than 140 girls from thirty-nine states attended with money raised by the National Girls' Coalition. According to Andrea Johnston, whose group Girls Speak Out helped to organize the conference, the United States Committee for UNICEF (the United Nations International Children's Fund) cosponsored the conference and brought girls from countries within Africa, Asia, Latin America, and Europe. The conference, which included a sleepover, was held at UNICEF House in New York City, across the street from the United Nations. Although adults such as Gloria Steinem and Marlo Thomas offered guidance, girls set the agenda and developed a Girls Global Plan of Action. Alongside girls' own activism are a spate of new organizations that want to foster the growth of girls, whether it's by teaching safety awareness and assertion at young ages or supporting girls to start their own businesses or to sing rock and roll. This chapter looks at ways in which individual girls and groups of girls are making their voices heard, whether by making zines, going online, or through organizations devoted to helping girls raise their voices. It also briefly considers the treatment of girls worldwide.

Awareness of issues that affect girls and girl advocacy is at a high point in the United States, and it's interesting to speculate where it will turn next. The world of education has engaged in much debate about single-sex schooling, with some people arguing that girls and boys are essentially different, and hence that they learn through essentially different modes. But does separating girls and boys during grade school or high school years bolster each gender, or does it create only more confusion about how to interact? And is the claim that no discrimination now remains against girls—they can do anything, be anything—really true? If it's popularly believed to be true, but not supported by legislation (such as the protection of Title IX) or other sets of cultural expectations (such as popular television shows with strong female figures), can girls really believe they can do or be anything? Or is this just another set of pressures to contend with? As this latest generation of girls is raised with the often-heard message, however practically contradicted, that gender is no longer a barrier to anything or even necessarily rigidly defined, what will these girls' adult lives as women look like and what will their daughters need? And just because a subset of girls has grown to see gender as unleashed from the strictures that once bound it, has society at large followed? Many girls believe their futures are open to whatever path they want to chart—but are all fields, jobs, and choices now open to all girls, giving them the support and opportunity they need to succeed? The glass ceiling, the "mommy track," the pink collar might still be real, but now at least they are visible. As girls look ahead to their futures, in the workforce, in their personal lives, as they effect change in the world, the futures they create will be as varied as the girls out there.

Zines: Chronicling Girlhood

In the 1960s the poet Muriel Rukeyser famously asked in her poem "Kathe Kollwitz": "What would happen if one woman told the truth about her life? The world would split open." Years later, Mary Celeste Kearney, in her book *Girls Make Media,* cites feminist scholar Lyn Mikel Brown as asking, "What would it mean for a girl—against the stories read, chanted or murmured to her—to choose to tell the truth of her life aloud to another person at the very point when she is invited into the larger cultural story of womanhood—that is, at early adolescence? To whom would a girl speak and in what context? Who would listen to the story she dares to author? What does she risk in the telling?"

Like Rukeyser, Brown asserts that there is another narrative being suppressed in service of larger societal mores, and zines—independently produced, often photocopied, stapled, self-made magazines and journals—are one place to find girls' other stories, those that put forward alternative narratives to the conventional script they're told they ought to follow.

"Zines"—short for magazine—have a long tradition as a place for alternative writing not found in the mainstream press. "Popular" magazines, such as *Seventeen,* often tout expected story lines: how to improve one's looks, handle romantic, heterosexual relationships, how to succeed socially. They are thick with advertisements, and it's no surprise that girls have often had a fraught relationship with their advice, both buying the publications and buying into the advice espoused, yet alternatively feeling as if the magazines generate a universe of rules that are impossible to keep up with (how to dress, how to act, how to look cute).

As the Riot Grrrl movement reached its peak in the early 1990s, a large part of the DIY (do-it-yourself) culture that the movement fostered included girls making zines that served as nontraditional spaces and represented alternative, feminist, and counterculture values. Zines became a place for girls to rebel against more traditional teen magazines, a way to claim media production themselves and create something that better addressed their own concerns and explored nontraditional conceptions of female identity; girls used them to put forward alternative views and stories about identity, sexuality, body image, and even more, and to experience the power that comes from media making. Although zinemaking fits, to some extent, with the encouragement girls often receive for reading and writing as approved activities (rather than playing rock and roll, for example), how they used the space was often to deliberately speak out against the strictures of femininity.

The sense of powerfulness that zinesters feel in creating their own media and making a place, literally, to share their stories is not to be underestimated. Zines provided a space for girls to write what was true to them and to clear away what was unwanted, either by reinscribing meaning to traditional concepts, or making fun of them, or simply by putting forward honest definitions about what their lives were really about. They also felt a sense of activism in taking hold of the means of media production and writing about topics that promoted girls and women in innovative ways. The handmade qualities of zines (photocopied or stapled or literally cutting and pasting with glue and tape) are another way in which zinesters reinforce their noncommercial press values, and revealing the actual "made-ness" of the zine is part of the appeal.

Zinemaking was (and still is) often one of the most accessible forms of media available to girls, although girls often must be privileged enough to have access to a photocopier or printer and be able to pay for paper and other materials. But zine producers also frequently relied on "illicit means of creating, reproducing, and distributing their texts," often using machinery, paper, and other materials from office jobs or other institutions, in part as a way to further usurp the means of production and "rebel against dominant social institutions" while exploring "counterhegemonic identities" even through issues of reproduction and distribution, Kearney says.

Sasha Cagen, cofounder of *Cupsize* in 1994, started her zine just out of college while interning at a major women's magazine. In typical zinester fashion, she co-opted the tools of the traditional media by using the copy machine and other resources while working on the carpet, literally cutting and pasting, during late hours after work. Cagen recollects that she and her coeditor very much felt part of an underground movement, especially as a "shameless intern, inside the media machine at a young age." "It was totally subversive," she says, "working at a mainstream magazine by day" and then putting out her own zine at night.

Cagen had thought of zines as "being distributed in record stores in NYC most made by pimply rock guys" until her friend Tara asked, "If all these boys are doing it, why not do one that represented our view of things?" Both shared, as she put it, "the advantages and disadvantages of being well endowed," so they named the zine *Cupsize* to reveal their own concerns and those of their contemporaries. They included articles about topics that varied from exploring bisexuality, picking toe calluses, or just "really kooky, weird details in life." One story described going to a peep show together, seeing other young women naked, and then thinking through class issues. "It was incredibly freeing," she says, "a place we could write anything we wanted." It also felt inspiring and unique that "you could have your own little magazine as a friend—you'd never get that opportunity at *Marie Claire*—not the way it worked."

The distributor Factsheet Five picked up *Cupsize*, and after that, Cagen says, they received requests for copies in the mail and often traded with other zinesters. Very gratifying, says Cagen, was making penpal friends around the world. "Each package was a work of art," she says, remembering the effort it took to print, collate, and then put

From the Personal to the Political:
Lauren Eggert-Crowe and "Galatea's Pants"

Lauren Eggert-Crowe was sixteen years old in 2000, the year she decided to start her zine, *Galatea's Pants*. Her inspiration first came, ironically, from *Seventeen* magazine, where she read a "queen of the zine" feature. She recollects thinking, *Cool! I want to do that*. Her title came from the story of Galatea (Pygmalion's statue), who became a real person once she put her own pants on. Since the zine's start, Eggert-Crowe has published three to four issues per year, with a few "one-shot zines" in the middle of this schedule. In 2008 she published issue 22, and for its tenth anniversary in 2010 she wants to do something big, although she was not yet sure what.

Although the zine maintains a webpage, she says, "I think it's really important to have something in your hand, that you can touch." She started *Galatea's Pants* in the same way most zinesters do, by writing about what was important to her at the time—her first kiss, movie reviews, current life events, and reproducing favorite poems that reflected her growing interest in creative writing. Also in typical fashion, she literally cut and pasted images from other sources and then photocopied everything for the zine, which, initially, she mostly gave to friends and family.

"Definitely, blogs are now out there in a way they weren't when I started," says Eggert-Crowe, who had a strong sense of participating in the history of the underground press. "Zines were big in the '70s and '80s with the punk rock ethic," she says. "A huge vein of the current zine scene was being part of that nerdy craft chic movement—that speaks to the non-web method of expressing oneself."

the zine in the mail. "It was never going to reach a lot of people that way," she admits, "but the relationships formed were more special." She comments that blogging might fill a similar need now for teenagers to write about their lives, but she insists that making your own zine is really empowering. "Blogging is great and so accessible—but there is still a pleasure in creating something tactile . . . and you also have

She says that she has always written most of the zine, with some contributions from others, and that it has made a dramatic arc from the solely personal to the political—a change that reflected her move to college and increasingly radical political stance, brought into sharper focus during the events of September 11, the Iraq War, and after finding herself on a politically conservative campus and being surprised to find out that "not everyone in the world was a feminist." Now the zine is almost totally devoted to radical politics. "It's always been my megaphone," she says. "I had a lot of things to say," and the zine was the place to do it.

Eggert-Crowe says that for many teenage girls, zining is making a diary of sorts, but one that is intended to be more public. "You knew other people were going to read it" (unlike one kept locked at home). "It could have a literary bent, or be as moody or loud as you wanted it to be, or be shy and secretive or confrontational. The gamut of zines for girls runs an emotional arc . . . they're all there."

Eggert-Crowe wrote her college honors thesis about the history of zines (in the form of a zine), and she connects the importance of girls making zines to the punk rock scene, which had been exclusively male until the early 1990s and the emergence of the Riot Grrrl scene, which included the female critique of punk and a whole new crop of girl zines.

When asked why girls make zines, or if zinemaking is a "quieter" version of the ways in which boys are encouraged to speak out, she replies that it's a "different externalization"—a girl's zine is very much meant to be seen and "a lot of zines are very loud!" Many girls' zines reflect the flooding of newfound adolescent consciousness, and they serve as a place to understand the "assaults between patriarchy and the personal." Eggert-Crowe insists that many girls are making brave statements within their zines and putting themselves forward. "It *does* have a transformative effect—it's not a passive space."

more control, and can share something with some people and [it's] not searchable forever." She points out another advantage to creating something that exists in print rather than forever available. "There is an intimacy when you hold it in your hand—it's more rare and special!"

In *Girls Make Media,* Kearney offers an overview of some of the other girl zines that emerged during the Riot Grrrl movement. She cites *Bikini Kill: A Color & Activity Book (Bikini Kill #1)* as one of the first zines associated with the movement. The first issue listed the zine's fundamental purposes, which included: "3.) To serve as a role model for other girls 4.) To show boys other ways of doing things and that we have stuff to say 5.) To discuss in both literal and artistic ways those issues that're really important to girls—naming these issues, specifically, validates their importance and other girls' interest in them—Reminds other girls that they aren't alone 6.) To make fun of and thus disrupt the powers that be."

The issue *Bikini Kill #2* emphasized taking back the means of producing media, Kearney says. In their manifesto, the zinesters write that part of their purpose is that "we must take over the means of production in order to create our own meanings. . . ." Once the floodgates were opened for expression of girls' interests and desires, it seemed a gaping need that had gone too long ignored. The manifesto also included this reason: "Riot grrrl is . . . because us girls crave records and books and fanzines that speak to us, that we feel included in and can understand our own ways. . . ."

The range of writing that emerged from this period reveals how thoroughly girls embraced the chance to write the stories of their real lives in a way that hadn't previously felt available. One author writing in *Bikini Kill #1* reveals the sense of urgency and relief she felt in having this medium available: "I was like, okay I can sit here in my apt. and be really pissed off . . . or I can get my anger out by making this little Xerox thing about what I was thinking, so I did. It made me feel a lot better, I mean if just one woman reads it and feels like she knows what I'm talking about, then it's totally worth it. I think the idea that one person can do stuff is totally important." Kearney also quotes Ciara Xyerra's comment about her zine *A Renegade's Handbook to Love & Sabotage*: "Riot grrrl . . . shook me out of my fear that i was too young, too inexperienced, too female, too stupid for people to want to hear my voice."

Kearney comments that most zinesters were white, despite the counterhegemonic and forward-thinking perspectives they often put forward. But that began to change in the 1990s. She writes, "Several girls of color have challenged the overwhelming whiteness of grrrl zine culture by foregrounding images of Asian, Latina, and African American females in their texts. For example, most issues of *Slant* and *Aim Your Dick* contain illustrations of their Vietnamese creator, Mimi Nguyen, and her Asian female friends. Similarly, Sabrina Margarita Sandata's *Bamboo Girl* regularly features drawings and photographs of Filipinas and other women of color." (Sandata now writes under the name Alcantara.)

Girls' zines of all persuasions explore many different topics, often thinking newly about beauty standards and body image, and often with the idea that "traditional" or "standard" understandings of beauty standards must first be addressed and then critiqued. Often, they spread the message that female identity in all forms must be affirmed and that this means breaking with the mold of traditional expectations for femininity. Zine titles also deviate from the need for catchy, salable phrases but rather reflect the zines' content. Some titles Kearney lists include: *Slant, Bamboo Girl, Mamasita, Blackgirl Stories, La Chica Loca, Hermana, Resist, Korean American Women with Attitude, Bi-Girl World, Lezzie Smut, The Adventures of Baby Dyke,* and *The Making of a Femme.* Other titles serve as rhetorical strategies through the reclaiming of particular words previously used to, as Kearney writes, connect girls with anger, such as: *Bitch, Bust, Rag Hag, Girl Germs, Angst Girl, Grrrl Trouble, Pretty in Punk, Barbie War, Housewife Turned Assassin.* Using new spellings, such as "womyn" or "boi," is another way in which zinesters seek to create a language (literally) that eschews patriarchal meaning and inscriptions. (A few zines that started small—*Bust* and *Bitch* are examples—have gone on to become more mainstream, taking in advertising and using more widespread distribution channels while still operating at a remove from the tenets of commercial publishing. Each has grown into a glossier, full-color publication that still strives to represent a diversity of topics about women's and girls' lives that mainstream media will not cover.)

Appropriating and reconfiguring the appearance of image was

important to most zinesters, given their oppositional stance toward dominant societal values. Kearney writes how some zinesters would take images from popular culture, such as "Lisa from *The Simpsons* animated television show, Angelica from Nickelodeon's *Rugrats* series, and Eloise from the popular children's book by the same name—thus refashioning such characters as role models for young girls." Other figures from popular media might be reconfigured; *Nerd Girl #4* features Lucy (of *Peanuts*) wearing a T-shirt bearing a feminist symbol, and a menacing Pippi Longstocking (from the Astrid Lindgren novels) flaunts a sword and a pistol. She writes, "Several grrrl zines, including *Quarter Inch Squares*, have attempted to expand Mattel's normative construction of young female identity by including a list of 'Barbies We Would Like to See,' such as Bisexual Barbie, Blue Collar Barbie, Gender Fuck Barbie, Homegirl Barbie, Rebbe Barbie, and Single Mom Barbie."

Weight is often frankly explored with various feelings of self-rejection in relationship to mass media expectations, Kearney says. Using images or text from traditional beauty and fashion magazines and reconfiguring them to show subtext or oppression is another way zinesters take back the standards they have been given to reinscribe their own. She cites Terry Moon writing in the special body images issue of her zine *Korespondances*: "We need a revolution whose aim is not merely changing property relationships, but one that aims to create new relationships, including relationships we have to ourselves and our bodies." Other zinesters address the discomfort of binding clothes or high heels, Kearney writes.

She cites *Nerd Girl #4* as an example of zinesters disrupting "commercial media messages" by "appropriating images of female beauty regimes and fashion practices . . . reconfiguring them in ways that reveal their oppressive characteristics." *Nerd Girl #4* shows several collages of bra advertisements, and fashion images from teen magazines "are juxtaposed with seemingly unrelated captions like 'She thinks high heels are comfortable.'" The editor writes, "i know that i've talked about this before, but it needs to be repeated over and over again . . . it's about how womyn and their bodies are portrayed in the media . . . it makes me sick that only a small percentage of womyn are represented, yet it is sold as a massive cultural ideal." Embracing nonnormative body sizes and imbuing different shapes with value, zinesters have sought to change cultural values for the audiences they are reaching.

Another example Kearney provides is from the zine *Skunk #4,* which includes a "full-page 'make-over' pictorial that shows Vikki, editor of *Psychedelic Wasteland* zine, getting her waist-length hair cut off and her head shaved." In high contrast to a "traditional" teen girl's magazine, which would valorize glossy hair and styling it, this shows a girl shaving it off. Similarly, Kearney points out, many zines include images of "tattoos, body piercings, unconventional haircuts, androgynous clothing, and work boots." She writes, "As these images reveal, many grrrl zinesters demonstrate their interest in developing a new body politics for young feminists" that eschews and moves beyond "conventional standards of female appearance promoted in commercial teen magazines."

Another common thread found within zines is the desire to tell "herstory" and to rewrite historical narratives that privileged men's experiences. Kearney reports *Ms. America #2* includes a page to "Riot Grrrandmas," mentioning Harriet Tubman, Virginia Woolf, Susan B. Anthony, and Anne Sexton, and another zine, *Marika 2,* contains Sojourner Truth's speech "Ain't I a Woman?" Raising awareness of girls and women who are at the forefront of contemporary change/barriers is a theme often found in zines, with Kearney offering examples of zines giving recognition to the first class to complete Hell Week at the Citadel, a military school that only recently admitted women, or to the All American Girls' Professional Baseball League. She writes that zines also have become a place to trade information about publications (books and articles) about girls that wouldn't otherwise find coverage in the mainstream media.

Zines also became a place to work out race relationships and connections between girls of different backgrounds. Kearney comments that grrrl zinesters' valorization of female rock musicians often reflected "their investments in whiteness," which unconsciously reaffirmed the "racial politics of rock culture, the zine community, and dominant society." *Bamboo Girl*'s Sabrina Margarita Alcantara frequently uses her zine to promote nonwhite female musicians. She says that she started her zine because she felt no one else was addressing race and gender in a way she could relate to. She says, "There definitely weren't any zines out there on being mixed blood Asian. As I continued creating my zine, I started to network with other ladies who were creating zines relating to race and gender, and so the community I found was comforting."

Alcantara comments that zines are the perfect vehicle for girls to make their voices heard. She writes, "As girls, we are bombarded with confusing images of what we're supposed to be, so when we feel we don't measure up to them, we question ourselves. It is such a great feeling to see something in print that you made yourself, because it validates you. And girls need that extra validation from themselves, their peers, and others, because it is not the norm that we receive growing up."

Although Alcantara maintains a web presence for her zine and acknowledges that it's cheaper and more immediate to have an online zine, like many other zinemakers, she insists, "I prefer being able to have something physical in my hands to sift through at my leisure. And no online zine can show the true creativity of a zinester who sews thread with care through their zine binding, or who cuts their zine to a specifically odd size, or who adds touches of obvious handiwork to it that makes it a collector's item." Despite the ease of the blog, the details she describes, and the desire to build community, are why those who love print and the physical object will continue zine making.

Girls Online

While girls go online almost as soon as they're old enough to navigate a computer keyboard, the online world is also one that is constantly changing, from Facebook updates to the growth of Twitter and the sudden ubiquitousness of text messaging. There's no doubt that going online can provide girls with all kinds of resources—particularly for those girls who might feel isolated or estranged from the communities they live in—but going online also poses dangers, not only from predators who pose under assumed identities to try to hook up with girls, but from cyberbullying and the ease with which harmful or hurtful information and photos can make their way around the web. In one well-publicized example, the parents of Megan Meier, a thirteen-year-old girl who committed suicide on October 17, 2006, after falling victim to an Internet hoax, have set up a foundation to work toward prevention of bullying and cyberbullying.

An ABC story about the Megan Meier case cites Nancy Willard, executive director of the Center for Safe and Responsible Internet Use: "When emotionally vulnerable young people get online, they can be very easily manipulated." Working out social hierarchies, friendships, and frictions online has led to a new construction of school connections for new generations and as the tools of the web increase, the web's usefulness can alter how relationships are played out. The story also reports that "in the information age, playground poundings have moved to online chat rooms and instant messages. Nearly half of all teenagers report they have been the victim of cyber attacks. Everything from text messaging to e-mail can be used to bully victims."

Yet, of course, there is a strong sense of connectedness and real resources girls can find and use online. Online peer counseling can connect a girl with an expert or an online friend with an efficiency not necessarily possible in real time. Many online sites are also an opposite model to the "girls are competitive" stereotype—rather, they emphasize cooperative sharing of information and inclusiveness. Girls reaching out through the web can foster a greater sense of global awareness about what it means to be a girl, such as girls sharing experiences of puberty, no matter where they live, or cultural rituals around girlhood milestones, such as having a *quinceañera,* bat mitzvah, or sweet sixteen party. A sampling of some girl-centered sites follows.

Still a presence but no longer as active as it once was, Girl-Mom (www.girl-mom.com) was the work of activist Allison Crews, who

Teen Sexuality—Help Is There, Online

Celebrating its tenth anniversary in 2008, Scarleteen (www.scarleteen.com) is a site founded by Heather Corinna, an advocate for straightforward and inclusive information about young adults' sexual health. Scarleteen's experts offer honest, direct information on any topic readers ask about while also encouraging readers to seek a diversity of sources and perspectives about sexuality. The site aspires to offer information to help girls—sexually active or not—develop their own values, in combination with the perspectives offered by "peers, schools, parents, other mentors and their overall culture and communities."

OutProud, the National Coalition for Gay, Lesbian, Bisexual and Transgender Youth (www.outproud.org), is one online resource that can help LBTQ girls who might not otherwise have access to information about sexuality. The site offers information about coming out to parents, and brochures such as "I Think I Might Be a Lesbian . . . Now What Do I Do?" in which girls who have come out describe their experiences and answer questions including, "What is it like to be young and a lesbian?" "How do we learn to like ourselves?" and "How can I meet other lesbians?" Another online brochure, "Watching Out for Yourself in Online Relationships," gives advice to teen girls about online interactions, particularly around keeping sex safe.

The organization Advocates for Youth (www.advocatesforyouth.org), based in Washington, DC, works to promote policies that "help young people make informed and responsible decisions about their reproductive and sexual health" by providing information and assistance to "youth-serving organizations" throughout the United States and in the developing world. Advocates for Youth hosts online groups such as YouthResource, which

died in 2005, at age twenty-two, of a seizure caused by medication. Crews founded the site and wrote candidly about becoming a teenage mother and her decision to keep her child at age fifteen. In her essay "When I Was Garbage," she writes about receiving the "Teen Mom Look" from strangers, about her many accomplishments, and concludes, "I am not a burden to society, my son is not a burden advocates for gay, lesbian, bisexual, and transgendered teens and argues that adolescents have the right to "balanced, accurate, and realistic sexuality education, confidential and affordable sexual health services," and "the tools they need to safeguard their sexual health." Advocates for Youth also hosts the website MySistahs (Mysistahs.org), a sexual and reproductive health information site created for young women of color; the organization offers online peer counseling with trained educators, comprising teenage and young adult women of color (ages thirteen to twenty-four) from all over the United States. Another sponsored site, ambienteJoven.org, offers Spanish-language sex and health information for Latino/a gay, lesbian, bisexual, and transgendered teens.

The Coalition for Positive Sexuality (CPS), established in Chicago in 1992 by high school students who sought open discussion and information, aims to "give teens the information they need to take care of themselves and in so doing affirm their decisions about sex, sexuality, and reproductive control" and to foster dialogue within schools about sex education and condoms. In 1995 the group established a website (www.positive.org), and in 2000 CPS reestablished itself as a virtual, Washington, DC–based organization. The group has described itself as "pro-safe sex, pro-teen, pro-choice, pro-queer, and pro-woman," and it states that its work is "predicated on respect: self-respect and respect for others." It also urges students to remember this basic principle: "It's about saying 'yes' to sex you do want, and 'no' to sex you don't . . . there's nothing wrong with you if you decide to have sex, and nothing wrong with you if you decide not to."

While not as immediate as having a peer, parent, or mentor figure guide girls through questions about sexuality, many good online sites can do this work, and especially for girls in circumstances where there are no outlets through which to acknowledge their feelings, can serve as a starting point to their sexual self-discovery.

on me." For nearly five years, Crews worked as the editor of the website, dedicated to empowering, educating, and supporting "young mamas." She encouraged these girls and women to meet online and in person and to share the trials and joys of parenting. Her website also offers suggestions on the best ways for teenagers to tell their parents about a pregnancy, tips on applying for government aid, and sharing information about how to find support for teenage parenting, legal rights, and much else, including contributions such as "Ten Ways to Have Fun for Under $2."

Crews's view was that "the only true epidemic associated with teen pregnancy is the overwhelming and universal lack of support available to young mothers." Her mission with Girl-Mom was to show that teenage girls are capable of mothering. "Girls like me have raised presidents," she writes. "We've raised messiahs and musicians, writers and settlers. Girls like me won't compromise, and we won't fail." She was adamant that "Girl-Mom in no way encourages teen pregnancy, as some critics have implied." Rather, she writes that it encourages "all young mothers to stand up for themselves, to fight for their children, to empower themselves and to defy the notion that being young means that you are unworthy of parenthood." Crews was named one of the Top 30 Under 30 Activists for Choice by Choice USA in 2003, and she helped launch the National Day to Support Teen Parents (October 11).

Hosted by Advocates for Youth (see sidebar), MySistahs (Mysistahs .org) is another site that seeks to empower young women, specifically young women of color, and it works with the premise that teenagers deserve accurate information and can be responsible. Created by and for young women of color to provide information and support on sexual and reproductive health issues, MySistahs offers monthly features, message boards, and online peer education to young women about varied topics that relate to activism, culture, and sexual health. For example, in an article about healthy body image, Ayanna writes: "It is a common myth that eating disorders only affect white middle and upper class females," going on to say how women of color are just as likely to be affected. Online peer support groups, working to change a teen model of rivalry and competition, instead help girls with models of friendship and counseling.

An iVillage site originally founded in 1996 at New York University, the web destination gURL (www.gurl.com) is flashy and filled with commercial ads, but it is also thorough in what it has to offer girls (listed as age thirteen and up). The gURL website says: "Through honest writing, visuals and liberal use of humor, we try to give girls a new way of looking at subjects that are crucial to their lives. We hope to provide connection and identification in a way that is not possible in other media. Our content deals frankly with sexuality, emotions, body image, etc. If this is a problem for you, you might not like it here." Along with a poetry section updated weekly and "comix" that focus on girls' lives, gURL provides an online encyclopedia of fast facts and sounding boards on different topics for girls to pose questions and receive feedback (such as "when girls like girls" or "being single"). A long list of "gURL guides" is available about a range of topics such as birth control, religion, gadgets, how to be a vegetarian, anxiety disorders, and much more. In the section "What Would You Do if You Were President?" one girl writes: "If I were president, I would try to make people understand that a size two is not the perfect way to be. Lots of girls who wear a size 20 are perfectly happy with their lives. Being little is not everything!" Other informative sections include what a first visit to the gynecologist is really like, frank talk about birth control, and more honest (than usual) inclusions such as "Mystery in Your Panties" and a fast-fact sheet about being a hermaphrodite. Another section called "Sucky Emotions" has information about depression, anxiety, and room for asking a range of questions.

Ophira Edut's site Adios Barbie (adiosbarbie.com) is a combination of playful satire and factual information mainly focused on body image, but also with resources about health, sexuality, and other topics. Edut started the site in 1999 and said she was inspired to do so after realizing how widely women and girls struggle with body image, particularly around ethnic stereotypes or expectations. She writes, "I think it's because our bodies symbolize everything that we feel intensely. They are our enemies and our only safety zones. They seem to act on their own will at times, betraying our brains' commands." While in college in 1992, with her twin sister and friends Edut cofounded *HUES (Hear Us Emerging Sisters),* a multicultural women's magazine, which they published until 1999. She also maintains a website for the anthology *Body Outlaws,* which also focuses on body image and self-acceptance.

Unique to Adios Barbie is her interactive. Feed the Model game and information about Barbie's latest incarnations and media buzz about the doll. Other highlights include her post "Seven Ways to Love Your Body—Through Thick and Thin" and essays such as "The Color of Hunger," which explores eating disorders for women and girls of color. Various features demonstrate women who love their bodies in all shapes and sizes, and a first-person essay discusses the politics of African American women's hair. Interesting is Edut's comment that some "skinny" girls have written to say that they feel left out on the website; Edut wants to emphasize that the site supports them too—loving one's body is still essential, whether thick or thin. The site is meant to help girls and women feel comfortable in their natural shapes, sizes, and colors and to speak out against impossible beauty standards.

Activist Groups for Girls

Helping girls is not a new idea, although girls' organizations have proliferated in the past ten years. It is interesting to see how openness about sexuality has changed in the information about sex that is provided to girls, and that girls are now counseled toward higher education and careers. The "home ec" classes girls were once channeled into so that they could learn the "domestic arts" are a thing of the past. A survey of what girls' organizations provide to girls reflects the changing course of the training and guidance now seen as essential to promoting girls and helping them make their way into their futures.

Girls Inc., founded in 1864, is one of the oldest organizations in the United States that works to promote girls, says its website. It first served young women who migrated from rural communities to the city during the Industrial Revolution in search of new job opportunities within textile mills and factories. Later, during the Great Depression, when many women sought work, Girls Inc. affiliates again provided a safe gathering place for girls where they "gave plays, made their own dresses and hats, danced and made lasting friendships." In the 1950s the group focused on more "traditional" understandings of girls' destinies: wife and motherhood. Yet, able to move with the times, Girls Inc. now uses the trademarked phrase, "inspiring all girls to be strong, smart, and bold," and offers programming to millions of American girls, especially those in high-risk and often underserved areas. It teaches girls how to be media literate and how to counter traditionally gendered messages, and its programs strive to reinforce a sense of potential to all girls and prepare them to enter into independent lives. Major programs address math and science education, pregnancy and drug abuse prevention, media literacy, economic literacy, adolescent health, violence prevention, and sports participation. Other programs offer girls development of economic skills and financial literacy, peer counseling, preventing pregnancy, and self-defense, among other issues, and its tip sheets vary from how to start your own girls' community to how to support girls' rights, advancement of which is Girls Inc.'s strongest goal and which include the rights to be respected, self-reliant, healthy, safe, and challenged.

Its national website lists a "Girls' Bill of Rights," which on the Los Angeles branch's homepage is then interpreted by girls themselves, emphasizing what each right personally means to a girl. About the right "Girls have the right to have confidence in themselves and to be safe in the world," Kira comments, "Although there have been vast improvements . . . girls are still being abused and taken advantage of. . . . And the sad truth is, it is often that very lack of confidence that invites others to mistreat these girls. They know that the girls will not say or do anything about how they are being treated because the girls do not feel that they can. They have been frightened into believing whatever they are told because they were not taught to believe in their own strength, their own power to make a difference." And next to the right "Girls have the right to prepare for interesting work and economic independence," Amanda writes, "What this bill means to me is that girls today have more choices when they grow-up. It also tells me that girls are just as equal as guys. We can do anything that guys can do if we want to."

Meanwhile, the program Girls in Government, with statistics on its website that sharply point out the disparity between men and women elected to government, works to create a next generation who will change these inequities. Describing itself as nonpartisan, it sponsors programs that teach leadership in schools, encourage girls to run for leadership positions, engage girls in the political process, and helps them work for change and to become responsible global citizens. Profiling "Girls Who Rule," the site highlights girls who embody these principles and aspire to careers in government and features opportunities for girls in government, such as how to apply to be a White House intern.

Now featured under the tab is Raven Robinson, a 17-year-old African American high school student in New York City who is president of her student government and ready to start campaigning now to be mayor of New York City in 2021. The site also provides basic background about government and the history of women's suffrage, with an interactive way to learn more about the women who insisted on securing the right to vote. Included is a suffrage timeline highlighting how far things have come, and where change is still needed. Broadening out from basic history, Girls in Government encapsulates what is going on for girls and women in current politics, whether it's an upcoming election or news of the first elected openly lesbian African American mayor (in Cambridge, Massachusetts) in 2008.

Many of the major organizations that serve girls began when it was clear that one generation of women missed having support they needed in a specific area. Or they realized that although they broke through a barrier, the glass ceiling (or wall, or door) was still barricading their progress. Not wanting the next generation to peer through the glass yet still feel blocked, they commited to changing the dynamic not only within a next generation of girls but to altering broader gender expectations that also contribute to keeping gender roles fixed and immutable.

In 1990, Judith Tomhave wrote her University of North Dakota master's thesis on young women and their experiences with the program Expanding Your Horizons (EYH). Tomhave questioned two sets of women nine years after they registered for or attended an Expanding Your Horizons conference. She found that those who attended the conference took more advanced math and science classes in school, planned to continue to higher education, and that they had more positive attitudes toward math and science than those who did not attend. The EYH network (formerly called the Math/Science Network) was begun in 1974 by a group of women scientists and educators in the San Francisco Bay Area who wanted to change low participation of girls in math classes. They coordinated efforts to strengthen what programs did exist and to found others. The first EYH conference took place at Mills College in 1976 and there have been more than 90 conferences per year for the past 15 years. As described on its website, EYH's programs are based on the assumptions that for more women to enter the fields of math, science, and engineering, more young women must have their interest cultivated in high school. Through organized conferences, held all across the United States and in Asia, girls gather to participate in workshops in which they explore a range of math and science topics, to meet each other, and to see women role models who are passionate about their fields.

Each EYH conference features hands-on activities with classes bearing titles such as "Let's Make Slime" or "Chemixtures and Chemysteries." Sample math classes include "My Name in Bits," where girls learn to represent their names in binary bits. In "Rock on!" girls learn how their favorite MP3 music is recorded onto a disc. "Something Fishy" leads girls to learn about marine biology and a class called "Tower of Power" teaches basics of engineering using everyday objects such as spaghetti noodles and hair dryers.

Other organizations have focused more on girl-led activism, often using peer groups, with some adult supervision, to encourage girls to serve and support each other. For example, the Center for Young Women's Development, based in San Francisco, describes itself as "run and led entirely by young women." Working with "the most marginalized" young women in San Francisco, many of whom have been part of the juvenile justice system, it has served more than 3,500 young women a year through street outreach. It encourages young women to advocate for other young women who have been in jail, and it claims that while young women and girls represent almost 30 percent of total juvenile arrests, they benefit from only a fraction of the programs aimed at prevention and alternatives to jail time that boys get. Through its internship program "Sisters Rising," the center helps girls work toward self-sufficiency, and another program helps young women develop skills for reintegrating into their communities. Its "Sister Circles" is a peer-led reentry program for young women released from detention, and in 2004, in response to requests, it launched the Sisters for Justice National Training Program (aka Through the Eyes of a Sister, or TES), which trains other community-based organizations how to best help young women coming out of the juvenile justice system and the street economy. The website strongly emphasizes that "it is time for low- and no-income young women to be recognized as experts on their own experiences."

The organization Girls for a Change, based in San Jose, California, is a national organization that teaches girls how to create social change. Girls design, lead, raise money, and carry out projects in their own neighborhoods; the organization provides partnerships, tools, and resources and focuses on girls from low-income communities. Teams of up to ten girls and two women volunteers "meet during the school year to identify an issue they want to change," and then design and carry out the project. The group reports that in 2008, it taught more than 2,500 girls. Bay Area projects in 2007–2008 included raising girls' self-esteem, fighting sexual harassment, educating about environmental issues and global warming, improving peer relationships, raising awareness about sexual harassment and rape, using creative writing as a tool for speaking out, stopping underage drinking, and changing body self-image for the better. Through partnerships with other nonprofits, it has had a global reach—teaching soccer to girls in Nicaragua and El Salvador and collaborating with Girls Helping Girls in India to work with young women who were victims of human trafficking, sexual exploitation, or are the children of sex workers.

Sista II Sista, based in Brooklyn, New York, first launched during the summer of 1996. According to its website, "Sista II Sista was created as a response to the lack of community spaces that focused on the experience of young women of color." The collective of women of color of differing ages strives to create new models that represent a vision of a society that is more just. Through different groups, the members devote their work to the "personal and political development of young women of color." Their "Big Mouth Project" offers workshops that explore ways to break silence about violence against women, and combating sexism and sexual harrassment in schools and the community. The workshop "The Revolutionary in You: Revolutionary Women of Color in History" explores the lives of women such as Audre Lorde, Sojourner Truth, and Mama Tingo and other powerful women. The group also offers a range of workshops and classes to encourage young women of color to "explore their braided identities in terms of gender, race/color, age, and class." For example, one session called "Herstory, Ourstory!—Growth Through SistaHood" has young women meet to share stories and "create a collective 'Herstory'" through "creative writing, drama, dance, video, and music," which is then presented to the local community.

Many other programs across the country also support girls' development. The Los Angeles organization WriteGirl, through teaching creative writing, strives to empower girls through self-expression. It offers one-on-one weekly mentoring for high school girls who are interested in creative writing, workshops at charter schools that serve pregnant and parenting teens, and monthly days of creative writing work that vary from teaching nonfiction and fiction to song- and playwriting. Launched in 2001, the nonprofit strives to "bring the skills and energy of professional women writers to teenage girls who do not otherwise have access to creative writing or mentoring programs" and to help "girls write their way to more positive futures."

Kore Press, in Tucson, Arizona, runs the Grrls Literary Activism Project, weekly workshops for girls and young women ages fourteen to eighteen in which they discuss other women writers' work as well as their own and then devise ways in which to bring their voices into the public sphere. Taking the concept that using written or spoken language "for public expression on a social or political issue" is important, the girls in each class devise a public project. Inspired by "foremothers" such as the Guerrilla Girls, past projects have included creating broadsides and zines, and girls have "printed poetry on door knob hangers, ironed their words onto t-shirts, made poetry 'fortune-tellers,' put their words and opinions on blogs, read out loud, and decorated a sanitary products machine full of tampons wrapped in poetry."

Still other groups focus on helping and supporting girls already at risk. Based in Florida, with numerous centers throughout the state, the nonprofit PACE Center for Girls (targeted to girls ages twelve to eighteen "who are identified as dependent, truant, runaway, delinquent, or in need of academic skills") advocates for girls by providing them with education, counseling, and training, in part through "gender-specific life management curriculum." Its goal is to "intervene and prevent school withdrawal, juvenile delinquency, teen pregnancy, substance abuse and welfare dependency in a safe and nurturing environment." It website says that it has served more than twenty-one thousand girls since its founding in 1983.

Alternatives for Girls is a nonprofit organization in southwest Detroit that serves "homeless and high-risk girls and young women." Since 1987 its program has helped them "avoid violence, teen pregnancy and exploitation" and to find opportunities necessary to be safe, strong, and to make positive changes through girls' clubs, the "Rise-N-Shine" summer program, and a focus on education and support. The AFG program focuses, in part, on improving self-esteem, rejecting drugs and alcohol, and connecting with a mentor. Its outreach program goes out into the streets to help young women in danger. Staff and volunteers look for young women "on the streets, in all seasons, during daylight and after dark, providing harm-reduction kits, a ride to AFG and other safe places—links to life-saving and support services."

Finally, some groups bridge cultural divides. In Union City, New Jersey, in the Project Provide a Home, a group of ten Muslim girls and ten Jewish girls came together to raise money for a homeless shelter for families. After having a group of Jewish volunteers work one week, and then another week a group of Muslims, it was suggested that the groups work together. After an initial awkwardness, the girls were described as "getting down to work" to raise money for the family shelter, leading to new friendships, understandings, and integration of the groups. As one fourteen-year-old participant said, "It's easier for us to do this because we're younger and listen to each other more."

The Importance of Title IX

It consists of just one simple sentence: "No person in the United States shall, on the basis of sex, be excluded from participation in, be denied the benefits of, or be subjected to discrimination under any educational program or activity receiving federal financial assistance." Passed on June 23, 1972, Title IX was part of the 1972 Education Amendments to the 1964 Civil Rights Act that was signed into law by President Richard Nixon on July 1, 1972. Title IX prohibits sex discrimination within any educational program or activity that receives federal funding. It applies to educational institutions from elementary school through the university level.

"Before Title IX, if you were discriminated against, all you could do is maybe transfer to another school—if they'd let you," says Bernice Sandler in the article "Schoolgirl Dreams" by Jennifer Hahn in the Fall 2007 issue of *Ms.* "Title IX [allowed students] to say," she continues, "'This is not only wrong; this is illegal.'" According to *Ms.*, Sandler became a specialist with the Special Subcommittee on Education in the U.S. House of Representatives and her discrimination suit against 250 colleges and universities, on the basis of discrimination in their hiring practices, brought these issues to the attention of Representatives Edith Green, from Oregon, and Patsy Mink, of Hawaii, the two founding members behind the amendment's birth. Green initiated congressional hearings on sex discrimination and Title IX passed quickly through Congress, to little media attention, something that changed once its impact was fully realized. Although primarily associated with creating equal opportunity within athletics, this law extends to many other areas: equality with hiring, course offerings and access, not denying girls or women education because of pregnancy (schools were previously allowed to expel pregnant girls and disallow pregnant teachers from the classroom), ensuring equality with standardized testing, and much more.

Since the passing of Title IX participation of girls within sports has grown substantially and "is one of the country's greatest success stories," according to the AAUW. "In 1971, seven percent of high school varsity athletes were young women but thirty years later, nearly 2.8 million young women representing 41.5 percent of high school varsity athletes were women. In 1972, fewer than 32,000 women competed in intercollegiate athletics. Women received only two percent of schools' athletic budgets, and athletic scholarships for women were nonexistent. Today, women receive 42% of the opportunities to play intercollegiate sports, and 32% of recruitment funds."

Among the many ways in which sports benefits girls, AAUW studies confirm that girls who participate in sports are less likely to get pregnant, to drop out of school, or to do drugs or smoke. Participating in sports has also been shown to help girls develop a strong work ethic and good school habits, which have been shown to have lasting effects in terms of understanding leadership within future careers. And according to the AAUW, "Graduation rates are significantly higher for female athletes (68 percent) than for female students in general (59 percent)." Offering girls the chance to participate in sports also means the possibility of winning scholarships to college, the pride of winning and achievement, the challenges and rewards of teamwork, and the lessons that competition brings.

Within the classroom, many standards that girls today may take for granted—that they can't be denied entrance to shop class in high school if they want to participate, or a medical school can't tell them that it will accept only a certain number of young women—were not realities before Title IX. Likewise, if a boy wants to take classes that had previously been considered aimed toward girls, he must be allowed entry. Before Title IX, it was considered standard for school counselors to track students into classes, and then careers, that were considered "appropriate" by gender, regardless of a student's ability or inclination. According to Jennifer Hahn, "Girls were barred from wood- and auto-shop classes and instead shunted into home economics. Counselors often advised girls not to take advanced math and science courses because they wouldn't need them for traditionally 'female' careers." To look at the scope of issues that the passing of Title IX changed is to realize what things were like "before" for girls and women—schools had the right to give priority to boys' sports and deny girls' teams, and they had the right to not offer funding, uniforms, or playing time to girls' teams at all. Title IX continues to hold an important line in fostering equality between boys and girls in school and its effects are large.

In her book *Let Me Play: The Story of Title IX,* author Karen Blumenthal shows the law's genesis from early suffragist movements through the civil rights and then women's movement of the 1960s. According to reviewer Bridget Booher, Blumenthal "documents Title IX's ripple effect on the professions women pursue and the changing landscape of the work force. Between 1971–72 and 2001–02, for example, the number of women entering medical schools increased from 1,653 to 7,784, she notes. During that same period, the number of women entering law school increased from 8,914 to 65,701." The Women's Educational Equity Act (WEEA) Equity Resource Center reports that "the number of high school girls participating in athletics increased from 300,000 in 1971 to 2.4 million in 1996." In 1996 it also reported, "The percentage of women earning first professional degrees has also increased dramatically: In dentistry the proportion rose from less than 10 percent in 1970 to 36 percent in 1996; in medicine it increased from less than 10 percent in 1970 to 41 percent in 1996; and in law it rose from less than 10 percent in 1970 to 44 percent in 1996."

Since its inception, Title IX has been challenged almost constantly. Strong opposition initially came from athletics groups that supported male teams. According to Booher, "The National Collegiate Athletics Association (NCAA), at the time dedicated to the advancement of men's athletics only, heard about the implications of Title IX for women's sports and, by extension, men's sports. The argument was no longer a moral one, it was financial: Men's athletics was big business, and the NCAA and its constituents feared that providing women with similar resources would drain money from men's sports programs." One widely perceived myth is that the passing of Title IX has meant schools were forced to cut programs for male athletes. This is not the case, although schools might do so in order to comply with Title IX or as a consequence of budget issues. Fundamentally, Title IX is meant to protect the rights of boys as well as girls, and cutting programs for boys is not its aim.

By mandating nondiscrimination on the basis of sex, Title IX changed discriminatory practices at their foundations. According to the WEEA Equity Resource Center, Title IX provided educators and advocates for equality to shift institutionalized imbalances and expand opportunities. Title IX barred sex-segregated classes and denial of admission to certain classes (often vocational) on the basis of sex, and it did away with having differing course requirements for boys and for girls. It also prohibited schools from forcing pregnant girls to drop out. Before Title IX, girls enjoyed a fraction of the athletic opportunities that boys did, and Title IX mandated equal opportunity and support for both sexes. Other ways in which Title IX leveled out gender differences, according to the WEEA Equity Resource Center, include offering equal access to school support programs, such as financial assistance, health and insurance benefits, and even housing. The reach of Title IX also extends beyond schools, and includes libraries, museums, and other resource centers that receive federal funding. Title IX compliance must be demonstrated, and violations of compliance can be filed. Lack of compliance will mean withdrawal of funding.

Title IX has also meant that sexual harassment is clearly illegal. Writes Hahn, "In the 1980s and 1990s, the U.S. Supreme Court issued rulings clarifying that the definition of sex discrimination under Title IX includes sexual harassment by peers or school employees. Before that, victims of sexual harassment in schools—including boys—had no clearly established way to seek justice of financial settlements." Hahn also reports that the PSAT and SAT have become less biased against girls because of Title IX, with the addition of a writing section to the PSAT in 1997, "which increased girls' overall scores and won them millions more in test-score-based scholarship money." Then, in 2005, a writing section was added to the SAT, "and by 2007 the gender gap favoring boys had decreased from 42 to 25 points."

Yet the fight for Title IX is not yet over. In 1984, the Supreme Court, according to *Ms.*, "succeeded in virtually overturning the law for four years—until feminists and civil rights leaders fought back with the Civil Rights Restoration Act of 1987." And more recently, "the Bush administration weakened Title IX with new rules allowing public, sex-segregated classes and schools"—which are generally believed to disadvantage girls. According to Booher, "Just months before she died in 2002, longtime Title IX advocate Patsy Mink, a U.S. representative from Hawaii, urged Congress to diligently protect the law, warning that those opportunities could be taken away just as quickly as they were created." The battle is ongoing.

Global Girlhood

While this book focuses on girlhood within the United States, it's worth broadening and contextualizing the discussion for a moment to briefly consider the struggles of girls worldwide. Girls' lives differ widely from country to country, household to household, and individual to individual, but some disturbing truths form a pattern. Worldwide, and generally speaking, girls often hold much lower status than boys and suffer from systemic discrimination that devalues their lives, leaving them vulnerable to sexual exploitation or physical abuse and at greater risk for disease or malnutrition. Girls are more likely to be denied education, pressed into service to help support their families, and offered by their families in marriage without their consent. Concern about the global treatment of girls is a cause gaining recognition with the realization that improving girls' status often has wide-rippling effects within a community, as girls who receive more education are likely to delay marriage and childbearing, work at higher-paid jobs, and significantly, feel a stronger sense of self-worth.

According to the humanitarian organization CARE, "Women and girls suffer disproportionately from the burden of extreme poverty—they make up 70 percent of the 1 billion people living on less than a dollar a day." The statistics continue: "Women work two-thirds of the world's working hours, produce half of the world's food, yet earn only 10 percent of the world's income and own less than 1 percent of the world's property." The organization points out that in developing countries, women and girls are increasingly at risk from HIV and complications relating to pregnancy and childbirth, and it says, "More than 850 million people—most of them women and children—suffer from chronic hunger or malnutrition." CARE also claims that one in three of the world's women will be physically or sexually abused at some point in her life.

Without economic opportunities, and living within a society that routinely devalues girls, girls often lack a sense of their own value and may not be protected by their families. On the website Captive Daughters, an NGO organization, Sarah M. Gonzales makes the link between poverty and sex trafficking and how this link persists worldwide, reporting, "What we do know is that poverty drives sex trafficking, and that sex trafficking as the delivery system for prostitution means that each day scores of young, poor women and girls will turn to sex trafficking and prostitution as a means to provide for themselves, and for their families, because they have no other choice."

She cites AnnJanette Rosga, a Fulbright researcher in Bosnia-Herzogovina commissioned by UNICEF in 2005; Rosga followed the cases of postwar poverty-stricken families who sent their daughters abroad to work as "waitresses" or "au pairs," and who sometimes knowingly, and sometimes unknowingly, sent their daughters into situations where they would work as prostitutes. Gonzales's report also mentions the estimate that of the sex workers in Philippine cities, 40 percent are from rural areas. She continues, "The only people profiting from these exploited women and girls are the traffickers, the bar and brothel owners and the government who touts their young sex workers as a tourist attraction." The site also offers findings on girls in Kenya, where rural dwellers have been forced, through drought or other environmental conditions, into cities to seek work with the disturbing effect of parents sending their daughters into towns to trade their bodies for money. Recent philanthropic attention and donations have brought new focus to this issue with the hope that offering more economic options for girls and women will end this cycle.

Stories of difficulty and denial of girls' rights are widespread. On UNICEF's website, Brigitte Stark-Merklein tells the story of fifteen-year-old Seng Srey Mach of Prey Veng Province, "a poverty-stricken area in Cambodia." The girl explains that she loves school but was forced to leave for two years when her mother was ill and too weak to work. Seng Srey, who lives alone with her mother, was able to continue in school through a program called OPTIONS, run by World Education with financial support from UNICEF and the U.S. Department of Labor. The article emphasizes how remaining in school helps to protect girls from being sexually trafficked or exploited and has far-ranging economic results. It ends, "Poverty is the main reason that keeps girls out of school in Cambodia," says Sok Kimsroeung of World Education, "but we also need to overcome other obstacles. Including the traditional perception that girls don't need higher education beyond Grade 6 or 9."

On the website Stop Child Poverty, Ilana Breitkopf asserts simply that education is the key to ending poverty, and yet, she writes, "Two thirds of all those who have no access to education are girls and women." Breitkopf mentions that at the UN Millennium Summit in September 2000, two of the eight Millennium Development Goals (agreed upon by all the world's countries and all the world's leading development institutions) were created to address this issue. One was the target that all boys and girls complete their "full course of primary schooling by 2015" and the other was to "promote gender equality and empower women, with the target of eliminating gender disparities in primary and secondary education by 2005 (this target has not been met), and in all levels of education by 2015."

Breitkopf offers a few brief examples of ways in which girls in developing countries are prevented from achieving an education: Some avoid walking to school for fear of being abducted for marriage, dowry systems force girls to leave school, the continuing problem of trafficking, and the effects of the AIDS epidemic, which forces girls to assume leadership roles within their families. These are just a few examples of the obstacles girls worldwide face in gaining an education. One link that has been made clear is that keeping a girl from school has long-ranging impact on her ability to provide for her present and her future family, on the economic growth of her society and even country, on gender balancing as girls eventually move into more positions of power and influence, and on her sense of self-worth. Breitkopf writes that commitment to increasing girls' education will require many adjustments, including changing school-day hours to accommodate girls' chores, as one example, but more important, changes in attitudes, "such as encouraging communities to rethink how much domestic work should be expected of school-age girls." That these central goals of education and rebalancing of gender inequity are being pursued worldwide is a hopeful sign, but it is also dismaying. It is clear the goal has not yet been achieved and many obstacles remain, as the interconnections between poverty, ethnic and cultural differences, social traditions, and perception of girls' status and inequities still need working out.

Yet girls are making changes and meeting with success. The Nike Foundation has launched a multimillion-dollar campaign directly linked to two of the UN Millennium Development Goals, poverty alleviation and gender equality, and is concentrating its efforts in specific countries. Called "The Girl Effect," the campaign offers strong statistics, such as that even an extra year of primary school education can boost a girl's future wages by 10 percent to 20 percent. And, "When girls and women earn income, they reinvest 90 percent of it into their families, as compared to only 30 or 40 percent for a man."

Another success story is that of Nujood Ali, reported in September 2008 by the *Los Angeles Times*. Ali, a 10-year-old Yemeni girl, managed to secure a divorce from a man three times her age, to whom she was given in marriage by her parents, and was able to return to school. She says, "I'm very happy to be going back to school. . . . I'm going to study Arabic, the Koran, mathematics and drawing. I will do that with my classmates and I will definitely make friends there." Her story made her something of an international celebrity, not for her age and the custom of selling child brides, but because of her rebellion and that she dared to fight that system. The reporters cite women's rights activists who say that child marriage is part of a vicious cycle, with girls dropping out of school when young and contributing to Yemen's high rate of female illiteracy. Nujood, however, "wanted to study hard, to be able to attend university and become a lawyer like Shada Nasser, the well-known Yemeni human rights advocate who helped her get her divorce."

In many places throughout the world, investing in girls is still a new idea. The surge of interest within the United States in girlhood seems part of broader concern about how girls' lives matter. Even more significantly, organizations have now identified how central education is for girls, and how far-reaching an impact girls' lives have within their communities and on a larger scale, for their countries.

Where Do Girls Go from Here?

The rise of girls' studies as a field has been steady since its birth. Yet defining as an academic field what constitutes girlhood is still in its own girlhood years, and one hopes, with a long growth spurt still ahead. Within popular culture, concerns about girls have always been present, whether that means defining a half century ago girls' conduct while in "mixed company" with boys, or more recently the extent to which girls should be able to obtain birth control on their own, or how girls exercise their sexuality—all topics that are explored through the law, parental control, and the ever-changing trends within any year. Speculation about the pressures and strictures that define girlhood and codes of femininity is always present—are girls still not outspoken enough, or are they too outspoken now?

Told that they can do anything but not supported in their quests? Or more pressured than ever to excel and achieve in all areas now that there are supposedly no barriers left? It's up to each generation, and individually, each girl, to find a place that's comfortable in negotiating the culture's tenets.

The field of girls' studies often seems diffuse. Classes can be found in gender and women's studies departments, or in history, or in American culture, or in education. But the interest in defining girlhood, no matter the home department, is growing with the recognition that study is needed, even as the terms still evolve. Within popular culture, defining girlhood has often played out in the past few years within arguments and philosophies about single-sex education—the idea that girls innately learn one way and boys another—along with the ever-present backlash that boys are left suffering through the attention given to girls.

One of Barack Obama's first acts as president was to sign into law the creation of the White House Council on Women and Girls. Obama said, "The purpose of this Council is to ensure that American women and girls are treated fairly in all matters of public policy." Not long before signing this bill, Obama had made one of his first real pieces of legislation the signing into law of the Lilly Ledbetter Fair Pay Restoration Act, changing the terms through which workers can sue employers for unfair gender discrimination. After signing the bill to establish the council, Obama said, "But I want to be clear that issues like equal pay, family leave, child care and others are not just women's issues, they are family issues and economic issues." His broadening of the argument—that issues that affect girls and women affect society at large—rings true. In tandem with his view of supporting girls and women, however, it is hard not to think of his two young daughters now in residence at the White House and all that as a parent he must wish for them. The faces and shapes of issues surrounding girls are as diverse and divergent as all girls are, and just as each new girl born brings her unique viewpoint to the world, so the issues that surround teaching femininity, expectations, and girls' rights will continue to change. But now that attention has been brought to how important and varied girlhood is, to its joys and its foibles, one can't help but feel the excitement and sense of possibility that accompany girls in their journeys as this field also grows up.

READER'S GUIDE

Questions for Discussion

Think back to your childhood and early years. Ask your parents and/or guardians what decisions they made about the clothes you wore, the toys you played with, who you played with, and so on. Ask them why they decided these things. Did gender play a role in any of them? How so?

Think about a recent occasion when you saw young children playing. What observations can you make about the way that little girls or little boys play? Who plays aggressively? Who plays quietly? Did you notice an adult telling them to behave one way or the other?

Think about your experience of going through puberty. Did you have the sense that you would have to assume different traits or habits as a teenager? How did it feel to go through these changes? If you were a girl, did you have a female figure to talk to about your body's physical changes? Did boys treat you differently? Did other girls treat you differently? If you were a boy, what were you told about what it means to "become a man"? Did you feel you had to assume certain roles?

When you were in elementary school and middle school, were boys and girls given equal treatment in the classroom? Were girls encouraged to work hard at subjects such as math and science? In your classes now, do both genders answer questions and call out equally?

When you were a child, were you ever told, or did you ever sense, that your gender, race, class, or disability would affect how people treated you? Did you have the sense that you had to fulfill certain expectations because you were female or male? What was your reaction? Did you notice receiving any of this treatment, explicitly or implicitly?

Think back to your adolescent years. When did you begin feeling pressure to change your appearance? What do you think influenced you? What sorts of things did you do? How did you see other kids of the opposite gender dealing with their appearance?

Think about your diet during your teenage years. Did you ever hear female friends talking about their weight and/or changing their diets? Did you eat what you liked without worrying about your weight or what other people would think?

When you were a girl, did you see female members of your race/ethnicity represented in TV commercials and/or magazine ads? Look at advertisements today in different media sources. What messages about gender and race/ethnicity are consistently conveyed?

If you believe that there is now complete equality between the genders, think of current instances within politics, business, the arts, or other fields in which there isn't equal representation. How could this change?

Topics for Research

Role Models with Gender

Ask several women in your family, school, or workplace: Did you have a female role model when you were a girl? Who was she and why did you admire her? Was there a moment when you were told you couldn't or shouldn't do something because you are female? What would you do differently if there were real gender equality when you were a girl?

Cultural Expectations

Find a man and a woman and ask, respectively: When you were little, what did you think it meant to be a woman/man? What sorts of physical changes or emotional changes did you expect? What are the ways in which you felt restricted by gender and how were you aware of this?

Media Awareness

Look through the pages of a contemporary magazine. How are girls and women consistently portrayed? How are boys and men represented? What races/ethnicities are most prevalent? What message does this send to young children who are learning about gender relationships? Similarly, note roles during a popular television show or film. What is consistent about the main characters' appearances and roles?

What Happens in the Classroom

Observe a classroom other than your own. Count how many times a female student calls out or answers a question and how many times a male student does. Are the male students more disruptive? Does the teacher respond to them more clearly? Is the curriculum (textbooks and lessons) representative of a range of races and ethnicities and abilities and genders?

The Impact of Language

Think about current slang and how it's used. Is it derogatory to call a boy "a girl"? Is it acceptable to call a group of girls "you guys" or a single girl "dude"? What about using derogatory terms for homosexuality? Reflect on how language is casually used and what larger cultural standards these terms represent.

FURTHER READING AND RESOURCES

BOOKS
Fiction

Cisneros, Sandra. *The House on Mango Street.* New York: Vintage, 1991.

Desai, Hidier, Tanuja. *Born Confused,* New York: Scholastic, 2003.

Diamant, Anita. *The Red Tent.* New York: Picador, 2007.

Fitch, Janet. *White Oleander.* New York: Back Bay, 2000.

Hesse, Karen. *Out of the Dust.* New York: Scholastic, 1997.

Hurston, Zora Neale. *Their Eyes Were Watching God.* New York: Harper Perennial Modern Classics, 1998 [copyright 1937].

Lamb, Wally. *She's Come Undone.* New York: Pocket, 1998.

Lemus, Felicia Luna. *Trace Elements of Random Tea Parties.* New York: Farrar, Straus and Giroux, 2003.

Lowry, Lois. *Number the Stars.* New York: Laurel Leaf, 1998.

Morrison, Toni. *Beloved.* New York: Alfred A. Knopf, 1987.

———. *Sula.* New York: Alfred A. Knopf, 1973.

Sebold, Alice. *The Lovely Bones.* New York: Back Bay, 2004.

Smith, Kirsten. *The Geography of Girlhood.* Boston: Little, Brown, 2006.

Tan, Amy. *The Joy Luck Club.* New York: Penguin, 2006.

Nonfiction

American Association of University Women. *Beyond the "Gender Wars": A Conversation About Girls, Boys, and Education.* Washington, DC: AAUW Educational Foundation, 2001.

———. *How Schools Shortchange Girls: The AAUW Report: A Study of Major Findings on Girls and Education.* New York: Marlowe and Company, 1995 [1992].

———. *Shortchanging Girls, Shortchanging America.* Washington, DC: AAUW, 1991.

———. *Voices of a Generation: Teenage Girls Report About Their Lives Today,* New York: Da Capo, 2000.

Baumgardner, Jennifer, and Amy Richards. *Manifesta: Young Women, Feminism, and the Future.* New York: Farrar, Straus and Giroux, 2000.

Bettie, Julie. *Women Without Class: Girls, Race, and Identity.* Berkeley: University of California, 2002.

Bettis, Pamela J., and Natalie G. Adams, eds. *Geographies of Girlhood: Identities In-Between.* Mahwah, NJ: Lawrence Erlbaum, 2005.

Blumenthal, Karen. *Let Me Play: The Story of Title IX: The Law That Changed The Future of Girls in America.* New York: Atheneum, 2005.

Brown, Lyn Mikel. *Girlfighting: Betrayal and Rejection Among Girls.* New York: New York University, 2003.

———. *Raising Their Voices: The Politics of Girls' Anger.* Cambridge, MA: Harvard University, 1998.

Brown, Lyn Mikel, and Carol Gilligan. *Meeting at the Crossroads: Women's Psychology and Girls' Development.* Cambridge, MA: Harvard University, 1992.

Brumberg, Joan Jacobs. *The Body Project: An Intimate History of American Girls.* New York: Vintage, 1998.

Chesler, Phyllis. *Letters to a Young Feminist.* New York: Four Walls, Eight Windows, 1997.

Currie, Dawn H. *Girl Talk: Adolescent Magazines and Their Readers.* Toronto: University of Toronto Press, 1999.

Douglas, Susan J. *Where the Girls Are: Growing Up Female with the Mass Media.* New York: Three Rivers, 1995.

Dowling, Collette. *The Frailty Myth: Redefining the Physical Potential of Women and Girls.* New York: Random House, 2000.

Edut, Ophira, ed. *Body Outlaws: Rewriting the Rules of Beauty and Body Image* (2nd ed.). Berkeley, CA: Seal, 2003.

Feuereisen, Patti, and Caroline Pincus. *Invisible Girls: The Truth About Sexual Abuse.* Berkeley, CA: Seal, 2005.

Findlen, Barbara, ed. *Listen Up: Voices from the Next Feminist Generation.* Berkeley: Seal, 2001.

Frank, Anne. *Anne Frank: The Diary of a Young Girl.* New York: Bantam, 1993 [copyright 1952].

Garbarino, James. *See Jane Hit: Why Girls Are Growing More Violent and What Can Be Done About It.* New York: Penguin, 2006.

Gilligan, Carol. *In a Different Voice: Psychological Theory and Women's Development.* Cambridge, MA: Harvard University, 1982, 1993.

Gray, Heather M., and Samantha Phillips. *Real Girl Real World: A Guide to Finding Your True Self.* Emeryville, CA: Seal, 2005.

Green, Karen, and Taormino, Tristan, eds. *A Girl's Guide to Taking Over the World: Writing from the Girl Zine Revolution.* New York: St. Martin's, 1997.

Greenfield, Lauren. *Girl Culture.* San Francisco: Chronicle, 2002.

Handel, Sherry S. *Blue Jean: What Young Women Are Thinking, Saying, and Doing.* Rochester, NY: Blue Jean, 2001.

Harris, Anita, ed. *All About the Girl: Culture, Power, and Identity.* New York: Routledge, 2004.

Harris, Anita. *Future Girl: Young Women in the Twenty-First Century.* New York: Routledge, 2004.

Hentges, Sarah. *Pictures of Girlhood: Modern Female Adolescence on Film*. Jefferson, NC: McFarland, 2005.

Hernández, Daisy, and Bushra Rehman, eds. *Colonize This! Young Women of Color on Today's Feminism*. Berkeley: Seal, 2002.

Hinshaw, Stephen, with Rachel Kranz. *The Triple Bind: Saving our Teenage Girls from Today's Pressures*. New York: Ballantine Books, 2009.

hooks, bell. *Bone Black: Memories of Girlhood*. New York: Henry Holt, 1996.

———. *Feminism Is for Everybody: Passionate Politics*. Boston: South End, 2000.

Howe, Florence, and Jean Casella, eds. *Almost Touching the Skies: Women's Coming of Age Stories*. New York: The Feminist Press at CUNY, 2000.

Jacob, Iris, ed. *My Sisters' Voices: Teenage Girls of Color Speak Out*. New York: Henry Holt, 2002.

Jesella, Kara, and Marisa Meltzer. *How Sassy Changed My Life: A Love Letter to the Greatest Teen Magazine of All Time*. New York: Faber and Faber, 2007.

Johnston, Andrea. *Girls Speak Out: Finding Your True Self* (2nd ed.). Berkeley, CA: Celestial Arts, 2005.

Kearney, Mary Celeste. *Girls Make Media*. New York: Routledge, 2006.

Kindlon, Dan. *Alpha Girls: Understanding the New American Girl and How She Is Changing the World*. New York: Rodale, 2006.

Lamb, Sharon. *The Secret Lives of Girls: What Good Girls Really Do—Sex Play, Aggression, and Their Guilt*. New York: Free Press, 2001.

Lamb, Sharon, and Lyn Mikel Brown. *Packaging Girlhood: Rescuing Our Daughters from Marketers' Schemes*. New York: St. Martin's, 2006.

Leadbeater, Bonnie J. Ross, and Niobe Way, eds. *Urban Girls: Resisting Stereotypes, Creating Identities*. New York: New York University, 1996.

Levin, Diane E. and Jean Kilbourne. *So Sexy So Soon: The New Sexualized Childhood and What Parents Can Do to Protect their Kids*. New York: Ballantine Books, 2008.

Luker, Kristin. *Dubious Conceptions: The Politics of Teenage Pregnancy*. Cambridge, MA: Harvard University, 1997.

Makhijani, Pooja, ed. *Under Her Skin: How Girls Experience Race in America*. Berkeley, CA: Seal, 2004.

Mam, Somaly. *The Road of Lost Innocence*. New York: Random House, 2008.

Monem, Nadine, ed. *Riot Grrrl: Revolution Girl Style Now!* London: Black Dog, 2007.

Nam, Vickie, ed. *YELL-Oh Girls! Emerging Voices Explore Culture, Identity, and Growing Up Asian American*. New York: HarperCollins, 2001.

Nash, Ilana. *American Sweethearts: Teenage Girls in Twentieth-Century Popular Culture*. Bloomington: Indiana University, 2005.

Odem, Mary E. *Delinquent Daughters: Protecting and Policing Adolescent Female Sexuality in the United States, 1885–1920*. Chapel Hill: The University of North Carolina, 1995.

Orenstein, Peggy. *Schoolgirls: Young Women, Self-Esteem, and the Confidence Gap*. New York: Anchor, 1995, 2000.

Perlstein, Linda. *Not Much Just Chillin': The Hidden Lives of Middle Schoolers*. New York: Ballantine, 2004.

Pipher, Mary. *Reviving Ophelia: Saving the Selves of Adolescent Girls.* New York: Ballantine, 1994.

Ryan, Joan. *Little Girls in Pretty Boxes: The Making and Breaking of Elite Gymnasts and Figure Skaters.* New York: Warner, 2000.

Sadker, Myra, and David Sadker. *Failing at Fairness: How Our Schools Cheat Girls.* New York: Touchstone, 1995.

Seely, Megan. *Fight Like a Girl: How to Be a Fearless Feminist.* New York: New York University, 2007.

Shandler, Sara. *Ophelia Speaks: Adolescent Girls Write About Their Search for Self.* New York: HarperCollins, 1999.

Siegal, Deborah. *Sisterhood, Interrupted: From Radical Women to Grrls Gone Wild.* New York: Palgrave Macmillan, 2007.

Simmons, Rachel. *Odd Girl Out: The Hidden Culture of Aggression in Girls.* New York: Harcourt, 2002.

———. *Odd Girl Speaks Out: Girls Write About Bullies, Cliques, Popularity, and Jealousy.* New York, Harcourt, 2004.

Sinclair, Carla. *Net Chick. A Smart-Girl Guide to the Wired World.* New York: Henry Holt, 1995.

Squires, Elisabeth. *bOObs: A Guide to Your Girls.* Emeryville, CA: Seal, 2007.

Stabiner, Karen. *Reclaiming Our Daughters: What Parenting a Pre-Teen Taught Me About Real Girls.* Emeryville, CA: Seal, 2007.

Sweeney, Kathleen. *Maiden USA: Girl Icons Come of Age.* New York: Peter Lang, 2008.

Tanenbaum, Leora. *Slut! Growing Up Female With a Bad Reputation.* New York: Perennial, 2000.

Tea, Michelle, ed. *Without a Net: The Female Experience of Growing Up Working Class.* Berkeley, CA: Seal, 2003.

Thompson, Sharon. *Going All the Way: Teenage Girls' Tales of Sex, Romance, and Pregnancy.* New York: Hill and Wang, 2005.

Valenti, Jessica. *Full Frontal Feminism: A Young Woman's Guide to Why Feminism Matters.* Emeryville, CA: Seal, 2007.

Vida, Vendela. *Girls on the Verge: Debutante Dips, Drive-bys, and Other Initiations.* New York: St. Martin's, 1999.

Weis, Lois, and Michelle Fine, eds. *Beyond Silenced Voices: Class, Race, and Gender in United States Schools.* Albany: State University of New York, 2005.

White, Emily. *Fast Girls: Teenage Tribes and the Myth of the Slut.* New York: Berkley, 2002.

Wiseman, Rosalind. *Queen Bees and Wannabes: Helping Your Daughter Survive Cliques, Gossip, Boyfriends, and Other Realities of Adolescence.* New York: Crown, 2002.

Wolf, Naomi. *The Beauty Myth: How Images of Beauty Are Used Against Women.* New York: HarperCollins, 2002 [1991].

Zimmerman, Jean, and Gil Reavill. *Raising Our Athletic Daughters: How Sports Can Build Self-Esteem and Save Girls' Lives.* New York: Doubleday, 1998.

ARTICLES, CHAPTERS, AND ESSAYS

Alcantara-Tan, Sabrina Margarita. "The Herstory of Bamboo Girl Zine." *Frontiers: A Journal of Women's Studies*, 2000, 21(1/2).

Archer, Louise, Anna Halsall, and Sumi Hollingworth. "Inner-City Femininities and Education: 'Race,' Class, Gender and Schooling in Young Women's Lives." *Gender and Education,* September 2007, 19(5).

Baumgardner, Jennifer. "Would You Pledge Your Virginity to Your Father?" *Glamour,* January 1, 2007.

Bayerl, Katherine. "Mags, Zines, and gURLs: The Exploding World of Girls' Publications." *Women's Studies Quarterly,* Fall/Winter 2000, 29(3/4).

Boodman, Sandra G. "For More Teenage Girls, Adult Plastic Surgery." *The Washington Post,* October 26, 2004.

Brody, Jane E. "Girls and Puberty: The Crisis Years." *The New York Times,* November 4, 1997.

Dancy, Denise O. "Dating Violence in Adolescence." *Family Violence Forum,* Winter 2003, 2(4).

Durham, Meenakshi Gigi. "Articulating Adolescent Girls' Resistance to Patriarchal Discourse in Popular Media." *Women's Studies in Communication*, 1999, 22(2).

Fudge, Rachel. "Girl, Unreconstructed: Why Girl Power Is Bad for Feminism." In Lisa Jervis and Andi Zeisler, eds., *BitchFest: Ten Years of Cultural Criticism from the Pages of* Bitch *Magazine.* New York: Farrar, Straus and Giroux, 2006.

Garrison, Ednie Kaeh. "U.S. Feminism—Grrrl Style! Youth (Sub)cultures and the Technologies of the Third Wave." *Feminist Studies,* Spring 2000, 26(1).

Goldberg, Carey. "After Girls Get the Attention, Focus Shifts to Boys' Woes." *The New York Times*, April 23, 1998.

Gottlieb, Joanne, and Gayle Wald. "Smells Like Teen Spirit: Riot Grrrls, Revolution and Women in Independent Rock." In Andrew Ross and Tricia Rose, eds., *Microphone Fiends: Youth Music and Youth Culture.* New York: Routledge, 1994.

Greenfieldboyce, Nell. "Girls' Math Skills Equal To Boys', Study Finds." *All Things Considered,* NPR, July 24, 2008, www.npr.org/templates/story/story.php?storyId=92881902.

Greenhouse, Linda. "Military College Can't Bar Women, High Court Rules." *The New York Times*, June 27, 1996.

Hernández, Daisy, and Pandora L. Leong. "Feminisms Future: Young Feminists of Color Take the Mic." *In These Times*, April 21, 2004.

Hodder, Harbour Fraser. "Girl Power: What Has Changed for Women—And What Hasn't." *Harvard Magazine,* January/February, 2008.

Hoff Sommers, Christina. "The War Against Boys." *The Atlantic Monthly,* May 2000.

Kearney, Mary Celeste. "The Missing Links: Riot Grrrl—Feminism—Lesbian Culture." In Sheila Whiteley, ed., *Sexing the Groove: Popular Music and Gender.* London and New York: Routledge, 1997.

———. "Producing Girls: Rethinking the Study of Female Youth Culture." In Sherrie A. Inness, ed., *Delinquents and Debutantes: Twentieth-Century American Girls' Cultures.* New York: New York University Press, 1998.

Mann, Judy. "Girls and the Single-Sex Classroom." *The Washington Post Education Review,* April 7, 1996.

McRobbie, Angela. "MORE! New Sexualities in Girls' and Women's Magazines." In *Back to Reality? Social Experience and Cultural Studies.* Manchester, UK: Manchester University, 1997.

Moore, Anne Elizabeth. "Meet Anne: A Spunky, Adventurous American Girl." In Lisa Jervis and Andi Zeisler, eds., *BitchFest: Ten Years of Cultural Criticism from the Pages of* Bitch *Magazine.* New York: Farrar, Straus and Giroux, 2006.

Moss, Gabrielle. "Teen Mean Fighting Machine: Why Does the Media Love Mean Girls?" In Lisa Jervis and Andi Zeisler, eds., *BitchFest: Ten Years of Cultural Criticism from the Pages of* Bitch *Magazine.* New York: Farrar, Straus and Giroux, 2006.

National Center for Education Statistics. *Trends in Educational Equity of Girls and Women: 2004,* Washington, DC: U.S. Department of Education, http://nces.ed.gov /pubs2005/equity.

Oler, Tammy. "Bloodletting: *Female Adolescence in Modern Horror Films.*" In Lisa Jervis and Andi Zeisler, eds., *BitchFest: Ten Years of Cultural Criticism from the Pages of* Bitch *Magazine.* New York: Farrar, Straus and Giroux, 2006.

Orenstein, Peggy. "What's Wrong with Cinderella?" *The New York Times Magazine,* December 24, 2006.

Poe, Marshall. "The Other Gender Gap." *The Atlantic Monthly,* January/February, 2004.

Reid-Walsh, Jacqueline, and Claudia Mitchell. "Girls' Web Sites: A Virtual 'Room of One's Own'?" In Anita Harris, ed., *All About the Girl: Culture, Power, and Identity.* New York: Routledge, 2004.

Rimer, Sara. "For Girls, It's Be Yourself, and Be Perfect, Too." *The New York Times,* April 1, 2007.

Ringrose, Jessica. "A New Universal Mean Girl: Examining the Discursive Construction and Social Regulation of a New Feminine Pathology." *Feminism and Psychology,* 2006, 16(4).

Rousso, Harilyn. *Strong Proud Sisters: Girls and Young Women with Disabilities.* Washington, DC: Center for Women Policy Studies, 2001.

Sjoblom, Yvonne. "Leaving Home Early: Passing from Girlhood to Womanhood." *Child and Adolescent Social Work Journal,* August 2006, 23(4).

Taft, Jessica K. "Girl Power Politics: Pop-Culture Barriers and Organizational Resistance." In Anita Harris, ed., *All About the Girl: Culture, Power, and Identity.* New York: Routledge, 2004.

Trotzky-Sirr, Rebecca. "Our Rights as Pregnant and Parenting Students." Girl-Mom, www.girl-mom.com/node/91.

Weiner, Stacy. "Goodbye to Girlhood: As Pop Culture Targets Ever Younger Girls, Psychologists Worry About a Premature Focus on Sex and Appearance." *The Washington Post,* February 20, 2007.

Weisbard, Phyllis Holman, and JoAnne Lehman, eds. [Girls' Studies Issues.] *Feminist Collections: A Quarterly of Women's Studies Resources,* 2007, 28(2/3/4).

FILMS AND VIDEOS

A Minor Altercation. Directed by Jackie Shearer, 1977.

Bend It Like Beckham. Directed by Gurinder Chadha. Twentieth Century Fox, 2003.

But I'm a Cheerleader. Directed by Jamie Babbit. Lions Gate, 2003.

Desire. Directed by Julie Gustafson, 2005.

Far from Home. Directed by Rachel Tsutsumi, 2005.

Freedom Writers. Directed by Richard LaGravenese. Paramount, 2007.

Girls Town. Directed by Jim McKay, 1996.

Girl Wrestler. Directed by Diane Zander, 2004.

Going on 13. Directed by Kristy Guevara-Flanagan and Dawn Valadez. Vaquera Films, 2008.

Grrlyshow. Directed by Kara Herold, 2000.

Hair Piece. Directed by Ayoka Chenzira, 1985.

Harriet the Spy. Directed by Bronwen Hughes. Paramount, 1996.

Incredibly True Adventure of 2 Girls in Love, The. Directed by Maria Maggenti. New Line Home Video, 1995.

It Starts with a Whisper. Directed by Shelly Niro and Anna Gronau. Canada, 1993.

I Was a Teenage Feminist. Directed by Therese Shechter. Canada/US, 2005.

Matilda. Directed by Danny DeVito. Sony Pictures, 1996.

Mean Girls. Directed by Mark Waters. Paramount, 2004.

Mirror Mirror. Directed by Jan Krawitz, 1990.

Mulan. Directed by Tony Bancroft and Barry Cook. Walt Disney, 1998.

Perfect Image? Directed by Maureen Blackwood, 1988.

Sisterhood of the Traveling Pants. Directed by Ken Kwapis. Warner Home Video, 2005.

The Education of Shelby Knox, The. Directed by Marion Lipschutz and Rose Rosenblatt. Incite Pictures, 2005.

Thirteen. Directed by Catherine Hardwicke. Twentieth Century Fox, 2003.

Tree Shade. Directed by Lisa Collins, 1998.

Troop 1500: Girl Scouts Beyond Bars. Directed by Ellen Spiro and Karen Bernstein, 2005.

Whale Rider. Directed by Niki Caro. Sony Pictures, 2002.

White Oleander. Directed by Peter Kosminsky. Warner Home Video, 2003.

WEBSITES

AAUW: www.aauw.org

> The American Association of University Women is dedicated to "advancing equity for women and girls through advocacy, education, and research."

About Face: www.about-face.org

> An organization that helps girls resist the harmful messages of beauty in the media.

A Girl's World: www.agirlsworld.com

> A cyber community filled with articles, stories, and quizzes written by girls and for girls and teens.

Ambiente Joven: www.ambientejoven.org
> This site provides information on safer sex and sexual health for Latin American GLBT youth.

Coalition for Positive Sexuality: www.positive.org
> The CPS provides the information that teens need "to take care of themselves and in so doing affirm their decisions about sex, sexuality, and reproductive control" and aims for "dialogue in and out of the public schools on condom availability and sex education."

Educating Jane: www.educatingjane.com
> "A national site for girls, their parents and educators, dedicated to helping girls grow with self-esteem, self-awareness, and involvement in the world."

Empowering Books for Girls: www.deebest.com
> A great book resource.

4Girls: www.4girls.gov
> Created by the Office on Women's Health, this is a website designed for giving girls health information and advice.

Girl-Mom: www.girl-mom.com
> An online community for teen mothers.

Girls Allowed!: www.girlsallowed.org
> A site providing girls with "information and tools for developing and maintaining healthy relationships with friends, partners, and others."

Girls Education and Mentoring Services (GEMS): www.gems-girls.org
> "GEMS provides preventive and transitional services to young women, ages 12–21 years, who are at risk for or involved in sexual exploitation and violence."

Girls, Inc.: http://girlsinc.org
> An organization that inspires young girls to be "strong, smart, and bold." Also a great source for fact sheets on a variety of girl-related topics.

Girls Leadership Institute: www.girlsleadershipinstitute.org
> Teaches girls how to be successful in areas of "self-expression, emotional intelligence, and conflict management."

Girls' Life: www.girlslife.com
> A magazine for girls that covers issues varying from advice for academic success to fun quizzes.

Girlstart: www.girlstart.org
> Founded in Austin, Texas, in 1997 "to empower girls to excel in math, science, and technology."

Girls Write Now: www.girlswritenow.org
> "New York's premier creative writing and mentoring organization for high school girls."

Global Grrrl Zine Network: http://grrrlzines.net/writingonzines.htm
> A site that lists links to resources and in-depth information about zines.

gURL: www.gurl.com
> "A teen site and community for teenage girls."

Hardy Girls, Healthy Women: www.hardygirlshealthywomen.org
"A nonprofit organization dedicated to the health and well being of girls and women."
Latinitas Magazine: www.latinitasmagazine.com
An online magazine written by Latina youth and for Latina youth.
Miss O and Friends: www.missoandfriends.com
A website made by girls and for girls "to provide a positive 'voice of authenticity' and
help build a sense of confidence for young girls growing up."
Moon Beam Sorority: www.moonbeamsorority.com
"Empowers young girls" by helping them learn to celebrate and embrace their
transition into womanhood.
MySistahs: www.mysistahs.org
This website is "created by and for young women of color to provide information
and offer support on sexual and reproductive health issues through education and
advocacy."
National Eating Disorders Association: www.nationaleatingdisorders.org
This nonprofit organization supports those who suffer eating disorders and their
families.
New Moon: www.newmoon.com
An ad-free magazine for girls ages eight to fourteen, produced by adult staffers and
a girls' editorial board, focusing on girls' voices and celebrating girls' diversity
and strength.
NOW and Young Feminism: www.now.org/issues/young/index.html
Committed to involving young girls in feminism.
NWSA—Girls Advocacy Board: www.nwsa.org
The National Women's Studies Association "leads the field of women's studies in
educational and social transformation."
Pooja Makhijani: www.poojamakhijani.com
The website for the editor of the book *Under Her Skin: How Girls Experience Race
in America.*
Rachel Simmons: www.rachelsimmons.com
The website of the founding director of the Girls Leadership Institute and author of
Odd Girl Out.
Rock'N'Roll Camp for Girls: www.girlsrockcamp.org/main
An organization that believes music creation and performance builds self-esteem in
girls.
Smart Girls at the Party: www.onnetworks.com/videos/smart-girls-at-the-party
Through a series of showcase interviews with girls, Amy Poehler, Meredith Walker,
and Amy Miles celebrate "extraordinary individuals who are changing the world
by being themselves."
Soy Unica! Soy Latina!: www.connectforkids.org/node/1253
A bilingual site designed for Hispanic girls.
Studio2B: www.studio2b.org
A site created by the Girl Scouts for girls seeking an online community.

What's Good for Girls: http://whatsgoodforgirls.blogspot.com
   A personal blog about girls and girls' issues.
Women Make Movies: www.wmm.com
   A nonprofit organization that produces independent films made by women and
   about women.
Women of Color Resource Center: www.coloredgirls.org
   A center based in San Francisco that "promotes the political, economic, social and
   cultural well being of women and girls of color in the United States."
Work4Women: www.work4women.org
   A website with tools and supportive strategies to help women work in nontraditional
   occupations.
WOW/EM: http://eamusic.dartmouth.edu/~wowem
   A site for young women and girls interested in media, art, homework help, and so on.
WriteGirl: www.writegirl.org
   "A nonprofit organization for high school girls centered on the craft of creative writing
   and empowerment through self-expression."
Zooey's Room: www.zoeysroom.com
   An online community for young girls to learn about science, math, and technology.

SOURCES

Chapter 1

America's Children: Key National Indicators of Well-Being, 2007. ChildStats.gov.www .childstats.gov/AMERICASCHILDREN/eco1.asp. Accessed October 4, 2008.

American Association of University Women. *Beyond the "Gender Wars": A Conversation About Girls, Boys, and Education.* Washington, DC: AAUW Educational Foundation, 2001, pp. 2, 25.

———. *How Schools Shortchange Girls: The AAUW Report: A Study of Major Findings on Girls and Education.* New York: Marlowe and Company, 1995 [1992], p. 83; "Executive Summary," pp. 1-3. www.aauw.org/research/schoolsShortchange.cfm. Accessed June 18, 2009.

———. *Shortchanging Girls, Shortchanging America.* Washington, DC: AAUW, 1991; "Executive Summary." pp. 5, 9, 14. www.aauw.org/research/sgsa.cfm. Accessed June 18, 2009

Anzaldúa, Gloria. *Borderlands/La Frontera: The New Mestiza.* San Francisco: Aunt Lute, 1987.

Benfer, Amy. "Lost Boys." *Salon.com,* February 5, 2002. www.salon.com/mwt/ feature/2002/02/05/gender_ed/print.html. Accessed May 12, 2009.

Bombardieri, Marcella. "Summers' Remarks on Women Draw Fire." *The Boston Globe,* January 17, 2005. www.boston.com/news/local/articles/2005/01/17/summer_remarks _on_women_draw_fire. Accessed September 10, 2008.

Brown, Lyn Mikel, and Carol Gilligan. *Meeting at the Crossroads: Women's Psychology and Girls' Development.* Cambridge, MA: Harvard University, 1992.

Dicker, Rory. *A History of U.S. Feminisms.* Berkeley, CA: Seal, 2008.

Gilligan, Carol. *In a Different Voice: Psychological Theory and Women's Development.* Cambridge, MA: Harvard University, 1982, 1993, pp. ix, xxi, xxiv

———. *The Birth of Pleasure.* New York: Alfred A. Knopf, 2002.

"Girlie Men." *Wikipedia.* http://en.wikipedia.org/wiki/Girlie_men. Accessed September 10, 2008.

Greenfield, Lauren. *Girl Culture.* San Francisco: Chronicle, 2002, pp. 55, 110.

Hoff Sommers, Christina. "The War Against Boys." *The Atlantic Monthly,* May 2000.

hooks, bell. *Ain't I a Woman?: Black Women and Feminism.* Boston: South End, 1999 [1981].

"Intersectionality." *Wikipedia.* http://en.wikipedia.org/wiki/Intersectionality. Accessed September 5, 2008.

Koehler, Robert. "The Hillary Nutcracker." *The Huffington Post,* February 21, 2008. www.huffingtonpost.com/robert-koehler/the-hillary-nutcracker_b_87779.html. Accessed May 21, 2009.

Kohlberg, Lawrence. *The Philosophy of Moral Development: Moral Stages and the Idea of Justice (Essays on Moral Development),* (Vol. 1) New York: Harper and Row, 1981.

Lamb, Sharon, and Lyn Mikel Brown. *Packaging Girlhood: Rescuing Our Daughters from Marketers' Schemes.* New York: St. Martin's, 2006, p. 212.

Mead, Sara. "The Evidence Suggests Otherwise: The Truth About Boys and Girls." *Education Sector,* June 27, 2006. www.educationsector.org/research/research_show. htm?doc_id=378705. Accessed May 12, 2009.

National Center for Children in Poverty. "Child Poverty." www.nccp.org/topics/ childpoverty.html. Accessed May 12, 2009.

Orenstein, Peggy. *Schoolgirls: Young Women, Self-Esteem, and the Confidence Gap.* New York: Doubleday, 1994, pp. xxvii.

————. "What's Wrong with Cinderella?" *The New York Times Magazine,* December 24, 2006.

Parker-Pope, Tara. "Sexual Harassment at School." *The New York Times,* May 1, 2008. http:// well.blogs.nytimes.com/2008/05/01/sexual-harassment-at-school. Accessed September 10, 2008.

Pipher, Mary. *Reviving Ophelia: Saving the Selves of Adolescent Girls.* New York: Ballantine, 1994, pp. 12, 19-23.

"Renfrew Center Expert Says Toys Aimed at Young Girls Can Damage Self-Esteem." KidSource Online, January 31, 1997. www.kidsource.com/kidsource/content2/news2 /girls_esteem.html. Accessed May 12, 2009.

Schor, Juliet. *Born to Buy: The Commercialized Child and the New Consumer Culture.* New York: Scribner's, 2004.

"Thai Police to Sport 'Hello Kitty' Armbands." MSNBC/Associated Press, August 6, 2007. www.msnbc.msn.com/id/20148953. Accessed October 1, 2008.

Thomas, Marlo, and Friends. *Free to Be . . . You and Me.* Arista Records, 2006 [1972].

Chapter 2

Advocates for Youth. "GLBTQ Issues." www.advocatesforyouth.org/index.php?option=com _content&task=view&id=37&Itemid=66. Accessed May 12, 2009.

————. "GLBTQ Youth of Color Need Culturally Competent Education, Programs, and Health Care." www.advocatesforyouth.org/index.php?option=com_content& task=view&id=425&Itemid=177. Accessed May 13, 2009.

Alabama Coalition Against Domestic Violence (ACADV). "Dating Violence." www. acadv.org/dating.html. Accessed May 12, 2009.

American Association of University Women. *Hostile Hallways: The AAUW Survey on Sexual Harrassment in America's Schools.* Washington, DC: AAUW Educational Foundation, 1993.

————. *Voices of a Generation: Teenage Girls Report About Their Lives Today,* New York: Da Capo, 2000, p. 37, 39, 45, 49.

American Association of University Women Educational Foundation. *Voices of a Generation: Teenage Girls on Sex, School, and Self.* New York: Marlowe and Company, 2000.

American Civil Liberties Union. "At ACLU Urging, FL High School Ends Discriminatory Graduation Dress Code." March 23, 2002. www.aclu.org/studentsrights/dresscodes /12771prs20020523.html. Accessed May 21, 2009.

American Psychological Association. "Executive Summary." *Report of the APA Task Force on the Sexualization of Girls.* Washington, DC: American Psychological Association, 2007. www.apa.org/pi/wpo/sexualization.html. Accessed May 12, 2009.

Banerjee, Neela. "Dancing the Night Away, with a Higher Purpose." *The New York Times,* May 19, 2008. www.nytimes.com/2008/05/19/us/19purity.html. Accessed May 12, 2009.

"Barbie." *Wikipedia.* http://en.wikipedia.org/wiki/Barbie. Accessed May 12, 2009.

Baumgardner, Jennifer. "Would You Pledge Your Virginity to Your Father?" *Glamour,* January 1, 2007. www.glamour.com/sex-love-life/2007/01/purity-balls. Accessed May 12, 2009.

Brumberg, Joan Jacobs. "Introduction." In Lauren Greenfield, *Girl Culture.* San Francisco: Chronicle, 2002, p. 6, 8.

————. *The Body Project: An Intimate History of American Girls.* New York: Vintage, 1998, pp. 46–47, 49, 61, 65-67, 70, 79, 99-100, 125-128, 160, 168.

Campaign for a Commercial-Free Childhood. "CCFC to Unilever: Ax the Axe Campaign if You Care About "Real Beauty."" www.commercialfreechildhood.org/pressreleases/ axtheaxe.htm. Accessed May 12, 2009.

Carroll, Rebecca. *Sugar in the Raw: Voices of Young Black Girls in America.* New York: Three Rivers, 1997, p. 37.

Centers for Disease Control and Prevention. "Nationally Representative CDC Study Finds 1 in 4 Teenage Girls Has a Sexually Transmitted Disease." March 11, 2008. www.cdc .gov/STDConference/2008/media/release-11march2008.htm. Accessed May 12, 2009.

————. "Preventing Teen Pregnancy. An Update in 2009." April 27, 2009. www.cdc .gov/Reproductivehealth/AdolescentReproHealth/AboutTP.htm. Accessed May 21, 2009.

Children's Defense Fund. *The State of America's Children, 2005.* Washington, DC: Children's Defense Fund, 2005, p. 159. www.childrensdefense.org/child-research -data-publications/data/the-state-of-americas.html. Accessed May 13, 2009.

Connolly, Ceci. "Federal Funds for Abstinence Group Withheld." *The Washington Post,* August 23, 2005. www.washingtonpost.com/wp-dyn/content/article/2005/08/22/ AR2005082201230.html. Accessed May 12, 2009.

Corcoran, Monica. "Sexy Costumes for Teens Can Give Parents a Fright." *Los Angeles Times,* October 26, 2008. www.latimes.com/features/health/la-ig-rage26 -2008oct26,0,6120151.story. Accessed May 12, 2009.

Damsky, Lee. "Beauty Secrets." In Ophira Edut, ed., *Body Outlaws: Rewriting the Rules of Beauty and Body Image* (2nd ed.). Emeryville, CA: Seal, 2003, p. 136-137.

"Diana, Princess of Wales: Diana's Lovers." *LondonNet: The Guide to London News and Entertainment.* www.londonnet.co.uk/ln/guide/themes/diana_lovers.html. Accessed May 21, 2009.

Dicker, Rory. *A History of U.S. Feminisms.* Berkeley, CA: Seal, 2008, p. 83.

Feldman, Deborah. "High Heels for Babies Hit the Market." King5.com, September 9, 2008. www.king5.com/lifestyles/stories/NW_090908LIFB_baby_heels_KS.5e106397 .html. Accessed May 12, 2009.

Garfinkle, Stacey. "On Parenting: Buh-Bye, Club Libby Lu." *The Washington Post,* December 5, 2008. http://voices.washingtonpost.com/parenting/2008/12/goodbye_ club_libby_lu.html. Accessed May 21, 2009.

Golding, Alan B., and Joneil Adriano. "I'm a Girl"—Understanding Transgender Children: Parents of Transgender 6-Year-Old Girl Support Her Choice. *ABC News,* April 27, 2007. http://abcnews.go.com/2020/story?id=3088298&page=1. Accessed May 8, 2009.

Greenfield, Lauren. *Girl Culture.* San Francisco: Chronicle, 2002, pp. 60.

Guttmacher Institute. "Strong Evidence Favors Comprehensive Approach to Sex Ed: New Analysis Confirms Abstinence-Only Programs Waste Tax Dollars." New York: Guttmacher Institute Media Center, May 23, 2007. www.guttmacher.org/media /nr/2007/05/23/index.html. Accessed May 12, 2009.

Healy, Melissa. "Sexy Halloween Costumes . . . For Little Girls?" *Los Angeles Times,* October 27, 2008. http://articles.latimes.com/2008/oct/27/health/he-sexy27. Accessed May 12, 2009.

"Homelessness in the United States: Health Problems of the Homeless." *Medscape Today,* 2004, 9(2). www.medscape.com/viewarticle/481800_2. Accessed October 3, 2008.

Jayson, Sharon. "Media Cited for Showing Girls as Sex Objects." *USA Today,* February 20, 2007. www.usatoday.com/news/health/2007-02-19-sexualized-girls_x.htm. Accessed May 22, 2009.

Keller, Bess. "Calif. District Agrees To Allow Women To Wear Slacks." *Education Week,* March 12, 1997. www.edweek.org/ew/articles/1997/03/12/24pants.h16.html?tkn=U MQFX59VFE7Zho66iH%2Fw6mvn3WWqzEKNSd2P. Accessed May 21, 2009.

Kilman, Carrie. "THIS Is Why We Need a GSA." www.tolerance.org/teach/printar .jsp?is=40&ar=778. Accessed May 12, 2009.

Kliff, Sarah. "The Changing Face of Abortion." *Newsweek,* September 23, 2008. www .newsweek.com/id/160401. Accessed May 21, 2009.

Lamb, Sharon, and Lyn Mikel Brown. *Packaging Girlhood: Rescuing Our Daughters from Marketers' Schemes.* New York: St. Martin's, 2006, pp. 23-24, 169-170, 217-218.

Levy, Barrie. *In Love and in Danger: A Teen's Guide to Breaking Free of Abusive Relationships.* Berkeley, CA: Seal, 2006, pp. 77.

"Menarche." *Wikipedia.* http://en.wikipedia.org/wiki/Menarche. Accessed May 16, 2007.

Mind on the Media. "Shocking Facts! Body Image." www.mindonthemedia.org/index
.php?type=static&page=shocking. Accessed May 15, 2008.

Naing, Eric. "Column: No Fat Chicks?" *DailyIllini.com,* August 29, 2005. www
.dailyillini.com/opinions/2005/08/29/column-no-fat-chicks. Accessed May 12, 2009.

National Alliance on Mental Illness. "Anorexia Nervosa." www.nami.org/Template
.cfm?Section=By_Illness&template=/ContentManagement/ContentDisplay
.cfm&ContentID=7409. Accessed May 14, 2008.

National Campaign to Prevent Teen and Unplanned Pregnancy. "Some Thoughts on
Abstinence." January 2009. www.thenationalcampaign.org/resources/pdf/Briefly
_Some-Thoughts-on-Abstinence.pdf. Accessed May 12, 2009.

———. Bill Albert, "TV and Teen Pregnancy." *Pregnant Pause,* November 3, 2008.
http://blog.thenationalcampaign.org/pregnant_pause/2008/11. Accessed May 13,
2009.

National Center for Health Statistics/Centers for Disease Control and Prevention.
"FastStats: Body Measurements." www.cdc.gov/nchs/fastats/bodymeas.htm. Accessed
May 12, 2009.

National Center for Missing and Exploited Children. "FAQ: Child Sexual Exploitation."
www.missingkids.com/missingkids/servlet/PageServlet?LanguageCountry=en
_US&PageId=2815. Accessed October 3, 2008.

O'Keefe, Lori. "Pediatricians Should 'Tune In' to Patients' Media Habits." *AAP News,*
January 2001. www.aap.org/advocacy/OKeefemediahabits.htm. Accessed May 13,
2009.

Orenstein, Peggy. "What's Wrong with Cinderella?" *The New York Times Magazine,*
December 24, 2006.

Pipher, Mary. *Reviving Ophelia: Saving the Selves of Adolescent Girls.* New York: Ballantine,
1994.

Popkin, Susan J., Tama Leventhal, and Gretchen Weismann. "Girls in the 'Hood:
The Importance of Feeling Safe." Urban Institute, March 1, 2008. www.urban.org
/publications/411636.html. Accessed October 2, 2008.

RAINN (Rape, Abuse, and Incest National Network). "Who Are the Victims?
Breakdown by Gender and Age." www.rainn.org/get-information/statistics/sexual
-assault-victims. Accessed May 12, 200.

Rennison, Callie Marie, and Sarah Welchans. *Special Report: Intimate Partner Violence.*
Washington, DC: U.S. Department of Justice/Bureau of Justice Statistics, May
2000.

Robinson, Matthew S. "Scared Not to Be Straight: Harassment of LGBT Teens Prompts
Antibullying Initiatives." *Edutopia,* January 10, 2008. www.edutopia.org/gay-lesbian
-antibullying. Accessed May 12, 2009.

Silver Ring Thing. "What Is SilverRingThing?" www.silverringthing.com/whatissrt.asp.
Accessed May 12, 2009.

Spiegel, Alix. "Two Families Grapple with Sons' Gender Preferences." *All Things Considered,*
NPR, May 7, 2008. www.npr.org/templates/story/story.php?storyId=90247842.
Accessed May 8, 2009.

Tanenbaum, Leora. *Slut! Growing Up Female with a Bad Reputation.* New York: HarperCollins, 2000, p. xix.

"Tina Brown Dives into Diana Details: 'Chronicles' Demonstrates Author Was Well Connected to Princess' World." MSNBC/Associated Press, June 20, 2007. www.msnbc.msn.com/id/19333815. Accessed May 21, 2009.

Tolman, Deborah L. *Dilemmas of Desire: Teenage Girls Talk About Sexuality.* Cambridge, MA: Harvard University, 2002, pp. 188, 199.

Traister, Rebecca. "Real Beauty—Or Really Smart Marketing?" *Salon.com,* July 22, 2005. http://dir.salon.com/story/mwt/feature/2005/07/22/dove/index.html. Accessed May 12, 2009.

Wereszynski, Kathleen. "Girl Culture Begets Backlash." FoxNews.com, April 22, 2004. www.foxnews.com/story/0,2933,117822,00.html. Accessed May 12, 2009.

White, Emily. *Fast Girls: Teenage Tribes and the Myth of the Slut.* New York: Berkley, 2002.

Wiseman, Rosalind. *Queen Bees and Wannabes: Helping Your Daughter Survive Cliques, Gossip, Boyfriends, and Other Realities of Adolescence.* New York: Crown, 2002, pp. 77, 87, 93, 129-130.

WomensHealth.gov/U.S. Department of Health and Human Services. "Body Image: Loving Yourself Inside and Out/Eating Disorders." www.womenshealth.gov /bodyimage/eatingdisorders. Accessed May 21, 2009.

Wong, Julia. "Mirror, Mirror." In Vickie Nam, ed., *YELL-Oh Girls! Emerging Voices Explore Culture, Identity, and Growing Up Asian American.* New York: HarperCollins, 2001, p. 121.

Chapter 3

Brown, Lyn Mikel. *Girlfighting: Betrayal and Rejection Among Girls.* New York: New York University, 2003, pp.4-6, 14-15, 17-18, 22, 29, 32, 70, 73, 86-88, 90, 95, 97, 107, 140, 142, 172-173, 181, 186, 191, 208, 212.

Hardy Girls, Healthy Women. "About Us." www.hardygirlshealthywomen.org/aboutus. php. Accessed May 13, 2009.

————. "Our Programs." www.hardygirlshealthywomen.org/ourprograms.php. Accessed May 13, 2009.

Kindlon, Dan. *Alpha Girls: Understanding the New American Girl and How She Is Changing the World.* New York: Rodale, 2006.

Lamb, Sharon. *The Secret Lives of Girls: What Good Girls Really Do—Sex Play, Aggression, and Their Guilt.* New York: Free Press, 2001, pp. 6, 142-144, 147, 150, 201-203, 205-207.

Meadows, Susannah. "Meet The GAMMA Girls: They're Not Mean. They Like Their Parents. They're Smart, Confident and Think Popularity Is Overrated. What Makes These Teens Tick." *Newsweek,* June 3, 2002. www.newsweek.com/id/64706/output/ print. Accessed May 13, 2009.

Mean Girls. Directed by Mark Waters. Paramount Pictures, 2004.

Pipher, Mary. *Reviving Ophelia: Saving the Selves of Adolescent Girls.* New York: Ballantine, 1994, pp. 293.

Simmons, Rachel. *Odd Girl Out: The Hidden Culture of Aggression in Girls.* New York: Harcourt, 2002, pp. 3, 18, 21, 30-31, 33-34, 55, 177-179, 268-270.

Smith-Rosenberg, Carroll. "The Female World of Love and Ritual: Relations Between Women in Nineteenth-Century America." *Signs,* 1975, 1(1). www.columbia.edu/cu/irwag/pdf-files/femaleworld.pdf. Accessed May 13, 2009.

Talbot, Margaret. "Girls Just Want to Be Mean." *The New York Times Magazine,* February 24, 2002. www.nytimes.com/2002/02/24/magazine/girls-just-want-to-be-mean.html. Accessed May 13, 2009.

Chapter 4

"Body Peace Treaty." *Seventeen.* www.seventeen.com/health-sex-fitness/body-types/body-peace-pledge?c_offset=2. Accessed May 13, 2009.

Douglas, Susan J. *Where the Girls Are: Growing Up Female with the Mass Media.* New York: Three Rivers, 1995, pp. 9-10, 13, 15-16, 20, 73, 78, 84, 86-87, 94, 98, 108, 120.

"Editorial Mission." *Muslim Girl.* www.muslimgirlworld.com/press_mission.cfm. Accessed May 13, 2009.

Free to Be . . . You and Me. Directed by Bill Davis and Len Steckler. Hen's Tooth Video, 2001 [1974].

Fudge, Rachel. "Girl, Unreconstructed: Why Girl Power Is Bad for Feminism." In Lisa Jervis and Andi Zeisler, eds., *BitchFest: Ten Years of Cultural Criticism from the Pages of Bitch Magazine.* New York: Farrar, Straus and Giroux, 2006, p. 160.

Gallup and Robinson. "Sex in Advertising" [4: Big Bang—Playboy]. www.gallup-robinson.com/tableofcontents.html. Accessed May 8, 2009.

Girls Inc. "Girls and Media." February, 2002. www.girlsinc.org/downloads/GirlsandMedia.pdf. Accessed May 13, 2009.

Handel, Sherry S. "Review." *Blue Jean: What Young Women Are Thinking, Saying, and Doing.* Rochester, NY: Blue Jean, 2001. www.bluejeanpublishing.com. Accessed May 22, 2009.

Herold, Kara. [Interview.] February 2009.

hooks, bell. *Talking Back: Thinking Feminist, Thinking Black.* Boston: South End, 1989, p. 8-9.

Jayson, Sharon. "Media Cited for Showing Girls as Sex Objects." *USA Today,* February 20, 2007. www.usatoday.com/news/health/2007-02-19-sexualized-girls_x.htm. Accessed May 22, 2009.

Jesella, Kara, and Marisa Meltzer. *How Sassy Changed My Life: A Love Letter to the Greatest Teen Magazine of All Time.* New York: Faber and Faber, 2007.

Kearney, Mary Celeste. *Girls Make Media.* New York: Routledge, 2006, pp. 12, 125, 129, 131, 191-192, 206, 210, 217-220, 224-225, 228, 231-233, 237.

Lee, Carol. "Teen Mag Editor Promotes Healthy Body Image." *Women's eNews,* March 2, 2002. www.womensenews.org/article.cfm/dyn/aid/833/context/journalistofthemoth.htm --march 2, 2002. Accessed May 8, 2009.

Masurat, Anastasia. "Why Not:? It's a New Golden Age of Young-Adult Fiction." *Bitch,* Fall 2008, Issue 41.

Means, Sarah. "Alternative Magazines Promote 'Positive View' of Womanhood." *Insight on the News,* October 20, 1997. http://findarticles.com/p/articles/mi_m1571/is_n38_v13/ai_19969867. Accessed May 13, 2009.

Media Awareness Network. "Beauty and Body Image in the Media." www.media-awareness.ca/english/issues/stereotyping/women_and_girls/women_beauty.cfm. Accessed May 13, 2008.

Mind on the Media. "Shocking Facts! Media." www.mindonthemedia.org/index.php?type=static&page=shocking. Accessed May 15, 2008.

Mulvey, Laura. "Visual Pleasure and Narrative Cinema." *Screen,* 1975, 16(3). In Laura Mulvey, *Visual and Other Pleasures.* Bloomington: Indiana University Press, 1989.

Nash, Ilana. *American Sweethearts: Teenage Girls in Twentieth-Century Popular Culture.* Bloomington: Indiana University, 2005, pp. 3-4, 17-19, 227-228.

New Moon Girls. www.newmoon.com. Accessed May 8, 2009.

Parker-Pope, Tara. "Books for Girls with a Health Message." *The New York Times,* October 13, 2008. http://well.blogs.nytimes.com/2008/10/13/books-for-girls-with-a-health-message. Accessed May 13, 2009.

———. "Healthful Messages, Wrapped in Fiction." *The New York Times,* October 13, 2008. www.nytimes.com/2008/10/14/health/14well.html. Accessed May 13, 2009.

Peterson, Latoya. "Oops, Where'd We Go? The Disappearing Black Girls in Young Adult Literature." *Racialicious,* May 4, 2007. www.racialicious.com/2007/05/04/oops-whered-we-go-the-disappearing-black-girls-in-young-adult-literature. Accessed May 13, 2009.

Pilkington, Ed. "Supermodels Launch Anti-Racism Protest." *Guardian,* September 15, 2007. www.guardian.co.uk/world/2007/sep/15/usa.fashion. Accessed May 13, 2009.

Roberts, Donald F. "Media and Youth: Access, Exposure, and Privatization." *JAH,* 2000, 27(2).

Rock'N'Roll Camp for Girls. "We Put the 'Amp' in Camp." www.girlsrockcamp.org/about. Accessed May 13, 2009.

Sheridan-Rabideau, Mary. *Girls, Feminism, and Grassroots Literacies: Activism in the GirlZone.* Albany: State University of New York, 2008, pp. 46, 49.

Sweeney, Kathleen. *Maiden USA: Girl Icons Come of Age.* New York: Peter Lang, 2008, pp. 129, 131-132, 134.

Thomas, Marlo, and Friends. *Free to Be . . . You and Me.* Arista Records, 2006 [1972].

"To Girls, 'Sassy' Meant Something More." *Talk of the Nation*/NPR, April 25, 2007. www.npr.org/templates/story/story.php?storyId=9826498. Accessed May 13, 2009.

Trebay, Guy. "Ignoring Diversity, Runways Fade to White." *The New York Times,* October 14, 2007. www.nytimes.com/2007/10/14/fashion/shows/14race.html. Accessed May 13, 2009.

Wolf, Naomi. "Young Adult Fiction: Wild Things." *The New York Times Book Review,* March 12, 2006. www.nytimes.com/2006/03/12/books/review/12wolf.html. Accessed May 13, 2009.

Chapter 5

Adios Barbie: A Bodylovin' Site for Every Body. adiosbarbie.com. Accessed May 13, 2009.

Advocates for Youth: Rights, Respect, Responsibility. www.advocatesforyouth.org. Accessed May 8, 2009.

Alcantara, Sabrina Margarita. [Personal correspondence.] March 19, 2009.

Alternatives for Girls (AFG). www.alternativesforgirls.org. Accessed May 8, 2009.

American Association of University Women. "AAUW's Position on Equity in School Athletics." www.aauw.org/advocacy/issue_advocacy/actionpages/titleix_athletics.cfm. Accessed May 14, 2009.

Blumenthal, Karen. *Let Me Play: The Story of Title IX: The Law That Changed the Future of Girls in America.* New York: Atheneum, 2005.

Booher, Bridget. "Let Me Play: The Story of Title IX, by Karen Blumenthal '81." [Review.] *Duke Magazine,* July-August 2005, 91(4). www.dukemagazine.duke.edu /dukemag/issues/070805/depbks.html. Accessed May 14, 2009.

Breitkopf, Ilana. "The Girl Child's Education." Stop Child Poverty. www.stopchildpoverty .org/learn/bigpicture/education/girlchild.php. Accessed October 1, 2008.

Cagen, Sasha. [Interview.] February 26, 2009.

CARE. "Ending Poverty—Why Empower Women and Girls?" www.aidemocracy.org /download/womenandgirls.pdf. Accessed May 14, 2009.

Center for Young Women's Development. www.cywd.org. Accessed May 13, 2009.

Coalition for Positive Sexuality (CPS): www.positive.org. Accessed May 8, 2009.

Eggert-Crowe, Lauren. [Interview.] March 11, 2009.

Expanding Your Horizons Network: Motivating Young Women in Science and Mathematics. www.expandingyourhorizons.org. Accessed May 13, 2009.

Girl Effect, The. "Why Should We Pay Attention to Girls?" www.girleffect.org/#/about. Accessed October 4, 2008.

Girl-Mom. www.girl-mom.com. Accessed May 13, 2009.

Girls for a Change. www.girlsforachange.org. Accessed May 13, 2009.

Girls in Government. www.girlsingovernment.org. Accessed May 13, 2009.

Girls Inc.: Celebrating Girls' Voices Since 1864. www.girlsinc.org/index.html. Accessed May 13, 2009.

Gonzales, Sarah M. "Poverty and Sex Trafficking: How Will Warren Buffett's $30.7 Billion Donation to the Bill and Melinda Gates Foundation, Earmarked to Fight Poverty, Affect Global Sex Trafficking, the Cause of Which Is Rooted in Poverty?" Captive Daughters. www.captivedaughters.org/gatesfoundation.htm. Accessed October 1, 2008.

Grrls Literary Activism Project (Kore Press). www.korepress.org/Grrrls.htm. Accessed May 14, 2009.

gURL. www.gurl.com. Accessed May 13, 2009.

Hahn, Jennifer. "Schoolgirl Dreams." *Ms.,* Fall 2007. feminist.org/education /TriumphsOfTitleIX.pdf. Accessed May 8, 2009.

Johnston, Andrea. *Girls Speak Out. Finding Your True Self* (2nd ed.). Berkeley, CA: Celestial Arts, 2005. www.feminist.com/resources/girlsyoungwomen/girls/gyw _johnston.html. Accessed May 13, 2009.

Kearney, Mary Celeste. *Girls Make Media.* New York: Routledge, 2006, pp. 61, 68-69, 135-136, 144, 163, 172-173, 179, 181-182, 185.

Minoui, Delphine, and Borzou Daragahi. "Yemeni 10-year-old Divorcee Nujood Ali Goes Back to School." *Los Angeles Times,* September 20, 2008. www.latimes.com /news/education/la-fg-nujood20-2008sep20,0,7766653.story. Accessed May 8, 2009.

MySistahs. Mysistahs.org. Accessed May 13, 2009.

Nike Foundation. "Nike Foundation and Buffetts Join to Invest $100 Million in Girls." www.nikefoundation.org/files/The_Girl_Effect_News_Release.pdf. Accessed May 8, 2009.

OutProud, the National Coalition for Gay, Lesbian, Bisexual and Transgender Youth: Be Yourself. www.outproud.org. Accessed May 8, 2009.

PACE: Believing in Girls. http://pacecenter.org/joomla. Accessed May 8, 2009.

"Parents: Cyber Bullying Led to Teen's Suicide." *Good Morning America*/ABC News, November 19, 2007. http://abcnews.go.com/GMA/Story?id=3882520. Accessed May 13, 2009.

Parry, Wayne. "Helping the Homeless Brings Muslim, Jewish girls Together." Associated Press, January 16, 2006. www.highbeam.com/doc/1P1-117381518.html. Accessed May 14, 2009.

Rukeyser, Muriel. "Kathe Kollwitz." *The Collected Poems of Muriel Rukeyser.* New York: McGraw-Hill, 1978, p. 482.

Scarleteen: Sex Ed for the Real World. www.scarleteen.com. Accessed May 8, 2009.

Sista II Sista/Hermana a Hermana. www.sistaiisista.org /main.html. Accessed May 13, 2009.

Stark-Merklein, Brigitte. "For Cambodian Girls, Education Is Antidote to Poverty and Sexual Exploitation." UNICEF. www.unicef.org/infobycountry/cambodia_27896 .html. Accessed October 1, 2008.

Stolberg, Sheryl Gay. "Obama Signs Equal Pay Legislation." *The New York Times,* January 29, 2009. www.nytimes.com/2009/01/30/us/politics/30ledbetter-web.html. Accessed May 8, 2009.

"Triumphs of Title IX, The." *Ms.,* Fall 2007.

WEEA Equity Resource Center. "Title IX and Education Policy." www2.edc.org /WomensEquity/resource/title9/index.htm. Accessed May 14, 2009.

———. "Title IX FAQ: Fact Sheet." www2.edc.org/WomensEquity/resource/title9 /t9faq.htm#fact. Accessed May 14, 2009.

White House, The. "President Obama Announces White House Council on Women and Girls." Office of the Press Secretary, March 11, 2009. www.whitehouse.gov/the _press_office/President-Obama-Announces-White-House-Council-on-Women-and-Girls. Accessed May 8, 2009.

WriteGirl: Empowering Girls Through Mentorship and Self-Expression. www.write girl.org. Accessed May 13, 2009.

INDEX

ACKNOWLEDGMENTS

If it takes a village to raise a child, it's taken a metropolis to bring this book into the world. This book would not exist without the dedicated support of so many, and I am deeply grateful for their help. My sincere thanks to the editors at Seal Press with whom I worked throughout this project: Jill Rothenberg, who got it all started, Denise Silva, Anne Mathews, the infinitely patient Brooke Warner, and finally, my deep gratitude to Karen Bleske for seeing me through the last mile. Thanks as well to Stephanie Malinowski in Seattle.

I am thankful for the institutional support I received at UC Berkeley through the Beatrice Bain Research Group and its wonderful participants, and for the good experience I gained teaching for the Department of Gender and Women's Studies. Most recently, I am glad to have found an academic home at UCLA with the Center for the Study of Women.

My great thanks to Jessica Taft and Allison Kimmich, who offered much-needed perspective just when I needed it. And endless thanks to Deborah Siegel, Shira Tarrant, and Laura Mazer for being sisters on this path through *Girl w/Pen* and beyond. This book would simply not exist if not for the guidance of Alexa Hagerty, whose genius for organization and buoying encouragement have been invaluable.

Finally, my greatest debt of gratitude to my loving parents and extended family, who saw me through my own girlhood to the person I am now. And my deepest thanks to Richard, whose love and perseverance through this project have been more priceless than I could have known.

ABOUT THE AUTHOR

ELLINE LIPKIN GREW UP IN MIAMI and attended Wesleyan University. She received her MFA in creative writing from Columbia University and her PhD in creative writing and literature from the University of Houston, where she completed the graduate certificate in women's studies. For two years she was a postdoctoral scholar with the Beatrice Bain Research Group on Gender at the University of California, Berkeley, where she also taught for the Departments of College Writing, Comparative Literature, and Gender and Women's Studies. She is now a research scholar with UCLA's Center for the Study of Women, where her work focuses on girls' studies and contemporary American women's poetry.

She is the author of *The Errant Thread*, and her poems have been published in *Crab Orchard Review, Margie, North American Review, The Texas Review*, and in *The Poets' Grimm: 20th Century Poems from Grimm Fairy Tales*. A contributing writer to *Girl w/Pen,* her nonfiction writing has appeared on Salon.com and in other contemporary sources.

SELECTED TITLES FROM SEAL PRESS

For more than thirty years, Seal Press has published groundbreaking books. By women. For women. Visit our website at www.sealpress.com. Check out the Seal Press blog at www.sealpress.com/blog.

A History of U.S. Feminisms: Seal Studies, by **Rory Dicker**. $12.95, 1-58005-234-7. A concise introduction to feminism from the late-19th century through today.

The Purity Myth: How America's Obsession with Virginity Is Hurting Young Women, by Jessica Valenti. $24.95, 1-58005-253-3. With her usual balance of intelligence and wit, Valenti presents a powerful argument that girls and women, even in this day and age, are overly valued for their sexuality—and that this needs to stop.

Laid: Young People's Experiences with Sex in an Easy-Access Culture, edited by Shannon T. Boodram. $15.95, 1-58005-295-9. This hard-hitting anthology paints a candid portrait of what sex is like—the good and the bad—for today's young people.

Girldrive: Criss-Crossing America, Redefining Feminism, by Nona Willis Aronowitz and Emma Bee Bernstein. $19.95, 1-58005-273-8. Two young women set out on the open road to explore the current state of feminism in the U.S.

Full Frontal Feminism: A Young Woman's Guide to Why Feminism Matters, by Jessica Valenti. $15.95, 1-58005-201-0. A sassy and in-your-face look at contemporary feminism for women of all ages.

Feminism and Pop Culture: Seal Studies, by Andi Zeisler. $12.95, 1-58005-237-1. Andi Zeisler, cofounder of *Bitch* magazine, traces the impact of feminism on pop culture (and vice versa) from the 1940s to today.